Anthropological Insights
for Missionaries

Anthropological Insights for Missionaries

Paul G. Hiebert

Baker Academic
Grand Rapids, Michigan

Copyright © 1985 by Baker Books
a division of Baker Publishing Group
P.O. Box 6287, Grand Rapids, MI 49516-6287
www.bakeracademic.com

ISBN 10: 0-8010-4291-7
ISBN 978-0-8010-4291-1

Library of Congress Catalog Card Number 85-071177

Twenty-second printing, November 2006

Printed in the United States of America

To
Frances,
Eloise and **Michael,**
Barbara and **Byron,**
and **John,**
who patiently taught me much about being a follower of Jesus Christ,
and to whom I owe more than I can ever express in words.

Contents

PART 4 **Cultural Differences and the Bicultural Community**

Preface

There is, today, in churches around the world a renewed vision of their responsibility to bring to people everywhere the Good News of salvation, and to minister to their needs. This can be seen not only in the revival of interest in missions which has occurred in the West, but also in the rapid growth of missionary outreach in the churches of Asia, Africa, and Latin America, the so-called Two-Thirds world.

With this renewal has come the realization that missions must be far more sensitive to people and their cultures. The modern mission movement was born during a time of Western colonial and technological expansion, and too often Western missionaries equated the gospel with Western civilization. Here and there individual missionaries identified closely with the people they served, and learned their ways. Many more showed their love for the people by their deep commitment to their ministries. They went abroad often knowing that they faced death in a few short years, and those who survived gave their whole lives to the task. But the identification of the gospel with Western power and technology made it foreign, and therefore unacceptable, to many people.

Today the young churches planted by the early missionaries are speaking out, calling us to be more aware of human cultures and their differences, and reminding us that God is not a tribal God, but the God of the world; that the gospel is for everyone; and that the church is one body that breaks down the walls of ethnicity, class, and nationalism that divide humans into warring camps. At the same time, there has been a growing awareness in the social sciences, particularly in anthropology, of the need to understand people in their cultural settings. Out of this has come the growing realization that missionaries today need not only a solid understanding of the Scriptures, but also a deep knowledge of the people they serve.

This book is an attempt to provide young missionaries with some basic tools for understanding other cultures and for understanding themselves as they enter these cultures. It is no substitute for a divine calling, or for biblical and vocational training. Every missionary must experience God's call to missions and be rooted in a love for God and his glory, and in a love for people, their salvation, and their well-being. This alone will keep him or her going when the going gets tough. Unfortunately in our day we are too often long on knowledge and short on lifelong commitment.

This book is also no substitute for solid training in the Scriptures and in the ministry in which the missionary serves, whether this be preaching, teaching, medicine, community development, or some other task. Rather, it is an attempt to introduce young missionaries to the third area in which they need expertise, namely, cross-cultural relationships and communication.

In many ways this book is autobiographical. It is based on long reflection on our years of ministry in India with the Mennonite Brethren Board of Missions and Services, and our many mistakes in that ministry. Unfortunately we cannot relive the past and undo our errors, but we can learn from them, and pass on our understandings to those who follow. It is also based on many lessons taught us by the church in India. In young churches there is often a freshness of the gospel message that has been lost through time in the older churches.

There are many who have made this book possible. I owe a particular word of appreciation to the Board of Trustees of Fuller Theological Seminary who granted me a sabbatical to complete the task. I also want to express my thanks to my colleagues at the School of World Mission who have often stimulated and critiqued my thinking, and to the staff at Baker Book House, particularly Betty De Vries, who took my rough manuscript and made it intelligible. Above all I want to thank my wife Frances, who listened and supported me patiently during the many long hours I spent in drafting the work.

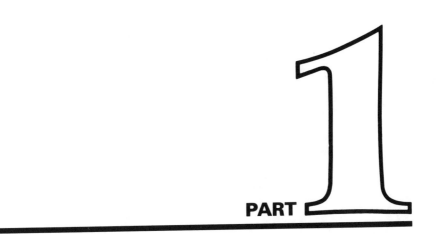

PART 1

The Gospel and Human Cultures

1

Missions and Anthropology

The Christmas pageant was over—or so I thought. Christ's birth to Mary and Joseph had been announced by angels, dressed in pure white. Their faces were brown and their message in Telugu, for we were in South India. The shepherds had staggered on stage, acting half drunk, but herding the smaller children down on all fours as the sheep. Not quite what I was reared to expect, but something I could explain in terms of cultural differences. Unlike Palestinian shepherds, who are known for their sobriety and piety, Indian shepherds are known for their drink and dancing. But the message was not lost, for at the sight of the angels the shepherds fell to the ground, frightened sober.

The wise men and Herod had appeared on stage in regal splendor. Now we sat cross-legged and crowded, as the shepherds, wise men, and angels gathered with Mary and Joseph around the manger. A fine ending to the Christmas story. Suddenly, out jumped Santa Claus! With a merry song and dance, he began to give out presents to Jesus and the others. He was the hero of the pageant. I sat stunned.

What had gone wrong? A case of syncretism, I first thought—a mixture of Hindu and Christian ideas that one might expect in new converts. The older missionaries had warned us that if drama were allowed into the church, it would bring in Hindu beliefs. But, no. Santa was a Western idea, brought by the Westerners along with the story of Christ's birth. What had happened?

13

Biblical Messages and Cultural Settings

In our preparation for missionary service, we are well trained in the Bible and the missionary message. When we go abroad, we assume that once we learn the local language we can preach, and the people will understand us. It comes as a shock that this is not so, that the task of communicating effectively in another culture is far more difficult than imagined. But what do we need to improve this?

There is a gulf between ourselves and the people to whom we go in service. There is an even greater gulf between the Bible's historical and cultural setting and contemporary life. How do we bridge these gulfs and make possible the effective cross-cultural and cross-historical communication of the gospel?

Clearly we need to understand the gospel in its historical and cultural setting. Without this, we have no message. We also need a clear understanding of ourselves and the people we serve in diverse historical and cultural contexts. Without this, we are in danger of proclaiming a meaningless and irrelevant message.

Too often, however, we are content to settle for only one of these goals (Figure 1). As evangelicals we emphasize knowledge of the Bible, but rarely stop to examine the people and cultures we serve. So the message we bring is often misunderstood and "foreign." The liberal wing of the church, on the other hand, has underscored knowledge of contemporary human settings, but downplays the importance of solid theological foundations based on biblical truth. This group is in danger of losing the gospel.

We need both approaches. We must know the biblical message. We must also know the contemporary scene. Only then can we build the bridges that will make the biblical message relevant to today's world and its people everywhere.

FIGURE 1

Bridging the Gulf of Historical and Cultural Differences

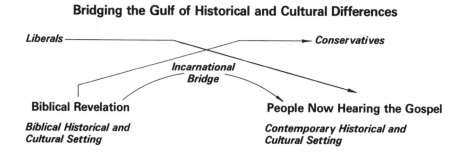

Anthropological Contributions to Missions

How can we know the biblical message? Clearly, we must study the Bible, theology, and church history. As missionaries we must also develop the skills of our ministry, whether this be preaching, teaching, medicine, development, radio, or writing.

How can we learn about the contemporary scene? Anthropology, sociology, history, and the other social sciences can help us here. They provide tools whereby we can examine the cultural settings within which we work and supply information about the contemporary scene. They can assist us in several ways.

First, anthropology can bring understanding of cross-cultural situations. For example, it can help us analyze the Christmas drama mentioned above. Recent studies show that people organize their ideas into larger blocks or domains. In this case it is clear that North Americans have a great many ideas associated with Christmas, but that they divide these into two distinct conceptual domains, resulting in two different Christmases. In one, the sacred sphere, they place Jesus, Mary, Joseph, angels, wise men, and shepherds. In the other, the secular one, they place Santa, reindeer, Christmas trees, stockings, and presents. They do not mix the two in their minds. Rudolph, the red-nosed reindeer, does not belong in the same picture as the angels and wise men. Nor does Santa belong on the same stage as Jesus. Missionaries introduced Indians to the basic concepts of "Christmas," but failed to communicate the implicit distinction between the two Christmases to their listeners. The Indians, therefore, did not separate Santa from the manger scene.

Second, anthropology can provide us with many insights into such specific mission tasks as Bible translation. Like missionaries, early anthropologists had to learn new languages, many of which had no written forms, grammars, dictionaries, or teachers. They developed techniques to learn languages quickly and accurately through local informants and to translate messages from one culture to another. These methods have been invaluable to missionaries in learning new languages and translating the Bible into these languages. Anthropologists have also examined the problems of cross-cultural communication, and the insights they have gained can help missionaries bring their message to other societies with a minimum of distortion and loss of meaning.

Third, anthropology can help missionaries understand the processes of conversion, including the social change that occurs when people become Christians. People are social beings, influenced by the dynamics of their social environments, and a familiarity with these psychological mechanisms is important to understanding the mission process.

Fourth, anthropology can help us make the gospel relevant to our listeners. As we have seen, there is a deep chasm between contemporary cultures and the sociological contexts in which the Bible was based. To bridge that chasm we need to understand both divine revelation within its historical and cultural settings and modern humans in their present-day environments. The latter we can gain in part through the social sciences.

Finally, anthropology can help us relate to people around the world in all their cultural diversity and assist us in building bridges of understanding between them. The gospel breaks down the barriers that divide people into Jews and Gentiles, slaves and masters, males and females, First World and Third World, Americans and Russians, "us" and "them." It calls Christians to be citizens of the kingdom of God, in which people from all nations and cultures are brought into common fellowship without destroying their ethnological distinctives.

In this book we will explore some of the insights that anthropology can bring to the missionary task. Since I am assuming that my readers have acquired a thorough familiarity with the Bible and have constructed their theological foundations upon that knowledge, we will not seek to lay these foundations again. Rather, we will look at what anthropology has to contribute to our study of different peoples in their historical and cultural contexts and examine the implications these insights have for our ministries. These are areas in which many evangelical missionaries are weak.

Before we do so, however, we need to look briefly at some of the hypotheses underlying this book. All studies are based on certain givens, and it is important to know what they are. First we will look at this book's theological assumptions and then at its anthropological assumptions, to see how both shape our thinking. Then we will seek to bring together biblical and anthropological insights to achieve a broader understanding of the missionary task. We must avoid a double vision that keeps us from seeing things clearly.

Theological Assumptions

What are the theological assumptions underlying this book, particularly as they relate to the missionary task? This is an important question, for we cannot divorce our anthropological models from our theologies. To do so is to imply a separation between the spiritual and eternal nature of human beings and their creaturely and temporal nature. Human history must be understood within the greater framework of cosmic events, and our anthropological models of humans must fit within our theological framework. It is biblical revelation that provides us with the ultimate foundations upon which we build our social and historical understandings of human beings.

God's Mission

A theology of missions must begin with God, not humans. It must begin with the cosmic history of the creation, the fall, and God's redemption of his creation. It must include God's revelation of himself to humans, the incarnation of Jesus Christ within history, the salvation he achieved through his death and resurrection, and the ultimate lordship of Christ over all creation. The history of humankind is first and foremost the story of God's mission to redeem sinners who seek his salvation, the story of Jesus who came as a missionary, and the story of God's Spirit who works in the hearts of those who hear.

It is in this context of God's activity within this world and throughout history that we must understand our task. The mission is ultimately God's, and we are but part of that mission. Our planning and strategizing are useless, even destructive, if they keep us from seeking first the guidance and empowerment of God himself.

Authoritative Scripture

The Bible is the fully authoritative record of God's self-revelation to humans. It is God's Word, and we turn to it not only to hear God's message of salvation, but also to see how he works in and through human history in accomplishing his purposes. Scripture is the standard against which we measure all truth and righteousness, all theologies and moralities.

Because the Bible is God's Word, it must be our message to a lost world. Our central task is to communicate it to people so that they understand and respond. We may be involved in many things—programs of preaching, teaching, giving of relief, healing, and development—but these are not a true part of Christian missions if they are not rooted in the Word and do not give expression to the gospel. Bearing witness to the gospel through proclamation and life is the heart of the mission task.

God's revelation is always given to humans in specific historical and cultural contexts. Consequently, to understand the Scriptures, we must relate them to the time and setting in which they were given. Even Christ came as a specific person within Jewish culture about two thousand years ago.

Christocentric

Scripture must be understood in the light of Jesus Christ. He is the center to which all revelation points. The Old Testament finds its fulfillment in him, and the New Testament bears witness to him. As Son of God, he is the perfect representation of God. And as Son of man, he is the perfect communicator of God's self-revelation to humans. Christ therefore becomes our exemplar, and his incarnation is the model for our mission. Not that we can save the world, but, like him, we must seek to identify with those to whom we go in order to bring to them the Good News of God's salvation in ways they can understand.

Our message, too, is centered on Christ. It is both the Good News of God's salvation through his death and resurrection and a call to Christian discipleship. It begins in a deep awareness of human sinfulness and ends in worship, when all in heaven and on earth will bow before him and recognize that Jesus is Lord.

Ministry of the Holy Spirit

Missions cannot be understood apart from the ongoing work of the Holy Spirit in the lives of his people and in those who hear the gospel. He prepares our hearts to receive and respond to the message of redemption. And the Spirit works within us to bring us to spiritual maturity by pointing us to Christ. It is through his power that we minister to those who are lost, to those who are broken in body and spirit, to those who are oppressed, and to those who are starving and homeless.

The Kingdom of God

The center of Christ's message was the kingdom of God, wherein God is still at work in creation and in history to redeem the world unto himself. The person of Christ is certainly central to that work, but it extends beyond him to the work of the Holy Spirit in the lives of people, and to the work of God in the affairs of nations and in all of nature. The scope of God's mission is not only his kingdom in heaven, but also his kingdom on earth. Although it has to do with the eternal destiny of humans, it also deals with their well-being on earth—with peace, justice, liberty, health, provision, and righteousness.

The Church

At the heart of the kingdom of God is the church, the people of God on earth. Through them he proclaims the Good News of his kingdom, and through them he strengthens those who enter that kingdom. In missions we need a strong theology of church as a corporate body, a community of the faithful. For the church is the discerning community within which the mission task must be understood. Missions is not first the responsibility of individuals; it is the task of the church as a whole.

Priesthood of All Believers

The church is a living body in which there are many members, each of whom has been given gifts to be used for the body as a whole. While members have different gifts, they all have the right to approach God and the responsibility to discern the message of God within the context of the church. All believers are priests!

This is a radical message, and its implications for missions are great. It means that converts in other lands have as much right as we to read and interpret the Scriptures. To deny them this is to deny the ongoing work of the Holy Spirit in their lives. Our task, then, is to bring them the Bible and help them discern within it God's message to them. We are to be models for them of God's people, living in obedience to his Word. Our challenge is also to allow them the greatest privilege we allow ourselves—the right to make mistakes and learn from them.

But the priesthood of believers forces us to differentiate between the Bible, God's revelation to us, and theologies, which are human understandings of that revelation in different cultural and historical contexts. Thus we speak of one Bible but of the theologies of Calvin, Luther, the Anabaptists, and others. As we will see in chapter 8, this distinction between the Bible and theological interpretations of the Bible does not relativize theology. A Christian theology has one foot in biblical revelation and the other in the historical and cultural context of the people hearing the message.

Since we are all given the right to read and interpret the Scriptures, our first task is to remain faithful to biblical truth. This begins with careful *exegesis*, in which the message of the Bible is understood within a specific cultural and historical context. Our second task is to discover what the meaning of the biblical message is for us in our particular cultural and historical setting and then determine what our response should be. This is *hermeneutics*. Although the message of the Bible is supracultural—above all cultures—it must be understood by people living within their own heritage and time frame.

Anthropological Assumptions

There are certain anthropological assumptions underlying this book which need to be made explicit. Theories of cultural evolution dominated anthropology until the first quarter of the twentieth century. In these, as in medieval Christian theology, the meaning of human experience was sought in terms of history. But in these theories history was explained purely in naturalistic rather than theistic terms. "Culture" was seen as a single human creation in various stages of development in different parts of the world. Societies were thought to progress from simple to complex organizations, from irrational to rational thought, and from magic to religion and finally to science.

This theory of cultural evolution was called into question after World War I. The optimism about human progress that preceded that war had been shattered. Moreover, research showed that far from being illogical, so-called primitive societies are as rational and complex as those of modern mankind, though in different ways.

A rejection of the idea of cultural "evolution" does not mean we must abandon diachronic or historical paradigms of explanation. The Bible itself explains humanity in terms of cosmic history, a drama in which there is a "plot" with a beginning, a development, and an ending. Scripture rejects the idea that human experience is a random set of events with no direction, no purpose, and hence no meaning. Moreover, it claims that the driving force behind history is not blind chance, but God's purposes and human responses. We need to understand people and divine revelation within the context of history.

By the 1930s theories of cultural evolution had largely been replaced, partly by structural functional theories that focused on the diversity of human societies and saw them as self-contained, integrated systems. Like living organisms, societies were thought to have many cultural traits, all of which contributed to the survival of the society as a whole.

Such theories have contributed much to our understanding of social structures and the dynamics of sociological change, and we will draw upon these insights here. In the extreme, however, these theories become deterministic and overlook the role of the human as a thinking, acting being. They then explain human thought in terms of social organization, and in so doing they relativize all systems of belief, including all religions and ultimately the body of science. In the end this relativism undermined the claims of the social determinists themselves. As Peter Berger notes (1970:42), "Relativizing analysis, in being pushed to its final consequence, bends back upon itself. The relativizers are relativized, the debunkers are debunked—indeed, relativization itself is somehow liquidated." Moving away from social determinism has not, as some anthropologists feared, led to a total paralysis of thought, but to a new flexibility and the freedom to ask questions of truth and meaning.

Another stream of thought that emerged after the rejection of theories of cultural evolution was cultural anthropology. This focused its attention upon systems of ideas and symbols. "Culture" came to mean not merely the aggregates of human thought and behavior, but both the systems of beliefs that lie behind specific ideas and actions and the symbols by which those ideas and actions are expressed. Cultures are seen as integrated wholes in which the many parts work together to meet the basic needs of their members.

Far from reducing beliefs and behavior to predetermined responses, this concept of culture makes rational human thought and choice both possible and meaningful. It has helped us to understand how people communicate with one another and build larger societies without which life would be impossible. It has also helped us to understand cultural differences, the nature of cross-cultural communication, and how societies change. These understandings are invaluable in the mission task.

Anthropologists have recently focused their attention on the fundamental assumptions that underlie explicit cultural beliefs. Each culture seems to have its own world view, or fundamental way of looking at things. If this is so, cross-cultural communication at the deepest level is possible only when we understand the world views of the people to whom we minister. It also means that people will understand the gospel from the perspective of their own world view. Consequently, missionaries must understand not only the explicit symbols but also the implicit beliefs in a culture if they are to communicate the gospel to its people with a minimum of distortion.

Finally, anthropologists have developed specialized theories that deal with specific aspects of human life, many of which are useful for missions. One of these is linguistics, which examines the structures of human languages and provides us with important insights into language learning and Bible translation. Another is psychological anthropology, which studies human personalities and their relationships to cultures and change.

In this book we will draw widely from those anthropological theories that have most relevance to the mission task. We will also seek to critique them from a Christian perspective and to integrate them with our theological understandings of the mission task.

Toward Integration

How do we integrate our theological and anthropological views of humans? We need to do this, and on a conscious level. So long as we use science in our everyday lives—in the form of electricity, automobiles, computers, modern drugs, and a thousand other of its creations—scientific assumptions will influence our theology. The same is true as we draw upon the social sciences. And if we leave these influences unexamined, our understanding of the gospel can be distorted.

Any attempt at integration must be wholistic in nature. It will not do to simply pick a few pieces of scientific thought and incorporate them into our Christian thought. If we wish to draw upon scientific insights, we must face head on the question of how science itself relates to biblical truth.

Here, in particular, we must look at scientific theories about human beings and compare these with biblical teachings about the nature of men and women, for how we look at people plays a crucial role in how we carry out the missionary task. Although we need to use scientific insights as these fit our understanding of the Bible, we must also seek an integration between what God has revealed to us through Scriptures and what he has shown to us through his creation.

The term *wholism* has many meanings today. For example, people speak of "whole earth" and "whole medicine." We will use the term in the anthropological sense of a broad, integrated understanding of human beings that deals with the full range of human existence.

The Variety and Unity of Humankind

Missionaries share with anthropologists an interest in all human beings. Most people do not, since they are concerned primarily with their own kinds of people, their own societies, or their own parts of the world. They ignore the rest of the world except when it affects them. Most of our newspapers are full of local news but carry little about the world at large. Universities offer numerous courses on the history and literature of Europe and the United States but almost none on India, Ghana, or Indonesia.

"All human beings" here has several dimensions. The term includes people in all parts of the world—China, Australia, Saudi Arabia, and Zambia. It refers also to people at all levels of society—the poor and weak just as much as the rich and powerful. It further includes people in all of history—those who lived in the past and those who will live in the future as well as those who are living today. Only within this broad picture can we begin to understand what it means to be "human."

This study of people in all their settings has made missionaries and anthropologists aware of the many differences between human beings. People differ in their biological and psychological makeup. They differ in the societies they organize and the cultures they create. As we will see, these differences raise profound philosophical and theological questions.

But missionaries, like anthropologists, are also concerned with human universals—what is common to all human beings. Clearly, humans share most physiological functions. They bear offspring, digest food, suffer illnesses, and respond to stimuli by the same biological processes. They experience joy and pain and share many of the same psychological drives. They organize societies and create cultures. Without such human universals, it would be impossible for people in one culture to understand or communicate with people in another. In fact, recognizing our common humanity with other people is the first step in building the relationship of love and trust that can bridge the deep differences that separate "us" from "them."

To these the Christian adds other human universals. All have sinned and fall short of the glory of God. And salvation is open to all through the death and resurrection of Jesus Christ. There is no other way for the rich or the poor, the American or the Chinese. Accordingly, we are concerned that all may hear and have an opportunity to respond to the gospel.

The church, too, is called to be one body of believers that transcends the differences of race and culture through the creation of a new humanity. There may be different languages but there is only one gospel. There may be different forms of worship but there is only one God. There may be different cultural settings but there is only one church.

A Wholistic Model of Humanity

We are interested in all people, but also in comprehensive ways of looking at them. We frequently take a fragmented approach to humans. When we see them as physical beings subject to the laws of motion, we can analyze what happens to their bodies when they are involved in car accidents. Or we may look at them in other ways—as biological creatures, when we examine how their bodies assimilate food, excrete wastes, reproduce, and respond to stress; as psychological beings, products of conscious and unconscious drives, feelings, and ideas; as sociocultural beings who create societies and systems of beliefs; or as sinners who need salvation.

Each of these models helps us understand something of what it means to be human. But how do we fit them all together? How do we avoid a fragmented view that breaks them up into parts and loses sight of the fact that they are whole humans—not just arms and legs, or bodies, or drives, or spirits?

Reductionism. The simplest and most common answer is reductionism. Although we may recognize many dimensions in human life, we reduce them all to one type of explanation. For example, in biological reductionism, we recognize that people find it hard to get along with one another or have times of spiritual depression, but we "explain" these in terms of biological causes such as hormonal imbalances and genetic tendencies. In psychological reductionism, we would explain them in terms of conscious or unconscious drives and human response patterns.

The danger of reductionism in missions is its overly simplistic approach to human need. We tend to see people only in terms of either physical or spiritual needs. Christ ministered to people in all their needs. Clearly, the eternal salvation of people is our highest priority, but we must bring them the whole gospel. Salvation, in the biblical sense, has to do with all dimensions of our lives.

In particular, we from the West must guard against a mechanistic reductionism. We tend to think in terms of cause and effect and believe that we can solve our problems and achieve our goals if only we have the right methods or answers. This approach has made us masters over much of nature, but it has also led us to see other people as objects that we can manipulate if we use the right formulas. In fact, even the social sciences can be seen as new "formulas" if they are misused. The gospel calls us to see people as *human beings*, and any effective mission action begins by building relationships, not programs.

A mechanistic approach also tempts us to seek to control God for our own purposes. We set the agenda and try to make God do our bidding. But Scripture always calls us away from this type of magic and toward worship and obedience. The missionary task is first the work of God, and we must follow his lead. This does not eliminate the need to plan or strategize. But it does mean that we must do so with an attitude of submission to God and a recognition that he acts when he chooses, often in ways that we cannot understand.

Stratigraphic approaches.   A second road to wholism is what Clifford Geertz has called the "stratigraphic approach." In this we simply stack different theories of human beings one upon the other, without any serious attempt to integrate them. Each model, whether theological or scientific, remains a self-contained explanation of some aspect of human life. The result is a collection of fragmentary understandings about people that are gathered by various methods of analysis. But, taken together, these do *not* give us a wholistic view of what it means to be a human (Figure 2).

We can, for instance, see starving people and introduce modern agriculture, or bring in hospitals for the sick, or build schools for the ignorant. But in so doing we often overlook the fact that these factors are all interrelated—that knowledge can prevent illnesses and help

FIGURE 2

A Stratigraphic Approach to Human Beings

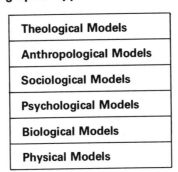

Theological Models
Anthropological Models
Sociological Models
Psychological Models
Biological Models
Physical Models

people to grow food, and that adequate food and health is needed for them to study. And we fail to tie starvation, illness, and ignorance to their roots in human sin. We also fail to see how they can lead to further sin.

Here, again, missionaries from the West must be on guard, for we grow up in a society that draws a sharp line between religion and science, between the supernatural and natural. This distinction is Greek, not biblical. It has led us to a stratified approach that explains material order in terms of autonomous natural laws and relegates God's activities to the miraculous. It separates human spirits from their bodies and makes a sharp distinction between evangelism and social concern. Evangelical missionaries too often see themselves as ministering in one or the other of these spheres. Doctors, teachers, and agricultural workers often see themselves as dealing with physical needs, and preachers often limit their concern to eternal salvation.

But broken, suffering, and lost people listen to doctors, teachers, and agricultural workers because these meet them where they hurt. The preacher's message often seems irrelevant to them at the moment. Consequently, they accept a secular science divorced from theology and reject Christianity. As John Stott points out, we must see humans as soul-bodies. We are not one or the other, but both in relationship to each other.

A stratigraphic approach to theology and science secularizes much of our lives by leaving them outside of theological critique. In the long run, this approach also undermines theology. Like it or not, so long as we use the benefits of science we absorb its views of reality, often uncritically. We need to deal consciously with the relationship of theological and scientific understandings of humans if we want to maintain our theological convictions.

Toward wholism. A wholistic approach to the understanding of humans cannot be gained by reductionist or stratified models. We must learn what theology and the sciences have to teach us about people and weave these insights into a comprehensive understanding of humans as whole beings, realizing that our knowledge is always imperfect and incomplete.

Such an approach must recognize the contribution different studies can make to our understanding of people. Anthropology does so in the social sciences by showing how the various insights each discipline brings relate to each other (Figure 3). For example, the physical characteristics of humans affect the cultures they create. If they were ten feet tall or if there were only one sex, their cultures and societies would be different.

On the other hand, cultures mold people's physical characteristics. Humans are remarkably imaginative in changing their bodies to fit their tastes. They drill holes in their ears, lips, cheeks, and teeth to support ornaments; bind heads and feet to change their shapes; put on glasses and hearing aids to improve their perceptions; paint and tattoo their skin, nails, and hair; cut their bodies and shape their hair in a thousand ways. Cultures also influence the ideas people have about health and beauty. In the West, where slim bodies are considered attractive, women diet to stay slender; in Tonga in the South Pacific, where beauty is measured by bulk, a woman eats to maintain a full figure.

Similarly the interaction of models must be studied in order to determine how people's biological systems affect them psychologi-

FIGURE 3

An Integrated Approach to the Study of Humans

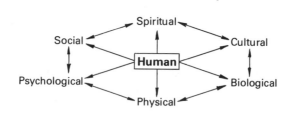

From Paul G. Hiebert, "Anthropological Tools for Missionaries" (Singapore: Haggai Institute, 1983), p. 1.

cally, how their psychological systems affect them physically, and how both affect and are affected by their culture.

While anthropology has worked toward an integrated view of human beings from the viewpoint of the sciences, we as Christians must ask a further question. How do scientific models of human beings relate to our theological understandings of them? Unfortunately, during the last century the relationship between scientists and theologians has often been one of confrontation. In part this has been due to reductionist approaches to knowledge. Both the sciences and theology have tended to claim a total and comprehensive view of reality, and each therefore ignored the other. We are becoming increasingly aware that reality is far more complex than our understandings of it—at best we can look at it from different perspectives. Like complementary sets of blueprints of the same building, different bodies of knowledge show us different aspects of reality. The sciences provide us with insights into various structures of empirical reality. Theology provides us with an overall picture of the building, the builder, and key events in its history.

Complementarity does not mean there will always be agreement between the sciences and theology. When disagreements do arise, we need to reexamine our science and our theology in the light of the Scriptures and creation. Since God is the source of both, proper understanding of each perspective will not lead to conflict.

The Missionary Task

> All authority has been given to me both in heaven and on earth. Therefore, as you go make disciples of all peoples by baptizing them in the name of the Father and the Son and the Holy Spirit, and by teaching them to observe everything which I have told you. And behold, I always will be with you to the end of your days and to the end of history (Matt. 28:18–20, trans. Hans Kasdorf).
>
> As the Father has sent me, so I am sending you (John 20:21).

With these words Jesus commissioned us to be his witnesses around the world. The Christian church was once largely in the Middle East and the West, with small pockets in Southwest India and in China for a time. Today the church is found in all parts of the world and is growing most rapidly in many of the younger churches in Africa, Asia, Latin America, and the Pacific Islands. Moreover, there is a growing interest in missions in these churches of the so-called Two-Thirds World. Missionaries from Korea are serving in Los Angeles, those from India in Europe, and those from one part of Africa in other parts of that continent. In fact, the most rapid growth in the missionary force today comes from these young churches.

We can, therefore, no longer equate missionaries with Westerners. When we use the word *missionary* in this study, we mean anyone who communicates the gospel in a cross-cultural setting, whether he or she is an African serving in India, or a Latin American in Spain. The illustrations used are slanted toward a Western audience, because this book will be used largely in the West. But the principles examined apply equally to missionaries from the Two-Thirds World. The reader need only think of local examples to replace the Western ones that are given.

Gospel and Culture

Missionaries face many dilemmas, none more difficult than those that deal with the relationship of the gospel to human cultures. Such questions are not new. In the Book of Acts, serious questions arose when the Gentiles began to enter the church not by ones and twos but by the thousands. Did they have to become Jewish proselytes and adopt such Jewish practices as circumcision and such taboos as the proscription of pork? If not, which of the Old Testament teachings should the church follow, and which parts of Jewish culture could be discarded?

The first great church council (see Acts 15) was called to answer questions that arose out of the missionary outreach of the early church. The same questions arise today wherever Christian missions are successful. So long as there are no converts, it is easy to continue the work. We can preach, teach, broadcast, and hand out tracts, without having to deal with new converts. But when people do become Christians in other cultures, we face numerous decisions. Can they keep several wives? Should they give food to their ancestors? And what should they do about their old religious customs? Should we teach them our rituals, or are these mainly Western? Should we as missionaries live like these people? Can we in good conscience participate in their songs and dances, or do these have non-Christian connotations?

Most of these questions have to do with the relationship between

29

the gospel and human cultures. On the one hand, the gospel belongs to no culture. It is God's revelation of himself and his acts to all people. On the other hand, it must always be understood and expressed within human cultural forms. There is no way to communicate it apart from human thought patterns and languages. Moreover, God has chosen to use humans as the primary means for making himself known to other humans. Even when he chose to reveal himself to us, he did so most fully by becoming a man who lived within the context of human history and a particular culture.

Before we can analyze the relationship of the gospel to human cultures, we need to look more closely at what those cultural patterns encompass.

The Concept of Culture

"Culture" is an ordinary English word. When we say, "She is a cultured person," we mean that she listens to Bach, Beethoven, and Brahms and knows which of the many forks and spoons to use at a banquet. Or we say, "Henry has no culture at all," meaning that he does not behave in a "civilized" way. When we use the word in this way, we are equating it with the customs of the elite members of a society—the rich, educated, and powerful. Implicitly, we assume that ordinary people, particularly the poor and marginal (those who are members simultaneously of two or more different cultures and do not identify fully with any of them), have no "culture" except as they emulate the elite.

Since anthropologists use the word in a different and more technical sense, there is considerable debate among them as to how the term *culture* should be defined. For our purposes, however, we will begin with a simple definition that we can modify later as our understanding of the concept grows. We will define culture as "the more or less integrated systems of ideas, feelings, and values and their associated patterns of behavior and products shared by a group of people who organize and regulate what they think, feel, and do."

Dimensions of Culture

Let us look at this definition and unpack some of its meanings. Note first that culture relates to "ideas, feelings, and values." These are the three basic dimensions of culture (Figure 4).

The cognitive dimension. This aspect of culture has to do with the knowledge shared by members of a group or society. Without shared knowledge, communication and community life are impossible.

FIGURE 4

The Three Dimensions of Culture

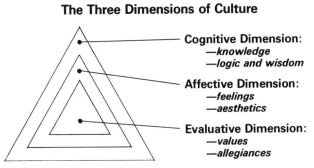

Cognitive Dimension:
—*knowledge*
—*logic and wisdom*

Affective Dimension:
—*feelings*
—*aesthetics*

Evaluative Dimension:
—*values*
—*allegiances*

Knowledge provides the conceptual content of a culture. It arranges the people's experiences into categories and organizes these categories into larger systems of knowledge. For example, Americans divide the rainbow into six basic colors: red, orange, yellow, green, blue, and violet. Telugus in South India see just as many colors, but divide the rainbow into two basic colors: *erras,* or hot colors (from red through orange); and *patsas,* or cold colors (from pale yellow through violet).

Knowledge also tells people what exists and what does not. For instance, most Westerners believe in atoms, electrons, and gravity, although they have never seen them. South Indian villagers, on the other hand, believe in fierce *rakshasas,* spirits with big heads, bulging eyes, fangs, and long wild hair, which inhabit trees and rocky places and jump on unwary travelers at night. Not all Indians believe in *rakshasas,* but those who do not must think about them, for they exist as a category within the culture. Similarly, atheists in the West are forced to deal with the concept of "God."

Cultural knowledge is more than the categories we use to sort out reality. It includes the assumptions and beliefs we make about reality, the nature of the world, and how it works. Our culture teaches us how to build and sail a boat, how to raise a crop, how to cook a meal, how to run a government, and how to relate to the ancestors, spirits, and gods.

Because our culture provides us with the fundamental ingredients of our thoughts, we find it almost impossible to break away from its grasp. Even our language reflects and reinforces our cultural way of thinking. Moreover, much of this influence is implicit; we are not even aware of it. Like colored glasses, culture affects how we perceive the world, without our being conscious of its influence. Only when the lenses become dirty, or we put on other glasses, are we aware of their power to shape the way we see the world.

Cultural knowledge is stored in many ways. Many of us store information in print. We turn to newspapers, books, billboards, cereal boxes, and even sky writing to retrieve it. Rarely are we aware of just how dependent we are on writing. Deprived of it, we soon starve intellectually, for we use so few other ways to store information. Most of us in the West know by memory only a few Bible verses and the first lines of a few hymns.

Although print is excellent for storing knowledge, it is not the only means. We often label those who cannot read "illiterate" and thus ignorant. The fact is, nonliterate societies have a great deal of knowledge and store it in other ways. They use stories, poems, songs, proverbs, riddles, and other forms of oral tradition that are easily remembered. They also enact dramas, dances, and rituals that can be seen.

This distinction between oral and literate societies and the ways they store and transmit information is of vital importance for missionaries. Since missionaries have generally been literate people, they have often misunderstood oral societies and their forms of communication. Consequently, they have generally concluded that the most effective way to plant churches in the mission field is to teach people how to read and write.

While literacy and education are important in the long run, particularly for preparing high-level church leaders, they are by no means the only or even the most effective ways of planting churches in oral societies. People do not have to learn to read to become Christians or to grow in faith. For example, P. Y. Luke and J. B. Carmen (1968) found that Christians in South India store their beliefs in songs—in what the authors call "lyric theology." In church and at home they often sing by memory ten verses of one song and fifteen of another. They also use dramas presented in an open square. While Hindu villagers soon become tired of preaching and leave, they will stay half the night to see a drama to its end. Christians in other parts of the world have made effective use of bardic performances, dances, proverbs, and other oral methods for communicating the gospel.

The affective dimension.   Culture also has to do with the feelings people have—with their attitudes, notions of beauty, tastes in food and dress, likes and dislikes, and ways of enjoying themselves or experiencing sorrow. People in one culture like their food hot, in another sweet or bland. Members of some societies learn to express their emotions and may be aggressive and bellicose; in others they learn to be self-controlled and calm. Some religions encourage the use of meditation, mysticism, and drugs in order to achieve inner peace and tranquility. Others stress ecstasy through frenzied songs, dances, and self-torture. In short, cultures vary greatly in how they deal with the emotional sides of human life.

The affective dimension of culture is reflected in most areas of life. It is seen in standards of beauty and taste in clothes, food, houses, furniture, cars, and other cultural products. Imagine for a moment a culture in which everything is only functional. All clothes would be the same drab color and style. All houses would look the same.

Emotions also play an important part in human relationships, in our notions of etiquette and fellowship. We communicate love, hate, scorn, and a hundred other attitudes by our facial expressions, tones of voice, and gestures.

Feelings find particular outlet in what we call "expressive culture"— in our art, literature, music, dance, and drama. These we create not for utilitarian purposes but for our own enjoyment and emotional release. This is obvious whether we attend a rock concert or an opera.

The evaluative dimension. Each culture also has values by which it judges human relationships to be moral or immoral. It ranks some occupations high and others low, some ways of eating proper and other ways unacceptable.

Value judgments can be broken down into three types. First, each culture evaluates cognitive beliefs to determine whether they are true or false. For example, Europeans in the Middle Ages believed that malaria was caused by a noxious substance in the air. Today they attribute it to sporozoan parasites. In other cultures people believe that malaria is caused by spirits that live around the village. In each of these cases the culture determines what people should accept as true.

Each cultural system also judges the emotional expressions of human life. It teaches people what is beauty and what is ugliness, what to love and what to hate. In some cultures people are encouraged to sing in sharp, piercing voices, in others to sing in deep, mellow tones. Even within the same culture likes and dislikes vary greatly according to settings and subcultures. Tuxedos and formal gowns are out of place at a skating party, and Country and Western music generally is inappropriate at a funeral.

Finally, each culture judges values and determines right and wrong. For instance, in North American culture it is worse to tell a lie than to hurt people's feelings. In other cultures, however, it is more important to encourage other people, even if it means bending the truth somewhat.

Each culture has its own moral code and its own culturally defined sins. It judges some acts to be righteous and others to be immoral. In traditional Indian society it is a sin for a woman to eat before her husband. If she does so, a village proverb says, she will be reborn in her next life as a snake. In China a person must venerate his or her ancestors by feeding them regularly. Not to do so is sin.

Each culture also has its own highest values and primary allegiances, each its own culturally defined goals. One pressures people to make economic success their highest goal; another assigns top priority to honor and fame, political power, the good will of the ancestors, or the favor of God.

These three dimensions—ideas, feelings, and values—are important in understanding the nature of human cultures, and we will refer back to them frequently.

The gospel in all three dimensions.   Missionaries should keep the three dimensions of culture in mind in their work, for the gospel has to do with all of them. On the cognitive level it has to do with knowledge and truth—with an understanding and acceptance of biblical and theological information and with a knowledge of God. It is on this level that we are concerned with questions of truth and orthodoxy.

The gospel also includes feelings. We feel awe and mystery in God's presence, guilt or shame for our sins, gladness for our salvation, and comfort in the fellowship of God's people.

Ultimately, the gospel has to do with values and allegiances. Jesus proclaimed the Good News of the kingdom of God, in which he rules in righteousness. His laws stand in contrast to those of our earthly kingdoms, and his perfection rules in judgment on our cultural sins. Jesus also calls us to follow him. To be a Christian is to give our ultimate allegiance to him. Anything else is idolatry.

All three cultural dimensions are essential in conversion. We need to know that Jesus is the Son of God, but knowledge alone is not enough. Even Satan must acknowledge the deity of Christ. We also need feelings of affection and loyalty toward him. But feelings, too, are not enough. Both knowledge and feelings must lead us to worship and submission, to obeying and following Jesus as the Lord of our lives.

All three must also be present in our Christian lives. We need both good theology—a knowledge of the truth—and emotions of awe and excitement. But these should lead to discipleship and to the fruits of the Spirit: love, joy, peace, and so on. Ironically, in the West we have reduced these to "feelings." In the Bible they are commitments and values. That is why Paul can command us to love, to rejoice, and to be at peace. In Christianity we are called to give ourselves to God and to others. Understandings and feelings often follow later.

We missionaries and church leaders tend to stress the cognitive aspects of the gospel. We are concerned with knowledge of the Bible and with theology. After all, this is the area in which we have received our training. Consequently, the methods we use, such as preaching and teaching, emphasize information and reason.

We often fail, however, to understand the importance of feelings and attitudes in the everyday lives of most people. Human beings spend much of their free time and resources in the pursuit of excitement and thrills or affection and tranquility—more perhaps than they do in gaining knowledge. They do almost anything to avoid pain, fear, and grief.

Emotions also play a crucial role in the decision making of most people. They choose their clothes, cook their food, and buy their cars as much by feelings as by reason. If this is true, we must present the knowledge of the gospel with feeling, so that people will believe and follow. We must teach the truth in a way that recognizes that many respond to the gospel not because they are rationally persuaded, but because they are freed from fears or experience forgiveness and joy in salvation. And we must persuade people to respond.

In the church we need good preaching and teaching so that young Christians will grow to maturity. We also need to provide ways for Christians to express themselves through music, art, literature, drama, dance, rituals, and festivals. Too often Protestant Christianity has had little appeal to Africans and Asians because it appears joyless, color-less, and drab in comparison to the religions they already have.

Our ultimate goal, however, is discipleship. We do not proclaim the gospel simply to inform people or to make them feel good. We are calling them to become followers of Jesus Christ.

Manifestations of Culture

Another part of our definition of culture involves "behavior and products." These are the manifestations of culture that we can see, hear, or experience through our other senses.

Behavior. To a great extent people are taught how to behave by their culture. In North America they learn to shake hands, to eat with their forks, to drive on the right side of the road, and to compete with one another for better grades or more money. In Japan they are taught to bow, to take off their shoes at the door, to sit on mats on the floor, to eat with chopsticks, and to assist one another in school and work.

Not all behavior, however, is culturally molded. In formal situations behavior is precisely defined. For example, at a banquet our clothes, behavior, and speech are carefully circumscribed. But everyday life is usually less formal, and we are allowed to choose from a range of permissible behaviors. Our choices reflect the occasion (swimming suits are out of place in the classroom) and our personalities. They also reflect our decisions of the moment, which are influenced by the economic, political, social, and religious circumstances of our lives.

In a sense our culture encompasses the set of rules governing the games of life that we and the members of our society play. Like players in most games, we often try to "bend the rules" a little and get away with it. If we are caught, we are punished; but if not, we gain some advantage or sense of achievement.

All cultures have ways to enforce their rules, such as gossip, ostracism, and force, but not all violators are punished. A society may ignore some transgressors, particularly those who are important or powerful. Or it may be unable to enforce a specific rule, particularly when a great many people break it. In such cases cultural ordinances may die, and the culture changes accordingly.

People in the same culture do not always agree on what the rules are. Like kids in a sandlot baseball game, they argue for one set of rules or another. In the end, those who can make their rules stick become the leaders and control the game to their own advantage.

Products.   Culture also includes material objects—houses, baskets, canoes, masks, carts, cars, computers, and the like. People live in nature and must adapt to it or mold and use it for their own purposes. They construct huts as shelter from the rain and cold, boats to cross the water, and hoes and digging sticks to farm the land. They sew clothes to keep warm and make weapons to kill game or to war with one another. They cut down forests, build roads, dam rivers, and tunnel through mountains. In the end, as their actions alter the environment itself, they in turn are forced to change their cultures.

People in simple tribal societies live in an environment largely formed by nature. Their culture may teach them how to make weapons to hunt game and how to build brush shelters and weave clothes to protect them from the elements. For the most part, however, they have to adapt to nature. In complex industrial societies most of a people's environment may be culturally molded. Electricity blurs the distinction between day and night; cars, planes, radios, and phones break the barriers of geographic distance; furnaces and air conditioners create artificial climates; and phonograph records freeze moments in history.

Material culture includes more than human responses to the environment. People make many things for their own use and to express their creative abilities. In simple nomadic cultures such things are few. In modern societies the number of different objects made is staggering. For example, a single Boeing 747 has more than 4,500,000 parts, and an average hardware store has more than 15,000 different types of objects for sale.

Human behavior and material objects are readily observed. Consequently, they are important doors for our study of a culture. We can begin our task by examining the things people make, who makes them and how, who uses them and for what purposes, what value the people place on their creations, and how they dispose of them. We can observe how people behave in different situations and with different people. In fact, if we do not take note of the behavior and products when we enter a new culture, they soon become so commonplace that we no longer notice them.

Symbol Systems

A third part of our definition is the word *associated*. Human behavior and products are not independent parts of a culture; they are closely linked to the ideas, feelings, and values that lie within its people. This association of a specific meaning, emotion, or value with a certain behavior or cultural product is called a symbol (Figure 5). In North America, for example, sticking out a tongue at someone signifies ridicule and rejection; in Tibet it is a symbol of greeting and friendship (Firth 1973:313).

In one sense a culture is made up of many sets of symbols. For instance, speech, writing, traffic signs, money, postage stamps, sounds such as sirens and bells, and smells such as perfumes are but a few of the sets of symbols in Western cultures. Even dress, in addition to its utilitarian value as protection and warmth, conveys feelings and meanings. In the United States a tuxedo or evening gown speaks of a formal occasion, just as jeans indicate informality. The uniforms of waiters and airline pilots announce their professions, just as the insignias of military personnel show rank.

FIGURE 5

Symbols Link Meanings, Feelings, and Values to Forms

A Symbol

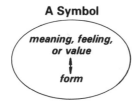

Form and meaning. The symbolic link between forms and meanings (or emotions or values) is complex and varied. Sometimes it is purely arbitrary. A company may choose to use a triple circle as its logo, or a college may make the husky its mascot.

Most cultural symbols, however, must be understood within their historical and cultural contexts. For example, the Greeks associated the word *polys* with the meaning "full" or "many." Over the centuries, as other languages evolved or borrowed from Greek, they kept that basic association. Today's English speakers use words like "polychromatic," "polygamy," and "polyhedron" that are, in part, products of their symbolic history.

Similarly, once created, symbols become parts of cultural systems. Rarely do they stand alone. They acquire meanings not only by the definitions we give to them, but also by their relationship to other symbols of the same set. For example, when we think of the word *red* we do so in relationship to all the other color categories we have. Thus, when in English we say "red," we also mean "not orange, not yellow, not purple," and so on. Symbols, therefore, carry both positive and negative meanings.

Many symbols are used in varied settings and so acquire a number of different but related meanings. For instance, we say of a house, "It is *red* [color]"; of a person, "He's a *Red* [political ideology]"; of ourselves, "I saw *red* [emotion of anger]"; of our friend, "Was he ever *red* [emotion of embarrassment]"; and of the stoplight, "It was *red* [command to stop]." These multivocal symbols help to integrate a culture by linking together various domains of thought.

Finally, for symbols to be part of a culture, they must be shared by a human community. Each of us has personal symbols that we use to communicate with ourselves. For example, we devise codes to remind ourselves of what we must do. But symbols become culture only when a group of people associate the same meanings with specific forms.

It is this shared nature of cultural symbols that makes human communication possible. We cannot transmit our thoughts into the heads of others. We must first code them into symbols that others understand. Although they receive only the forms of these symbols (our behavior, speech, or products), they can infer our meanings because they share with us a common set of symbols (Figure 6).

Because cultural symbols are shared and because they continue over time, people can transmit their knowledge and feelings from one to another and from one generation to the next. It is this that accounts for both stability and change in cultures. We are the recipients of a culture developed by previous generations. Although we begin with it, we in turn change it and transmit this modified form to the next

FIGURE 6

Symbols Make Communication Possible by Turning Meanings into Forms

generation. This transition from one generation to another also accounts for the cumulative nature of culture. New information is added and new products created, and it is important to remember that cultures are both social and historical in nature.

The fusion of form and meaning. The link between form and meaning in some symbols is so close that the two cannot be differentiated. This is often true with historical symbols. For Muslims, Mecca has strong religious meanings because it was the birthplace of Muhammed. Similarly, for Christians the cross stands for Christ's death, for the simple reason that Christ was crucified on a cross. We may choose other symbols to speak of that death, but we cannot change the facts of history.

Forms and meanings may also be equated in ritual symbols. For instance, worshipers in some cultures use images simply as forms to remind them of their gods. In other cultures they believe that their gods inhabit the idol. But worshipers in yet other cultures equate the two—the idol *is* their god. Many Western Christians differentiate forms and meanings in their rituals. The Lord's Supper reminds them of Jesus' last meal with his disciples, and the bread and the wine *represent* symbolically Christ's body and blood. They say, "We go to church *in order to* worship." In other words, the act of going to church is not itself an act of worship. Worship is an inner feeling they have in church. Other Christians do not make such a distinction. To them, the Eucharist *is* to eat with Christ, and the bread and wine are seen as his body and blood. They say, "In going to church we *are* worshiping." They do not separate the outer act of going to church from the inner thoughts and feelings that led them to do so.

People in the West, in particular, tend to separate forms and meanings, whereas traditional and peasant cultures tend to equate them. Consequently, rituals often have little meaning in the West, although they are vital to the lives of people in other parts of the world. We need to recognize this as Western missionaries, lest we misunderstand the place of rituals in the lives of the people we serve.

As we shall see in chapters 5 and 6, it is important that missionaries understand the nature of cultural symbols, not only when we translate the Bible and its message into a new language, but also when we plant the church and contextualize its symbols and rituals within a new cultural setting.

Patterns and Systems

Cultures are more than random assortments of symbols that people use piecemeal. As noted in our definition, symbols are used in specific ways. For example, North Americans use forks when they eat most foods. This association of a specific symbol with a particular use or context is called a cultural trait, groupings of which are linked to one another in larger patterns sometimes referred to as cultural complexes. When dining, Americans use forks together with spoons, knives, plates, cups, glasses, chairs, tables, and often linen. Moreover, the silverware must be used in certain ways, depending on the occasion. In contrast to this, Indians use their fingers and eat from brass, aluminum, or leaf plates while seated on the floor.

Not all behavior, however, is patterned. When a teacher drops her book or a student slips on the ice, most likely these are accidents and not prescribed by culture. Moreover, some patterns are personal and have no significance or meaning in a society. One individual may eat only sour foods or dress only in brown. Cultural traits and complexes, on the other hand, are patterns that have meaning for the members of a given society.

The practice of some traits may be limited to a single person. A king, for example, may be the only one allowed to wear a crown or sit on a throne, but even these customs are understood by others in his court. Many traits, however, are practiced by specific groups of people within a society. Baseball players, secretaries, college students, and even missionaries have their own patterns of cultural behavior. So do women and men. Finally, some traits are practiced by most or all people in a society. For example, in the United States, everyone is expected to wear clothes in public, and, with few exceptions, those who do not will be punished.

It is not always easy to distinguish between patterned and unpatterned human behavior, because cultures are constantly changing as new traits are added and old ones dropped. Accidental or creative acts may be copied by others and so incorporated in the culture. An example of this is the American missionary in India who decided to treat the American missionary children in his area to a Christmas celebration. Dressed as Santa Claus and riding a bicycle, he went to their homes with gifts. Unfortunately, on the way he slipped in the mud while crossing an irrigation ditch. Each year thereafter, the children waited at the ditch to see him fall, and he never disappointed them!

Cultural traits and complexes are organized around systems of beliefs. For instance, the medical system in the West includes a great many beliefs about the nature of diseases and their cures, about the nature of healers as professionals, and about the way health care should be organized. These beliefs provide doctors, nurses, and patients with blueprints for their behavior and for the kinds of hospitals they build. On the other hand, by acting in the culturally prescribed ways, they reinforce their own systems of belief.

In complex societies, such as the United States or Canada, it is hard to speak of a single culture. Some beliefs and practices may be accepted by all, such as driving on the right side of the road. But the differences are also significant. In such societies it is useful to speak of "cultural frames." A cultural frame is a social setting that has its own subculture—its own beliefs, rules for behavior, material products, symbols, structures, and settings. For example, a bank is a subculture that has its own information, feelings, and values, and corresponding symbols, property, and patterns of behavior. Similarly, supermarkets, hospitals, and churches are cultural frames. The ways people think and relate, their values and goals and the products they use, vary considerably from one of these institutions to another.

In simple tribal societies the number of cultural frames is few and the differences between them minimal. Among the Arunta of the Australian desert, men hunt and have secret rituals that no women can attend, and women share certain other activities by themselves. Much of the time, however, men and women are together in the camp, interacting within the same cultural frame.

In modern cities, on the other hand, there are many frames, and the differences between them are great. Religious, social, political, educational, economic, aesthetic, and recreational institutions form their own subcultures. In fact, there are even significant cultural differences between grade schools, high schools, colleges, and seminaries and to a lesser extent between one college or seminary and another.

People in urban societies take part in different institutions, but find their primary identity in only one or two of them. An individual may be a regular customer at one supermarket and a particular bank and occasionally attend an opera or professional baseball game. But his or her deepest commitment may be to a job as teacher or businessperson or doctor, to a role at home as mother or father, to a church as deacon or choir director or lay person, or even to a bowling team or yacht club. It is here that the individual will invest time and seek to gain community recognition.

The diversity of cultural frames in modern societies reflects their growing complexity and the increasing specialization of their institutions. In simple societies many of the functions of life such as instructing the young, raising food, caring for the sick, and performing religious rituals are carried out by the family and by groups of relatives. In complex societies these tasks are given over to schools, agribusinesses, hospitals, and churches. But such diversity also reflects the growing social hierarchy in these societies. The cultural frames of the rich are vastly different from those of the poor, as different as a country club is from a ghetto bar, or a corporate penthouse office is from the face of a coal mine.

Although modern societies are made up of astonishingly diverse subcultures, they are larger systems held together by webs of communication and transportation, by ties of trade and common government, and by networks of social relationships.

Cultural Integration

Cultures are held together not only by economic, social, and political organization, but also—at the deepest levels—by fundamental beliefs and values shared by the people. Much of the knowledge of a culture is explicit. In other words, there are members of the culture who can tell us about it. But behind such knowledge are basic assumptions about the nature of things that are largely implicit. Like foundations, they hold up the culture, yet they remain largely out of sight. Those who challenge these assumptions are considered crazy, heretical, or criminal, for if these underpinnings are shaken, the stability of the whole culture is threatened. (See Figure 7.)

We can illustrate cultural integration by investigating our practices of sitting and sleeping. For the most part, North Americans try to avoid sitting on the floor. In an auditorium they find small platforms on which to sit. Latecomers who find no vacant seats stand along the walls or leave. At home, large amounts are spent to purchase special platforms suitable for various rooms and occasions: couches, recliners, rockers, dining-room chairs, bar stools, and lawn chairs.

North Americans also try to avoid sleeping on the floor. When they travel, they are afraid to be caught at night without a bed in a private room. So, in addition to travel reservations, they make certain they have bookings in hotels. Interestingly enough, they make no such reservations for meals—they assume they can find food somewhere or, if necessary, do without. Caught in an airport at night, they try to sleep

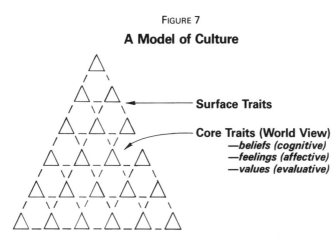

FIGURE 7

A Model of Culture

From Paul G. Hiebert, "Anthropological Tools for Missionaries" (Singapore: Haggai Institute, 1983), p. 4.

slumped in a chair rather than stretched out on the carpeted floor, since they would rather be dignified than comfortable.

In short, platforms are seen everywhere in the United States. People sit on them, sleep on them, build their houses on them, store their goods on them, and even put fences around them for their babies. Why this obsession with platforms? Traditional Japanese sit comfortably on mats on the floor. And Indians know that all you need for a good night's rest is a sheet to keep you clean and a flat place to lie down—and the world is full of flat places: airport lounges, train aisles, sidewalks, and parks.

Why then, do North Americans insist on sitting on chairs and sleeping on beds? Most of them have not given much thought to the matter. If they did, they might argue that these are the most "natural" and comfortable ways to sit and sleep. But this is not true. Rather, their behavior is linked to a fundamental attitude they have about floors, namely, that floors are "dirty." And because dirt is bad, they must avoid contact with floors as much as possible.

This assumption also helps us to understand other patterns of our behavior. If a boy drops a potato chip on the floor and then pops it into his mouth, his mother is upset. The moment the chip touches the floor, no matter how clean the floor, the chip turns into dirt. And when people enter the house, they keep their shoes on. After all, the floor is already dirty.

Is it possible to build a culture on the assumption that floors are clean? We would sit and sleep on cushions on the floor and leave our shoes at the door. We would let our children play on the floor. This, in fact, is the pattern of traditional Japanese culture.

"More or less."   Cultures and cultural frames are never fully integrated. Consequently, we must use such qualifiers as "more or less" and "tend to be." Human beings are creatures of curiosity and explore different areas of the world around them, not only to meet personal needs but also to understand them. They develop theories about nature, the weather, diseases, crops, fishing, birth, human origins, and why the sun crosses the heaven. They also seem to need some measure of consistency between these theories—a harmony found partly in the underlying world view. But human beings and their beliefs are never fully consistent. There are gaps and internal contradictions in their theories, just as there are in their behavior.

There is another way in which cultural integration is incomplete, particularly in complex societies. Groups and individuals in the same society may hold different theories. The rich, for instance, see things differently from the poor, or one ethnic group from another. There are differences between the folk beliefs of the common people and theories of the specialists regarding religion and medicine. There are also disagreements among specialists. For instance, an agnostic scientist and a Christian minister may offer different explanations of the same event.

A. F. C. Wallace (1956) points out that the differences in beliefs from one individual to another in modern complex societies are so great that we must talk about personal, rather than cultural, world views. People in these societies often experience a crisis of belief when they have no group assurance that what they think is right. When everyone disagrees with them, they begin to question their own convictions.

World views help us to understand cultural stability and resistance to change. In tribal and peasant societies, people generally share fundamental beliefs and assumptions that are constantly reinforced by the group. They also teach their world view to their children and so assure its perpetuation. Change is often resisted in such settings, because the whole society is unified in its beliefs. Individuals who adopt new ideas are ostracized. Consequently the first converts to Christianity are often rejected by their people.

Internal contradictions, on the other hand, often lead to changes in world view. When these are minor, the people may revise their beliefs or modify their behavior. If a tribesman finds that his amulet no longer protects him from danger, he throws it away and finds a new one. A modern woman faced with gas shortages may buy a smaller car or take the bus. Similarly, medieval scientists believed the sun revolved around the earth and made constant adjustments to the Ptolemaic system of astronomy to make it fit their experimental findings.

Integration is limited by the fact that all cultures are constantly changing, some rapidly, and some more slowly. New traits are added, and in time their impact is felt on other areas of culture. Meanwhile, other traits are dropped. All these changes call for a new cultural synthesis.

Inconsistencies, competing theories and changes in customs undermine the internal harmony of a culture, but as long as a minimal cultural integration exists, organized social life is possible.

World view. People perceive the world differently because they make different assumptions about reality. For example, most Westerners assume that external to themselves is a real world made of lifeless matter. People in South and Southeast Asia, however, believe that this external world does not really exist; it is an illusion of the mind. And tribal peoples around the world see the earth as a living organism to which they must relate.

Taken together, the basic assumptions about reality which lie behind the beliefs and behavior of a culture are sometimes called a world view (Figure 8). Because these assumptions are taken for granted, they are generally unexamined and therefore largely implicit. But they are reinforced by the deepest of feelings, and anyone who challenges them becomes the object of vehement attack. People believe that the world really is the way they see it. Rarely are they aware of the fact that the way they see it is molded by their world view.

There are basic assumptions underlying each of the three dimensions of culture. Existential assumptions provide a culture with the fundamental cognitive structures people use to explain reality. These structures define what things are "real." In the West they include atoms, viruses, and gravity. In South India they include *rakshasas, apsaras, bhutams,* and other spirit beings. In central Africa they include ancestors who after death have continued to live among the people.

Existential or cognitive assumptions also furnish people with their concepts of time, space, and other worlds. For instance, we in the West assume that time is linear and uniform. It runs like a straight line from a beginning to an end, and it can be divided into uniform intervals such as years, days, minutes, seconds, and nanoseconds. Other cultures see time as cyclical: a never-ending repetition of summer and winter; day and night; birth, death, and rebirth; and growth and decay. Still others see it as a pendulum. It goes forward and it goes backward, it moves at different rates, and sometimes it stops moving altogether. This, in fact, corresponds in some ways with our personal experience

FIGURE 8

A Model of World View

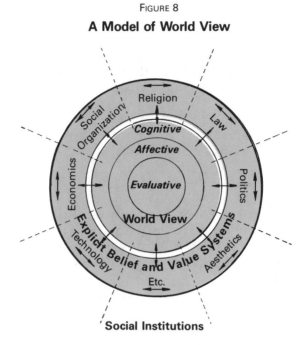

Social Institutions

of time. A good movie is over too quickly, and a boring lecture drags on forever. And sometimes, when we have deep experiences of worship of God, time seems to stop.

Cognitive assumptions perform many other tasks. They shape the mental categories people use for thinking; they play a vital role in determining the kinds of authority people trust and the types of logic they use. Taken together these assumptions give order and meaning to life and reality.

Affective assumptions underlie the notions of beauty, style, and aesthetics found in a culture. They influence the people's tastes in music, art, dress, food, and architecture as well as the ways they feel towards each other and about life in general. For example, in cultures influenced by Theravada Buddhism, life is equated with suffering. Even joyful moments create suffering, for one realizes that they will come to an end. There is, therefore, little use in striving for a better life here on earth. By contrast, in the United States after World War II, many people were optimistic. They believed that with hard work and planning they could achieve a happy, comfortable existence during their lifetime.

Evaluative assumptions provide the standards people use to make judgments, including their criteria for determining truth and error, likes and dislikes, and right and wrong. For instance, North Americans assume that honesty means telling people the way things are, even if doing so hurts their feelings. In other countries, it means telling people what they want to hear, for it is more important that they be encouraged than for them to know the truth.

Evaluative assumptions also determine the priorities of a culture, and thereby shape the desires and allegiances of the people. During the past century North Americans have placed a high value on technology and material goods, and business is their central activity. Their status is determined largely by their wealth, and their culture is focused on economic themes. The skylines of modern American cities are dominated by bank and insurance buildings. In the Indian countryside, on the other hand, people place a high value on religious purity, and the greatest honor is given to members of the priestly caste. Their culture is organized around religious themes, and temples are the centers of their villages. Medieval towns, with their kings, vassals, lords, and knights, focused on power, conquests, and politics. Castles and forts were their dominant structures.

The fact that different cultures have different standards of morality creates many cross-cultural misunderstandings. In North America the cardinal sin among Christians is sexual immorality, and missionaries from that part of the world have placed a great deal of emphasis on proper sexual behavior. Those who went to South Asia, however, often did not know that a cardinal sin in that part of the world is losing one's temper. They were unaware of the consequences when they became impatient or angry with Indian servants, students, and pastors.

The fact that moral systems differ from culture to culture raises many difficult questions in missions. How do we deal with the existing ethical beliefs of the people, and how do we introduce biblical concepts of sin? What, in fact, is the biblical view of sin, and to what extent are we in danger of forcing our own cultural values on others?

Moreover, what happens when we do not live up to the norms of the people? For instance, in many societies barrenness is seen as a curse of God upon those who are evil, so a man must take a second wife if his first one bears him no children. In these societies, what should a missionary couple do if they have no children? To take a second wife violates their beliefs about sin, but to have no children undermines trust in their witness.

Taken together, cognitive, affective, and evaluative assumptions provide people with a way of looking at the world that makes sense out of it, that gives them a feeling of being at home, and that reassures them that they are right. This world view serves as the foundation on which they construct their explicit belief and value systems, and the social institutions within which they live their daily lives.

World-view functions. Taken together, the assumptions underlying a culture provide people with a more or less coherent way of looking at the world. One's world view serves a number of important functions.

First, our world view *provides us with cognitive foundations* on which to build our systems of explanation, supplying rational justification for belief in these systems. In other words, if we accept our world-view assumptions, our beliefs and explanations make sense. The assumptions themselves we take for granted and rarely examine. As Clifford Geertz points out (1972:169), a world view provides us with a model or map of reality by structuring our perceptions of reality.

Second, our world view *gives us emotional security.* Faced with a dangerous world full of capricious and uncontrollable forces and crises of drought, illness, and death, and plagued by anxieties about an uncertain future, people turn to their deepest cultural beliefs for emotional comfort and security. It is not surprising, therefore, that world-view assumptions are most evident at births, initiations, marriages, funerals, harvest celebrations, and other rituals people use to recognize and renew order in life and nature.

One powerful emotion we face is the dread of death. Another is the terror of meaninglessness. We can face death itself as martyrs if we believe it to have purpose, but these meanings must carry deep conviction. Our world view buttresses our fundamental beliefs with emotional reinforcements so that they are not easily destroyed.

Third, our world view *validates our deepest cultural norms*, which we use to evaluate our experiences and choose courses of action. It provides us with our ideas of righteousness—and of sin and how to deal with it. It also serves as a map for guiding our behavior. A city map, for instance, not only tells us about the street names, but also enables us to choose a route that will take us from our hotel room to a recommended restaurant. Similarly, our world view provides us with a map *of* reality and also serves as a map *for* guiding our lives. World views serve both predictive and prescriptive functions.

Fourth, our world view *integrates our culture.* It organizes our ideas, feelings, and values into a single overall design. In doing so it gives us a more or less unified view of reality, which is reinforced by deep emotions and convictions.

Finally, as Charles Kraft (1979:56) points out, our world view *monitors culture change.* We are constantly confronted with new ideas, behavior, and products that come from within our society or from without. These may introduce assumptions that undermine our cognitive order.

Our world view helps us to select those that fit our culture and reject those that do not. It also helps us to reinterpret those we adopt so that they fit our overall cultural pattern. For example, villagers in South America began to boil their drinking water, not to kill germs, but (as they saw it) to drive out evil spirits. World views, therefore, tend to conserve old ways and provide stability in cultures over long periods of time. Conversely, they are resistant to change.

But world views themselves do change, since none of them are fully integrated, and there are always internal contradictions. Moreover, when we adopt new ideas they may challenge our fundamental assumptions. Although we all live with cultural inconsistencies, when the internal contradictions become too great, we seek ways to reduce the tension. Normally, we change or let go of some of our assumptions. The result is a gradual world-view transformation of which we ourselves may not even be aware.

Sometimes, however, our old world view no longer meets our basic needs. If another and more adequate one is presented to us, we may reject the old and adopt the new. For example, some Muslims and Hindus may decide that Christianity offers better answers to their questions than their old religions. Such world-view shifts are at the heart of what we call conversion.

Implications for missions. The integration of cultural traits, complexes, and systems into a single culture whole has considerable significance for missionaries. First, as we shall see later, the more integrated cultures are, the more stable they are—but also the more they resist change. Second, when we introduce change into one part of a culture, there are often unforeseen side effects in other areas of the culture.

Jacob Loewen in a lecture cited one example of such unintended consequences of introducing change. The people in one part of Africa kept their villages swept clean. When they became Christians, however, their villages were soon littered with trash. On investigation, the missionary found that formerly they feared the spirits, which they believed were in the forest and came to the village, hiding behind old rags, stones, broken pots, and other litter. Consequently, they kept the village clean so that the spirits would not enter the compound and harm them. But, when they became Christians, they no longer feared these spirits and had no reason to remove the dirt and debris.

Polygamy is another case in point. In many parts of the world, men frequently die young. To provide companionship and care for a widow and her children, the people marry her to the brother or closest male relative of her dead husband, regardless of whether or not that relative is already married. If the church then forbids polygamy , it must make other arrangements for widows and orphans, since the people can no longer turn to their traditional solutions. Missionaries need to realize that changes they introduce often have far-reaching consequences in other areas of the people's lives, and they must be sensitive to unintended side effects.

Cultural Education

By definition, we restrict "culture" to learned beliefs and behavior. In so doing, we differentiate it from biologically instinctive responses. For example, when a North American girl accidentally touches a hot stove, she jerks her hand away and says "Ouch," "Blast it," or something similar. The former reaction is instinctive; the latter is learned. An Indian girl says "Array" or "Abbow."

If culture is learned, it must also be taught. All people are born helpless—without language, culture, or the ability to survive alone in the external world. Yet, within a surprisingly short time, the same person can be molded into a Canadian, Dutchman, Chinese, or member of one of a thousand other societies. One of the important discoveries of the social sciences has been the crucial importance of childhood years in the formation of the human personality and in the transmission of culture from one generation to the next. As one wit put it, each generation must civilize the barbarian hordes that are constantly invading it from below.

Each society has its own ways of "enculturating" its young, of teaching them its cultural ways. All, however, use a combination of pressing them on the one hand and pulling them on the other. The pressures are often obvious. Parents discipline their children for bad behavior, and the society punishes adults for serious violations of the cultural norms. Other pressures are not so obvious—gossip, snide remarks, social ostracism, and withholding rewards—but these are equally effective in enforcing a society's rules.

Societies pull people by giving them cultural heroes, ideal characters and models for the various roles found within the society, and by rewarding good behavior. A Western child is taught by example what it means to be a good teacher, preacher, or truck driver. She or he is also similarly taught how to behave as a wife or husband, mother or father.

"Shared by a Group of People"

Finally, a culture is "shared by a group of people." It summarizes the beliefs, symbols, and products of a society.

Humans are social creatures and dependent upon one another for survival and meaningful existence. They need care during their long childhood and often in their old age. Since they find their greatest joy and fulfillment in the company of others, social isolation is among the greatest punishments they can inflict upon one another.

All human relationships require a large measure of shared understandings between people. They need a common language, whether verbal or nonverbal, a shared set of expectations of one another, and some consensus of beliefs for communication to take place. In other words, they must share to some extent in a common culture. The more they have in common, the greater the possibilities of interrelating.

We need to clarify what we mean by "society," and how it relates to "culture." A society is a group of people who relate to one another in orderly ways in different settings. The basic order that underlies these relationships is called a social organization or structure. A social structure is how people actually relate to one another. This is linked to, but different from, their culture, which encompasses their beliefs about relationships.

People do not always act as their culture says they should. For example, most Christians believe that they should attend church on Sunday, but many find excuses when they want to stay home. Interestingly enough, when they want to break the cultural rules, their culture tells them how to do so. It is all right for them to tell the pastor that they were sick or out of town. But they should not tell him they hate his sermons or cannot stand another member in the church.

Even suicide, the supreme act of social rejection, is culturally molded. Men in Western cultures think of guns or autocide and women may use drugs, while Indian women drown themselves in open wells and Indian men may choose hanging.

The relationship between a society and its culture is dialectical. People develop structures in order to carry out their lives. In turn they teach these to their children as part of the culture that will mold their lives. People also create new ideas and products that—if they are accepted by the society—influence the way people relate to one another. The car, for example, has led to greater mobility, which in turn has led to the flight of the affluent to the suburbs.

Social and cultural boundaries are clearly defined in tribal societies. Here a group of people shares a distinct culture and often the same territory and language and "culture" and "society" are closely linked.

In complex peasant and urban areas, however, cultural and social boundaries become fuzzy, and the relationship between them is more complex. For example, there are many subcultures in Los Angeles, even though the people in that city participate in many of the same social structures, such as the government, political parties, and banks and markets. On the other hand, people who share the same culture, such as Korean immigrants, take part not only in the activities of the Korean community, but also in schools, factories, and neighborhoods made up of people from many different cultures.

In such situations, what constitutes a culture or a society? Here we need to return to our concept of cultural frames. Each social institution, for example, is a cultural frame—it has its own community of people, social structure, and subculture. In a school, members of a group relate to each other through respective roles, be they teachers, students, administrators, staff, and caretakers. They share beliefs and feelings about how these relationships should be carried out. They also share a common body of knowledge, much of it stored in libraries; common ways to express their feelings; and common values and rules.

In a bank, on the other hand, another group of people interrelates in other ways, using roles such as client, teller, office manager, and bank president. They, too, have certain knowledge, feelings, and norms in common. A hospital provides yet another case of a cultural frame having its own community of people and local culture.

Individuals in complex societies move from one frame to another, from one group to another, and from one culture to another, "shifting gears" as they move. Depending on the frame, they may wear different clothes, change their ways of speaking, express different attitudes, and talk about different things. To an outsider they often seem to be different people in the various contexts.

Cultural frames are linked to each other in local cultures. The schools, banks, hospitals, and churches in a city are not only made up of many of the same people, they are also related by systems of laws, economic trade, and networks of communication.

Local cultures are integrated into larger regional and national cultures. For instance, people and institutions in the United States share a common cultural history and beliefs in freedom and democracy, use the same money and postage stamps, and have other cultural ties. In this sense we can speak of different levels of cultural integration, beginning with cultural frames at the bottom and ending with national or even international cultures at the top.

The Gospel and Culture

If cultures are the ways different people think, feel, and act, where does the gospel fit in? Is it not itself part of a specific culture? If we say yes, what culture must we adopt to become Christians? Obviously not European or North American cultures, for these came late in history and certainly are not essentially Christian. The answer must be the Jewish culture of the time of Christ. But here is the question raised by Gentile converts in the Book of Acts. Must they become Jews in order to become Christians?

The early church struggled with this question. The answer they gave was no. Although the gospel was given within the context of Jewish culture from Abraham to Christ and must be understood within that context, the Good News was God's message given *within* that culture. It is not limited to that cultural frame.

Since then, however, the debate has continued. Each Christian community is tempted to equate the gospel with its own culture. This has led churches to split on the basis of cultural differences alone.

The consequences have been equally devastating in missions. By equating Christianity with Western culture, we have used the gospel to reinforce our sense of cultural superiority, and we have made the gospel foreign to other cultures by asking people to convert to our culture to become Christians.

What, then, is the gospel, and how does it relate to human cultures? Here we will speak of the gospel as God's revelation of himself—in history through his deeds, and supremely through his incarnation. The definitive record of this revelation is found in the Bible. The relationship of God's revelation in the Scriptures to human cultures is complex and can best be understood by analogy to Christ's incarnation. Just as Christ was fully God, but became fully human without losing his deity, so also the gospel is God's revelation, but is communicated by means of human cultures without losing its divine character.

There are three principles we need to examine to help us understand the dynamic tension between the gospel and human cultures.

The Gospel Versus Culture

First, the gospel must be distinguished from all human cultures. It is divine revelation, not human speculation. Since it belongs to no one culture, it can be adequately expressed in all of them.

The failure to differentiate between the gospel and human cultures has been one of the great weaknesses of modern Christian missions. Missionaries too often have equated the Good News with their own cultural background. This has led them to condemn most native customs and to impose their own customs on converts. Consequently, the gospel has been seen as foreign in general and Western in particular. People have rejected it not because they reject the lordship of Christ, but because conversion often has meant a denial of their cultural heritage and social ties.

A second danger in equating gospel and culture has been to justify Western imperialism. Christians in the newly formed United States believed that God had blessed their country in a special way and that they were God's chosen people. Pietism and patriotism were blended together. Political parties and the national government used Christian sentiments and symbols for their own purposes. When religion is used to justify political and cultural practices, it is "civil religion."

Early Americans believed that God was on the side of their country, making it different from and better than all others. For them the purposes of their nation and of God became one. Colonialism and military actions were justified as ways of Christianizing the world. It should not surprise us that in many parts of the world, Christianity is equated with militarism and imperialism.

A third danger in equating gospel and culture has been a growing sense of relativism with regard to sin. All cultures have their own definitions of what constitutes sin. As cultures change, so do their ideas of sin. For example, it was once considered evil in the West for women to wear trousers. Today it is widely accepted. Formerly, young couples were publicly condemned if they lived together without marriage, but this no longer raises comment in some modern circles.

Because cultural definitions of sin change, many argue that sin is relative, that there are no moral absolutes. They point out that churches that once forbade their young people to go to movies now hold youth outings there. Who is to say, then, that the premarital sexual relations still generally condemned may not one day be accepted? As cultural definitions of sin change, if we do not distinguish biblical norms from those of our culture, we cannot affirm the absolute nature of biblically defined standards.

As Christians, we affirm that there are God-given standards of righteousness by which all humans and cultures will be judged. The Good News is that there is forgiveness for sin.

The Gospel in Culture

Second, although the gospel is distinct from human cultures, it must always be expressed in cultural forms. Humans cannot receive it apart from their languages, symbols, and rituals. The gospel must become incarnate in cultural forms if the people are to hear and believe.

On the cognitive level, the people must understand the truth of the gospel. On the emotional level, they must experience the awe and mystery of God. And on the evaluative level, the gospel must challenge them to respond in faith. We refer to this process of translating the gospel into a culture, so that the people understand and respond to it, as "indigenization," or "contextualization."

The whole Bible is an eloquent witness of God's meeting humans and conversing with them in their own cultural contexts. God walked with Adam and Eve in the Garden in the cool of the day. He spoke to Abram, Moses, David, and other Israelites within a changing Hebrew culture. And he became the Word who lived in time and space as a member of the Jewish society. Similarly, the early church presented the apostolic message in ways that the people understood. Peter's sermon at Pentecost and Paul's address to the Areopagus in Athens show how they tailored the message to fit their audiences. The Gospels and the Epistles likewise address people in different cultures in different ways. All authentic communication of the gospel in missions should be patterned on biblical communication and seek to make the Good News understandable to people within their own cultures.

All cultures can adequately serve as vehicles for the communication of the gospel. If this were not so, people would have to change cultures to become Christians. This does not mean that the gospel is fully understood in any one culture, but that all people can learn enough to be saved and to grow in faith within the context of their own culture.

Not only are all cultures capable of expressing the heart of the gospel, but each also brings to light certain salient features of the gospel that have remained less visible or even hidden in other cultures. Churches in different cultures can help us to understand the many-sided wisdom of God, thereby serving as channels for understanding different facets of divine revelation, truths that a theology tied to one particular culture can easily overlook.

The Gospel to Culture

Third, the gospel calls all cultures to change. Just as Christ's life was a condemnation of our sinfulness, so the kingdom of God stands in judgment of all cultures (Figure 9).

FIGURE 9

The Gospel Must Be Both Contextualized and Prophetic

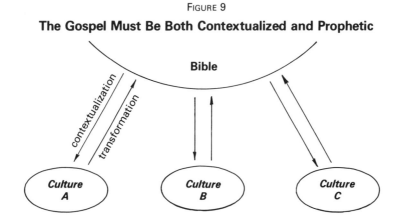

Not everything in human culture is condemned. Humans are created in the image of God, and as such they create cultures, each of which has much that is positive and can be used by Christians. Every culture provides a measure of order that makes life meaningful and possible.

But, because of human sinfulness, all cultures also have structures and practices that are evil. Among these are slavery, apartheid, oppression, exploitation, and war. The gospel condemns these, just as it judges the sins of individuals.

A truly indigenous theology must not only affirm the positive values of the culture in which it is being formulated, but it must also challenge those aspects which express the demonic and dehumanizing forces of evil. Kenneth Scott Latourette (Minz 1973:101) points out, "[I]t must be noted that Christianity, if it is not hopelessly denatured, never becomes fully at home in any culture. Always, when it is true to its genius, it creates a tension."

The gospel serves a prophetic function, showing us the way God intended us to live as human beings and judging our lives and our cultures by those norms. Where the gospel has lost this prophetic voice, it is in danger of being wedded to beliefs and values that distort its message. Charles Taber (1978:73) notes:

> This is precisely one of the most flagrant failures of western theology: it has too often tended to emasculate the gospel, to accept, uncritically, profoundly unbiblical values and principles—and even to provide guilt edged justifications for some of the grossest evils of human history.

The same can happen in young churches that seek to contextualize the gospel uncritically within their culture. Nirmal Minz (1973:110) warns:

> There is a very subtle kind of bondage in which the indigenous church may live. Revival of national heritage and various forms of neo-paganism might creep into the church and may dominate its life and work. The Batak Church in Indonesia had [for a time] almost succumbed to this temptation and lived under the bondage of nationalism and neo-paganism. . . . Such indigenous churches are false to the teaching and Spirit of Jesus Christ.

All Christians and all churches must continually wrestle with the questions of what is the gospel and what is culture—and what is the relationship between them. If we fail to do so, we are in danger of losing the gospel truths.

Suggested Exercise: Gospel and Culture

This exercise is intended to help you test your own theological consistency on a number of issues that Protestants in various denominations have felt important. As a Christian in a cross-cultural setting, you will need to learn the differences between those elements essential to the church in every culture, and those elements which are not.

Part One

Separate all the items that follow into two categories, based on these definitions:

Essential. These items (commands, practices, customs) are essential to the church in every age. [Mark these *E* on the list.]

Negotiable. These items (commands, practices, customs) may or may not be valid for the church in any given place or time. [Mark these *N* on the list.]

1. Greet each other with a holy kiss.
2. Do not go to court to settle issues between Christians.
3. Do not eat meat used in pagan ceremonies.
4. Women in the assembly should be veiled when praying or speaking.
5. Wash feet at the Lord's Supper (Eucharist).
6. Lay on hands for ordination.
7. Sing without musical accompaniment.
8. Abstain from eating blood.
9. Abstain from fornication.
10. Share the Lord's Supper (Eucharist) together.
11. Use only real wine and unleavened bread for your Eucharist meals.
12. Use only grape juice for Eucharist meals.
13. Anoint with oil for healing.
14. Women are not to teach men.
15. Women are not to wear braided hair, gold, or pearls.
16. Men are not to have long hair.
17. Do not drink wine at all.
18. Slavery is permissible if you treat slaves well.
19. Remain single.
20. Seek the gift of tongues.
21. Seek the gift of healing.
22. Lift your hands when you pray.
23. People who don't work don't eat.
24. Have a private "devotional time" every day.
25. Say *Amen* at the end of prayers.
26. Appoint elders and deacons in every congregation.
27. Elect the leaders.
28. Confess sins one to another.
29. Confess sins privately to God.

30. Give at least ten per cent of your income/goods/crops to God.
31. Construct a building for worship.
32. Confess Christ publicly by means of baptism.
33. Be baptized by immersion.
34. Be baptized as an adult.
35. Be baptized as a child/infant.
36. Do not be a polygamist.
37. Do not divorce your spouse for any reason.
38. Do not divorce your spouse except for adultery.

Part Two

Reflect on the process by which you distinguished the "essential" from the "negotiable" items. What principle or principles governed your decision? Write out the method you used, in a simple, concise statement. Be completely honest with yourself and accurately describe how you made your decisions. Your principle(s) should account for every decision.

Part Three

Review your decisions again, and answer the following questions:

Are your "essential" items so important to you that you could not associate with a group that did not practice all of them?

Are there some "essential" items that are a little more "essential" than others?

Are there any items that have nothing explicitly to do with Scripture at all?

"The Temporary Gospel," *The Other Side* magazine, Nov.-Dec. 1975. Reprinted with permission from *The Other Side* magazine, 300 W. Apsley St., Philadelphia, Pa. 19144. Copyright (c).

PART

Cultural Differences and the Missionary

3

Cultural Differences and the New Missionary

Every new missionary feels it—the excitement of travel and the romance of foreign sights. We sample esoteric foods, ride rickshaws, and buy finely embroidered blankets in the bazaar. We wander hesitantly through temples and watch devotees offer sacrifices to strange gods. We expected it all to be like this!

Then reality sets in. The realization dawns that this is now our home. Here our children will grow up as natives. And we must become one with these people with their unintelligible tongues and foreign ways before we can effectively share with them the Good News of the gospel. Suddenly, things that seemed romantic and exciting become strange and threatening. Questions arise. Can we really make this culture our own? Can we really identify with these people and plant a church among them? Will we even survive? When this shift occurs, we come face to face with one of the central concerns of all new missionaries: the problem of cultural differences.

Cultural Differences

People create a great variety of cultures. They eat different foods, build different kinds of houses, speak different languages, and greet each other in different ways. Yap women wear grass skirts reaching to

61

their ankles; Dinka men coat their bodies with ash; Muslim women are hidden in public in *burkas;* and some South Sea Islanders wear only lip plugs. The Masais of Kenya draw blood from a cow through hollow arrows and consider it a great delicacy, often mixing it with fresh milk. Chinese for the most part reject dairy products but are fond of pork. Muslims and Orthodox Jews abhor pork and like milk. Some African tribes make butter, but smear it on their bodies for decorative purposes (Nida 1975:77–78).

Less obvious yet more profound are differences in the ways people relate to one another and how they think about their world. American farmers raise crops to feed their families. Men in the Trobriand Islands raise crops to feed their sisters and their sisters' children. These men and their children, in turn, live on food provided by their wives' brothers. The Shilluks of Sudan speak of scorpions and crocodiles as their relatives; the American Indians of the Southwest eat peyote buttons to have visions of guardian spirits; and aged Eskimos used to walk out on the ice to die so as not to consume food, which was scarce in winter. All people see the same world, but they perceive it through different cultural glasses. And they are often unaware of their culture and how it colors what they see (Figure 10).

A study by Edward Hall (1959) illustrates how different cultures can be in their perceptions of time. Since all people live in time, we might assume that everyone sees it in the same way. Not so, says Hall. Americans, for example, place a premium on punctuality and define being "on time" as from five minutes before to five minutes after the set time. Someone arriving fifteen minutes after an appointed hour must offer an apology, but need give no explanation. Those arriving

FIGURE 10

Cultures See the World in Different Ways

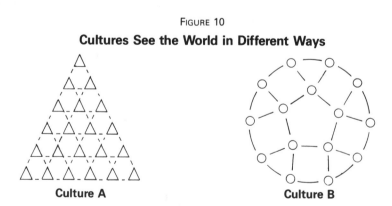

Culture A   **Culture B**

From Paul G. Hiebert, "Anthropological Tools for Missionaries" (Singapore: Haggai Institute, 1983), p. 9.

more than a half hour "late," however, are "rude" and must offer a credible excuse (Figure 11).

In traditional Egypt, Hall points out, servants are expected to show up at the set time as an act of obedience. Men of equal rank, however, need to show their independence, and they do so by arriving at the "proper" time, an hour later. Only those who arrive a half hour after that must offer apologies.

There is no confusion when two Americans or two Egyptians meet, because they understand one another, but there is confusion when an Egyptian pastor and an American missionary meet. The American arrives "on time" at the set hour, and the Egyptian "on time" an hour later. The former is frustrated and complains (wrongly) that the Egyptians lack a sense of time, and the Egyptian is perplexed at the apparent subservience of the missionary.

Cultural differences can lead to humorous situations. Eugene Nida (1975:5–6) tells of early missionaries to the Marshall Islands who received their mail once a year, when a sailing boat made its rounds of the South Pacific. One year the boat was a day ahead of schedule, and the missionaries were away on a neighboring island. The captain of the boat left the mail with the Marshallese, who finally had in hand what the missionaries spoke about so often and with such anticipation. Unacquainted with the strange ways of the foreigners, they tried to find out what made the mail so attractive. They concluded that it must be good to eat, so they cooked the letters and found them unpalatable.

FIGURE 11

Use of Time Differs with Cultures

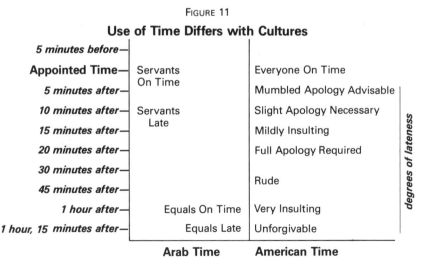

	Arab Time	American Time	
5 minutes before—			
Appointed Time—	Servants On Time	Everyone On Time	
5 minutes after—		Mumbled Apology Advisable	
10 minutes after—	Servants Late	Slight Apology Necessary	
15 minutes after—		Mildly Insulting	*degrees of lateness*
20 minutes after—		Full Apology Required	
30 minutes after—		Rude	
45 minutes after—			
1 hour after—	Equals On Time	Very Insulting	
1 hour, 15 minutes after—	Equals Late	Unforgivable	

From Paul G. Hiebert, *Cultural Anthropology,* 2nd ed. (Grand Rapids: Baker, 1983), p. 34.

When the missionaries returned, they found their year's mail turned into mush.

Cultural differences also create difficulties. For instance, two missionary women working in central Mexico were circumspect in their relationships with men, but thought nothing of drinking lime juice at breakfast for their health. The Indians, however, were certain the young women had lovers, for the locals used lime juice, which they called "baby killer," to produce abortions (Nida 1975:8).

In the next three chapters we will look at the effects of cultural differences on *missionaries*. In chapters 6 through 8 we will examine their influence on the *message*. In chapters 9 through 11 we will see how they affect the *bicultural community* within which the missionaries and nationals work.

How do cultural differences affect the missionary? We will look first at some of the difficulties young missionaries experience. In chapter 4 we will examine in more detail the ongoing problems that missionaries face in cross-cultural ministries.

Culture Shock

We are all excited and a little fearful when we enter a new culture. When the letter of appointment arrives, our level of personal satisfaction is high (see Figure 12). Our dreams have come true. This is what we have been planning and training for over the past few years.

The farewell at the church is even more satisfying. All our lives we may have occupied the pews but now we are center stage. Even the pastor takes second place. The good-byes at the airport are even more exciting, a sweet mix of sad partings and the thrill of new adventure.

Landing in a strange city abroad, our satisfaction is still high. We are tired from the flight, but there is the excitement of new sights and strange customs. We are really here. We can hardly believe it!

We stop at a restaurant and order lunch. But when it comes, we recognize only half of it as food. The other half looks inedible—like worms or even ants. Hungry, we stop at the market and ask for some oranges, but the woman in the stall does not understand us. We suddenly realize that all people do not speak English. Desperate for something to eat, we point like children to our mouths and stomachs and then to the oranges. When the vendor finally understands and gives us fruit, we face another problem. How are we going to pay for it? We cannot understand her, and the new coins make no sense to us. Finally, in desperation, we hold them out and let her take what she wants. We are sure we are being cheated. To make matters worse, the children nearby are making fun of us, obviously amused that these wealthy and

FIGURE 12

Culture Shock

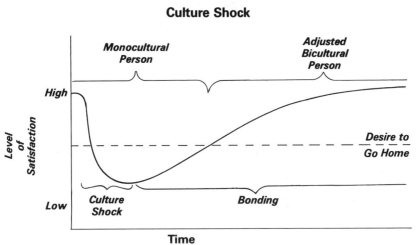

From Paul G. Hiebert, *Cultural Anthropology*, 2nd ed. (Grand Rapids: Baker, 1983), p. 40.

educated people cannot speak a language any local three-year-old knows well. Inside we are angry and want to tell them how learned we really are, but to no avail. Our education is of little use to us here.

The next day our host sends us across town on a bus, with instructions to get off after five miles at the stop with a big brown house on the left and a small green one on the right. We set out confidently, but a few stops later we see a big brown house on the left and a small green one on the right. We know we must go further, but every stop thereafter is the same. Suddenly we are afraid of getting lost, but we cannot turn back now. We have visions of spending the rest of our lives riding around a strange city in a bus.

Later we get sick and are taken to a local doctor. We are afraid, for are not all foreign doctors witch doctors? Can they really cure us?

As anxieties multiply, we seem to get little done beyond keeping ourselves alive. Everything is strange, everyone looks alike, we have few friends to whom we can turn for help, and we cannot admit defeat and go home. Unlike the tourists, we cannot even go to the local Hilton and its familiar settings. What has happened to our dreams?

Causes of Culture Shock

What causes this psychological unrest when we enter a new culture? It is not, as we might suspect, the sight of poverty and dirt. Nor is it the fear of illness, although those in culture shock are often preoccupied with cleanliness and health. Culture shock is the disorientation we experience when all the cultural maps and guidelines we learned as children no longer work. Stripped of our normal ways of coping with life, we are confused, afraid, and angry. We rarely know what has gone wrong, much less what to do about it.

Culture shock strikes most people who enter deeply into new cultures and afflcts not only Westerners who go abroad. Africans experience it when they move to the United States, just as do Koreans when they move to Indonesia. Some have serious cases of it. Others have mild attacks. The severity depends upon the extent of the differences between the cultures, the personality of the individual, and the methods used to cope with the new situations.

What are some of the symptoms and causes, and how does the disease progress? (Myron Loss [1983] has given us an excellent summary of culture shock, and I owe much here to his insights.)

Language Shock

The first shock we often experience in a new culture is our inability to communicate. Ever since our early childhood, we have talked, gestured, written, and talked some more—until we are no longer aware of the communication processes themselves. They have become almost automatic.

Suddenly, as strangers in a new world, we are stripped of our primary means of interacting with other people. Like children, we struggle to say even the simplest things, and we constantly make mistakes. Describing this, William Smalley (1978:698) writes:

> Even after weeks of study [the missionary] is unable to discuss much more than the price of a pound of potatoes. He is unable to display his education and intelligence, the symbols which gave him status and security back home. He meets intelligent and educated people but he responds to them like a child or an idiot because he is not capable of any better response. . . .
>
> The language learner has the uneasy feeling that people are laughing behind his back—and they are. His study is tiring, boring, frustrating. Nothing seems to go logically or smoothly, because logic is identified with familiar ways of talking and thinking. It is based on his language and academic tradition.
>
> Many an overseas American who started out to learn a language has ended by rejecting it. The pattern of rejection sometimes means less and less study; the development of more and more English contacts. Sometimes it means illness, genuine physical illness.

Some people believe they simply cannot learn a new language. Others have a mental block against practicing things they do not understand or cannot do well. But you cannot learn a language without making mistakes and without practicing it until you are familiar with it. Language shock can catch people in a vicious cycle—unable to learn, unable to get along without learning. Trapped, they seek some way out. Smalley continues:

> [They] cling to the crutch of translation and desperately try to find out how to translate the things they want to say from English into the local language, and they let this substitute for a knowledge of the language, fooling themselves into thinking that because they have learned how to make the equivalents of some English statements (even "preaching" full sermons), they know the language. Through this process they have missed whole portions of it, having cut these off by their insistence upon approaching it through English. And the portions they have missed are ever-present sources of anxiety as they miss much of what is going on around them.

Some never learn the local language and work all their lives abroad through translators—in some cases for forty years or more!

Changes in Routine

Another frustration we face in culture shock is change in daily routine. In our home culture we carry out efficiently such tasks as shopping, cooking, banking, laundering, mailing, going to the dentist, and getting a Christmas tree, leaving ourselves time for work and leisure. In a new setting, even simple jobs take a great deal of psychic energy and more time, much more time. It takes two or three times as long to cook our meals in some countries, because we must light wood fires, and the chickens are still running around when we buy them. Elisabeth Elliot (1975:41) writes:

> Then there were the simple things which, for safety's sake one ought not to overlook. They only take a minute. Like washing lettuce. "Avoid raw vegetables" is good advice for a tourist, but if you are going to live in a place (it was living we were aiming for, not mere tropical survival), you want raw vegetables sometimes. The book said to dip everything, lettuce included, in boiling water for a few seconds. This could be counted on usually to kill amoeba and always to kill one's zest for salad.

Life during the first year in a new culture is often a struggle simply to survive. All our time seems spent in cooking, washing clothes, marketing, and building or repairing our houses. No time is left for the work we came to do. Frustration mounts as the months pass and we are unable to do much teaching, preaching, counseling, or Bible translation. And there seems little we can do about it.

Changes in Relationships

Human lives are centered around relationships with relatives, friends, colleagues at work, bosses, bank tellers, clerks, and even strangers. Through these we gain our identity within a society and an image of ourselves. When our self-perceptions conflict with the images others have of us, we work desperately to change what they are thinking. If this fails, we are forced to change the ideas we have of ourselves. Few of us can sustain our beliefs or sense of worth without constant reinforcenment from others. Even gossip is better than not to be noticed at all.

Maintaining relationships in our own culture, where we understand what is going on, is hard enough. In another culture, the task seems almost insurmountable. Our spouses and children have their own problems adjusting to a new language and culture, and they need extra attention at the very time we are crying out for help. They get on our nerves (and we on theirs), for we are thrown together in stressful situations with few outside relationships to sustain us. Other missionaries, if they are around, are often of little help because they are busy and seem so well adjusted and we are afraid to admit our weaknesses to them. After all, we now are "missionaries." Obviously, it is we who are at fault for our inability to adjust easily to the new culture. So we draw apart, afraid to share our deep anxieties.

Building relationships with the local people is even more stressful. We can barely speak their language and do not understand the subtle nuances of their relationships. Their humor escapes us, and ours makes them frown. Trying to listen to them in normal social activities drains our energies. Even going to church, which first excited us with its novelty, becomes tedious and contributes little to our own spiritual nourishment. We are lonely and have no one with whom we can share our self-doubts.

Added to all this is our loss of identity as significant adults in the society. In our own society we know who we are because we hold offices, degrees, and memberships in different groups. In the new setting our old identity is gone. We must start all over again to become somebody. Richard McElroy (1972:inside cover) writes:

> During the first week of language study the new missionary experiences "role shock." In North America he was a leader, successful and secure. Suddenly, he is a learner, with a high school graduate teaching him Spanish phonetics—and correcting, correcting, correcting him. If the missionary does not make the role switch, he feels insecure, self-conscious and threatened. The experience brings out the worst in some students: stubbornness, rudeness, withdrawal, and hyper-criticalness.

Another shock is having servants around the house. They are often necessary to heat the laundry water, kill and pluck the chickens, and do other tasks that we could handle in the West by mechanical servants and pre-prepared food. Moreover, we soon find that we would have no time left to work if they were not around. And we are criticized if we refuse to give jobs to household workers. But how do we relate to servants? As Christians we want to be egalitarian, so we invite the servants to eat with us like guests. Yet this conflicts with the local understandings of the position of workers in the house and makes the servants feel uncomfortable. Since we also prize the personal privacy of our homes, we find the presence of servants around the house an intrusion.

Even participation in native life can be traumatic. When we try our hand at some of the local crafts or participate in some strange sports, we are slow and awkward, and our performance is like that of children. We also tend to see some dangerous religious significance in every doubtful activity.

Loss of Understanding

To become truly human is to learn a culture and understand what is going on. It is to know what to expect in life and what is expected of us. A North American knows to drive on the right side of the road, not to bargain with the clerk for sugar, and to stand in line at the ticket counter. An Indian knows the worth of a rupee, the way to bargain for a sari, and the meaning of *Tirupathi Venkateswara*. We need such knowledge to understand what is happening around us and to find meaning in our lives.

In a new culture much of our old knowledge is useless, if not misleading. When we point at something with a finger, the people are offended, for we have made a dirty sign. We offer help and keep quiet if the people reject it. Only later do we learn that in many societies people must always demur on the first offer and that we are expected to offer it a second time. The result is often embarrassment and confusion. William Smalley (1978:693) gives another example:

> When I first went to Paris to study French, I and many other Americans like me found it dfficult to know when and where to shake hands. French people seemed to us to be shaking hands all the time, and very unnecessarily so from our point of view. We felt silly shaking our hands so much, and we passed around among us the stories that we heard, such as the one about how French children shake hands with their parents before going to bed every night. . . . This small and inconsequential difference of habit in shaking hands was enough to bring uneasiness,

and combined with hundreds of other uncertainties brought culture shock to many.

When our knowledge repeatedly fails us, we become desperate, for our lives seem to be careening out of control. In the long run, it is the sense of meaninglessness arising out of this confusion that can be the most damaging consequence of culture shock. We seem to have lost our hold on reality.

Emotional and Evaluative Disorientation

Culture shock has a cognitive dimension, but it also involves emotional and evaluative disorientation. On the emotional level, we face both deprivation and confusion. The music we hear often sounds dissonant, the food strangely spiced, and the entertainment unintelligible. We long to hear recognizable music, eat familiar food, watch the evening news on television, and go out for the type of entertainment we have "at home." And long after we understand meanings in the new language, its fine emotional nuances such as humor, irony, sarcasm, poetry, and double entendre escape us.

We also face feelings of frustration that arise out of the cross-cultural setting. After the initial excitement of being abroad, we become homesick and begin to dislike the unfamiliar ways. We feel guilty because we cannot live up to our own expectations. We are angry because no one told us it would be this way and because we make such slow progress in adjusting to the new culture.

On the level of values, we are incensed at what appears to be a lack of morality: the lack of proper dress, the insensitivity to the poor, and what to us is obviously stealing, cheating, and bribing. We are even more shocked to learn that the people consider *our* behavior just as immoral. In New Guinea, for example, the nationals accused missionaries of being stingy because they did not freely share their foodstuffs and such belongings as clothes, blankets, and guns with those around them. After all, everyone must share. The local people, too, would share with the missionaries if they ran out of food.

Indian people considered the dress of missionary women immoral. In their society, the sexiest parts of a woman's body are the calves of their legs. Proper women, therefore, wear ankle-length saris—but missionary women wore knee-length skirts.

Symptoms of Culture Shock

The first days in a new culture are a chaotic mixture of fascinating new sights and shocking experiences. North Americans in India are terrified at the sight of salamanders on their bedroom walls (they keep down the mosquitos) and snakes in the grass, remembering that twenty thousand Indians (out of seven hundred million) die of snakebite each year. Indians in the United States are equally terrified of freeway traffic, knowing that forty thousand Americans (out of two hundred thirty million) die each year from automobile accidents.

Bad as they may seem, these initial shocks are not serious. The real problem in culture shock is the psychological distortion that comes undetected while we think we are functioning normally. This twists our perceptions of reality, and wreaks havoc with our bodies. What are the symptoms of this cross-cultural malady?

Rising Stress

We all live with stress. Indeed, without it we would enjoy or achieve little in life. But too much of it can be destructive. How much is too much? It is hard to measure stress precisely, but Thomas Holmes and M. Masusu (1974) have given us a rough scale by which to estimate the stress created by various experiences in life. The scale runs from "no stress" to a maximum of 100 points for the death of a spouse (Table 1).

Stress is cumulative and persists long after the events that caused it have passed. To measure the present tensions we are experiencing, we need to total the stress points we have logged over the past year. Holmes and Masusu found that only one-third of those who scored less than 150 stress points were likely to become seriously ill in the following two years. But one-half of those who had accumulated more than 150 stress points, and four-fifths of those who had more than 300, were likely to have significant health problems within that time.

By these measures, most missionaries should be basket cases, particularly during their first term of service. In their first service year, new missionaries have usually experienced marked changes in their financial status, occupation, geographic location, recreation outlets, church routine, social activities, and eating habits. If they are young, they may have just been married or had a child. In addition, they face the stresses that arise out of moving into radically different cultures— tensions that Holmes and Masusu have not even attempted to measure. For example, James Spradley and Mark Phillips (1972) estimate that learning to use a new language in everyday activities alone adds more than 50 points of stress to the new missionary's life. It should not surprise us, then, that many first-term workers have scores that run over 400 points.

TABLE 1

The Stress Produced by Changes in Life

Nature of the Event	Points of Stress Due to Change
1 Death of a spouse	100
2 Divorce	73
3 Death of a close family member	63
4 Personal injury or illness	53
5 Marriage	50
6 Change in the health of a family member	44
7 Pregnancy	40
8 Gain of new family members	39
9 Change in financial state	38
10 Change to a different line of work	36
11 Change in responsibilities at work	29
12 Change in living conditions	25
13 Change in work hours or conditions	20
14 Change in residence	20
15 Change in recreation	19
16 Change in church activities	19
17 Change in social activities	18
18 Change in number of family get-togethers	15
19 Change in eating habits	15

From Thomas H. Holmes and M. Masusu, "Life Change and Illness Susceptibility," in *Stressful Life Events: Their Nature and Effects*, ed. Barbara S. Dohrenwend and Bruce P. Dohrenwend (New York: Wiley, 1974), pp. 42–72, © John Wiley & Sons, Inc.

Physical Illness

One common consequence of high stress is physical illness. Among the more common sicknesses caused by prolonged stress are chronic headaches, ulcers, lower back pain, high blood pressure, heart attacks, and chronic fatigue. Stress also impairs our ability to concentrate and makes us accident prone. Cecil Osborne (1967:198) writes:

[Emotional] stress creates a chemical imbalance resulting in mal-function of glands and other organs. The body then becomes unable to provide resistance to germs which are normally held in check. Since the mind tends to hand its pain, guilt and grief over to the body by an unconscious process, we find it easier to incur physical illness than mental anguish. For one thing, we receive sympathy, which is a form of love, when we are physically ill; but the person suffering from mental anguish or depression is likely to be told to "snap out of it" or to "pull yourself together."

Illness in a foreign setting, however, only increases our anxiety, particularly if the medical services we are used to are not available. In strange settings we easily become obsessed with health and cleanliness and magnify every symptom. Nor are such fears totally unfounded. We often do face strange diseases and dangers, and it is our lives that are at stake.

Psychological and Spiritual Depression

The most serious consequences of stress are often depression and a sense of failure. Caught unaware, we are unable to cope with the problems of living in a new culture. We are overwhelmed by constantly having to face confusing situations and the strain of learning a new way of life. There is little time for leisure—after all, is it proper for missionaries to relax when there is so much to do? Our support systems are gone. We are part of a missionary community made up of strong-willed strangers to whom we do not dare admit weakness, and there may be no one to pastor us when we fail.

There also hangs over us the sword of unrealistic expectations. The public's image of a missionary is a hardy pioneer who suffers great deprivations; a saint who never sins; an outstanding preacher, doctor, or personal worker who overcomes all obstacles—in short, a person who is creative, brave, sensitive, and always triumphant. When we are young, we almost believe that we can become such persons when we cross the ocean.

It is not surprising, then, that we face depression, often severe, when we discover that we are still very human. Going abroad has neither changed our weak and sinful natures nor given us new talents. Levi Keidel (1971:67) echoes the experience of many missionaries when he writes:

> I began to stand my various manifestations of unchristlikeness up on a row to take a good look at them: bad temper, chafing against unavoidable circumstances, enslaving myself to legalistic motivation, ill will towards those who impeded my program.
>
> To these I added recurrent terminal exhaustion. . . . I remember the counsel of my pastor when we first left for Congo: "Now Levi, you don't have to accomplish everything during your first term." Before I com-

pleted two years on the field I was taken to a hospital. . . . I was a bowl
dipped empty and scraped raw by the ravenous appetite of demand.

Unfortunately, if we think we are failing, we work harder to maintain our self-esteem. But this only multiplies our problems, for the
fear of failure itself saps our energies. Defeated, we conclude that we
are faulty and not acceptable for God's service.

Sometimes we put on masks to disguise our weaknesses. For a time
we can deceive others, even ourselves, but in the long run we know
these are worthless self-images. Dwight Carlson (1974:65) writes:

> Like other unresolved conflicts, the mask requires a lot of energy and
> leads to a host of problems besides fear, such as irritability, worry, anx-
> iety, fatigue, excusing ourselves, blaming others, and, not infrequently,
> frank lying and deceit. . . .
>
> When we refuse to remove our masks, we not only create internal
> conflict and fatigue, but we also hinder our own growth and the growth
> of others. Individuals grow by relating to other genuine people and seeing
> how they deal with life's problems. Christian leaders must be willing to
> first remove their own masks before they can ever expect others to do
> likewise. Only as we Christians are willing to expose our feet of clay will
> others feel (and maybe only then) safe to expose themselves and their
> needs.

The Cycle of Culture Shock

It is consoling when we are in culture shock to know that we are
normal human beings and that in time the traumas of adjusting to a
new culture will end. Furthermore, a knowledge of how culture shock
progresses can help us to deal with it and turn it into a positive experience that prepares us for our future ministry. The first year or two
is crucial in our adaptation to a new culture. How we adjust during
this time will color our ministry for the rest of our lives.

Kalervo Oberg (1960:177–182) traces the steps we normally take in
learning to live in a new cultural setting.

The Tourist Stage

Our first response to a new culture is fascination. We live in hotels,
with other missionaries, or in homes not too different from what we
are used to, and we associate with nationals who can speak our language and are gracious to us as foreigners. We spend the days explor-
ing new sights and sounds and retreat at night to places insulated in
part from the strange culture outside. We may be taken to see the local
attractions and to meet important people who welcome us. And we

will respond with words of goodwill and appreciation for the local culture.

This honeymoon stage may last from a few weeks to several months, depending on the circumstances. Ordinary tourists leave before this phase comes to an end and return home to tell stories about the strange ways of the people. But as missionaries we have come to stay, which means we must begin the difficult journey of becoming members of a new culture.

Disenchantment

The tourist stage ends when we move from being outside visitors to becoming cultural insiders. This takes place when we establish our own homes, take responsibility for ourselves, and start making a contribution to the local community. It is here that frustrations and anxieties arise. We have language problems, shopping trouble, transportation woes, and laundry mixups. We are concerned about the cleanliness of our drinking water, food, and bedding and afraid of being cheated or robbed. We also feel left alone. Those who welcomed us so warmly have gone back to their work and now seem indifferent to our troubles.

The result is disenchantment. No longer is the strange culture exciting. Now it seems inscrutable and impossible to learn. Our normal response is hostility because the security of our lives is threatened. We find fault with the culture and compare it unfavorably with our own. We criticize the people and see each shortcoming as proof of their laziness and inferiority, developing stereotypes that caricature the host country in negative ways. We withdraw from the culture and take refuge in a small circle of foreign friends, or stay in our homes where we try to re-create the culture of our native land.

This stage marks the crisis in the disease. How we respond to it determines whether or not we stay and how we will ultimately adjust to the new culture. Most new missionaries drop below the "go home" line during this time (see Figure 12). We look for mail and talk about things we will do when we return "home." We write letters of resignation but do not mail them. After all, what would our friends or church say if we were to return?

Another process, however, is also at work during this stage, one we hardly notice. We are learning how to live in the new culture. We begin to realize that we can learn how to shop in the new language and use the local currency. As we make friends among the people, we start having good days. With a word of encouragement from older missionaries and national leaders, most of us throw away our letters of resignation and begin the long task of learning the language and adjusting to the new culture. Those who cannot make this transition may have to leave before they experience a nervous breakdown.

Resolution

The emergence of humor often marks the beginning of recovery. We begin to laugh at our predicaments and crack jokes about the people instead of criticizing them. We begin to sympathize with others who we think are worse off than ourselves. Although we may still take a superior attitude, we are beginning to learn new cultural ways.

How we relate to the people and culture at this stage is particularly crucial, for the patterns of adjustment we form here tend to stay with us. If we develop positive attitudes of appreciation and acceptance of the host people, we have laid the foundations for learning their culture and becoming one with them. On the other hand, if we remain negative and aloof, chances are that we will remain foreign and never identify ourselves with the nationals. And since we are models of the gospel for these people, it, too, will appear to them as distant and foreign.

Not only is our first year, indeed our first month, crucial in molding our lifelong relationship to a culture, it is also the time when we are most adaptable to it. We have few preconceptions of what we should do and a strong idealism that has motivated us to come. Since we have not yet settled into comfortable routines that blind us to what is going on, we are willing, at this stage, to identify closely with the people and make their culture our own. In this sense, culture shock is not simply an experience to be endured. As the Brewsters point out (1982), it is, in fact, one of the most significant and formative periods in our whole missionary experience. To use their term, it is a time when we are "bonded" in one way or another to the new culture.

Adjustment

The final stage of culture shock comes when we feel comfortable in the new culture. We have now learned enough to function efficiently in our new setting without feelings of anxiety. We not only accept the local foods, dress, and customs, but actually begin to enjoy them. We cherish the friendship of the people and can begin to feel constructive in our work. If we take time to think about it, we realize that we will miss the country and its people when we leave.

We can adjust to the new culture in a number of ways. We can, for example, keep our distance and build a Western ghetto from which we sally forth to do our work. Or we can reject our past and try to "go native." A third possibility is to identify ourselves with the culture and work for some type of integration with our own. (We will look at these alternatives and how they affect our ministry in the next chapter.)

Are Missionaries Unbalanced?

T. Norton Sterrett

Are missionaries unbalanced? Of course they are. I'm one. I ought to know.

A missionary probably began as an ordinary man or woman. He dressed like other people. He liked to play tennis and listen to music.

But even before leaving for the field he became "different." Admired by some, pitied by others, he was known as one who was leaving parents, prospects and home for—a vision. So he seemed to be a visionary.

Now that he's come home again he's even more different. To him some things—big things—just don't seem important. Even the World Series or the Davis Cup matches don't interest him especially. And apparently he doesn't see things as other people see them. The chance of a lifetime—to meet Isaac Stern personally—seems to leave him cold. It makes you want to ask where he's been.

Well, where has he been?

Where the conflict with evil is open and intense, a fight not a fashion—where clothes don't matter, because there's little time to take care of them—where people are dying for help he might give, most of them not even knowing he has the help—where the sun means 120 in the shade, and he can't spend his time in the shade.

But not only space, time too seems to have passed him by. When you talk about the Rolling Stones he looks puzzled. When you mention *Star Wars* he asks what that is. You wonder how long he's been away.

All right, how long has he been away? Long enough for thirty million people to go into eternity without Christ, with no chance to hear the gospel—and some of them went right before his eyes: when that flimsy riverboat overturned; when that cholera epidemic struck; when that Hindu-Muslim riot broke out.

How long has he been gone? Long enough to have had two sieges of amoebic dysentery, to nurse his wife through repeated attacks of malaria, to get the news of his mother's death before he knew she was sick.

How long? Long enough to see a few outcast men and women turn to Christ, to see them drink in the Bible teaching he gave them, to struggle and suffer with them through the persecution that developed from non-Christian relatives, to see them grow into a sturdy band of believers conducting their own worship, to see this group develop an indigenous church that is reaching out to the community.

Yes, he's been away a long time.

So he's different. But unnecessarily so now, it seems. At least, since he's in this country, he could pay more attention to his clothes, to what's going on around the country, to recreation, to social life.

Of course, he could.

But he can't forget—at least most of the time—that the price of a new suit would buy three thousand Gospels, that while an American spends one day in business, five thousand Indians or Chinese go into eternity without Christ.

So when a missionary comes to your church or your Christian group, remember that he will probably be different. If he stumbles for a word now and then, he may have been speaking a foreign tongue almost exclusively for several years, and possibly is fluent in it. If he isn't in the orator class, he may not have had a chance to speak English from a pulpit for awhile. He may be eloquent on the street of an Indian bazaar.

If he doesn't seem to warm up as quickly as you want, if he seems less approachable than a youth evangelist or college professor, remember he's been under a radically different social system since before you started high school, and maybe is unfamiliar with casual conversation.

Sure the missionary is unbalanced.

But by whose scales? Yours or God's?

Originally appeared in *HIS,* student magazine of Inter-Varsity Christian Fellowship, ©1948, 1960, 1967, 1982 and used by permission.

Reverse Culture Shock

The idea that we experience reverse culture shock when we return "home" after a long residence abroad may surprise us. After all, we are returning to a culture with which we are familiar. But that culture has changed, and so have we—more deeply than we know. Research shows that individuals who have adjusted most successfully to a new culture have the greatest difficulty in readapting to their old one (Brislin and Van Buren 1974).

In many ways readjusting to our native culture is like entering a new society. At first there is the excitement of returning. We are back with loved ones—relatives, friends, and colleagues. We are the object of much attention, pride, and excitement, and people listen as we tell of our strange experiences. We go out for the hamburger and Dairy Queen that we have dreamed about while we were abroad. In short, we expect to pick up our lives where we left off.

After this initial excitement subsides, we begin the serious business of reestablishing ourselves in the local culture. It is now that we begin to experience irritation and frustration. Things that once seemed so natural now look extravagant and insensitive in a world of need. People seem so parochial. They soon lose interest in our stories and turn to more important topics of conversation—changes in the latest models of cars, local politics, neighborhood gossip, and sports. We even find it hard to relate to our friends and relatives because they will not listen, or they listen politely but do not seem to understand what we are trying to say. They keep asking ridiculous questions such as "Do people in Guatemala know what telephones are?"

Our frustration is intensified by the fact that all this is so unexpected. We have become strangers in our own culture! We are put into new roles that we did not expect. We are out-of-step with the lifestyles that once seemed so important but now seem so extravagant and self-centered.

Our initial response is defensive. We become angry and critical about local customs. Assuming an attitude of superiority, we withdraw from local events. Sometimes we wish we had not returned "home." We begin to realize that no place is home the way it used to be, that we are pilgrims here on earth.

Joseph Shenk (n.d.:5) describes this feeling:

> "Vacuum" is a good word to describe the first six months we are home. We go from being the center of a lot of activity to being the center of nothing. We are on no committees. We have no community connections. At church people are a bit afraid they might say something which will trigger a speech from us about injustice or something so conversations are kept as superficial as possible. Evenings are quiet unless we are being put on display somewhere.
>
> "Slippage" is another good word. While overseas economically and technologically we have stagnated. Our vocabularies have shrunk. We do not have clothes or vehicles or appliances or homes to match our contemporaries. Since individual worth in the United States and Canada is largely measured by these things it is very possible that we will experience sobering moments of self doubt. In that gasp of lostness we mortgage everything in order to acquire those trappings of relevance which are so important here. Then we discover that we are locked into very tight economic parameters for the next score of years.

Our second response is to try to change the culture. About a year after getting back, we are in danger of being sullen, angry people. We cannot comprehend the wealth around us and are eager for any opportunity to tell the "natives" how poor the rest of the world is. But the people do not seem to want to listen. This only reinforces our frustration and leads us to seek the company of people from other cultures or other returnees.

In time, however, we readjust in one way or another to our original culture. Sometimes our modes of adjustment are destructive to ourselves and others. We become abusive or withdrawn or we leave our home communities.

Normally, however, we again find our place in the society. We learn enough about sports and local politics to participate in neighborhood conversations. We catch up on the latest music and styles of dress so that we no longer stand out in a crowd. We discover that we can build meaningful lives again in our original culture. Above all, we discover that we are not the same persons who left this culture—that profound changes have taken place within us in our years abroad, and that we will never fully fit back into our first "home."

In readjusting, it helps to look at our original society as a foreign community and to enter it the way we entered the culture abroad. Often we are more tolerant of people in other societies than in our own. We need to learn from the "natives," and identify ourselves with them as much as we can, without negating who we now are. We need to realize that they cannot fully understand us, for they have not experienced what we have.

Learning to Adapt to New Cultures

All of us experience dislocation in moving into new settings—some more than others. Tourists can minimize the shock by returning each night to a Hilton hotel, an island of Americana in the middle of an ocean of strange customs. There they feel at home and recover for another day of adventure. Missionaries, however, have come to make this new setting their home.

Culture shock is rarely terminal. With experience and patience, we all learn to live in one way or another in new cultural settings. We learn to eat the local foods and even like them. We find we can ride buses, and even if we are lost, we can find our way back home. We learn the language well enough to carry on ordinary conversations and order oranges in the market. We gain a feel for the value of the local currency. We make friends and discover that the local people do not all look alike. We find that the native doctor can heal us and that we are not going to die from our first sickness. In short, we learn not only how to survive, but also how to live and enjoy the new culture. Our level of satisfaction begins to rise. This place has become "home."

Individuals differ greatly in the extent to which they suffer shock in new cultural settings. In part this depends upon their personalities. Some people are flexible and can live with a great deal of ambiguity, and thus find adapting to new ways quite easy. Others are rigid and need to have a great deal of control over their lives. The severity of shock depends partly upon the differences between their first culture and the culture into which they move. The deeper the differences, the more they must change to fit into the local scene.

But culture shock also depends on the methods used to deal with cultural differences. We can learn methods that help us minimize the tensions of adapting to a new culture and that can, in fact, make it an exciting and growing experience. We can identify with the people in ways that will make our ministry more effective.

Recognizing Our Anxieties

The first way to minimize culture shock is to recognize our anxieties. It is perfectly normal to be afraid of new situations because of the uncertainties they contain. Fear is an important human response that alerts us to respond to immediate and specific dangers. In the long run, however, fear can turn into anxiety—a feeling of uneasiness and dread of some vague, unknown danger. In a sense it is a fear of the uncertainties we face in new settings. It is this anxiety, not specific fears, that is the most damaging part of culture shock.

How can we deal with anxiety when we do not even know what the enemy is? One way is to pinpoint specific anxieties, to recognize them so that we can deal with them. When we consciously look at our dreads, we find that many of them are unfounded. Others can be eliminated by making changes in our lifestyles, since most of them will leave if we learn how to live in the new culture. It helps greatly to know that we are normal when we experience anxieties, and that we can learn ways to deal with anxieties instead of covering them up and hoping they will go away.

Learning the New Culture

Learning a new culture can be either a terrifying ordeal or an exciting new experience. The difference often is the attitude we bring to the situation. If we are afraid of the unknown, we will tend to withdraw into a small circle of friends made up largely of missionary colleagues and national Christians. We will try to reconstruct as best we can an island of Western culture where we can live. The result is a small Christian community largely isolated from the world around it. Here we can carry out our mission work with a minimum of dislocation but with a minimum of witness to the people around us.

On the other hand, we can venture out to learn the new culture. At first this increases our anxieties, but we soon learn that the risk pays off. As our knowledge of the culture grows, our fears of the unknown decrease. We find, moreover, that studying a strange culture and meeting new people can be an exciting and fulfilling experience. We discover that many of the people want our friendship and are delighted when we make the simplest efforts to learn their ways. They are all too ready to be our cultural teachers if we are willing to be honest students.

We learn a culture best by being involved in it. Although it helps to read all we can about a culture before we arrive, there is no substitute for participating in the lives of the people. For example, rather than buying a week's supply of groceries, we can go to the store daily and purchase a few items at a time. We can sit with people in the coffee shop or visit with them in the village square. We can invite them to our homes—after all, they are as curious about our culture as we about theirs—and accept invitations to visit them. We will find that friendships and opportunities to participate in the local culture multiply rapidly if we take time to relate to the people on a personal level.

It is important that we enter into a culture immediately, before we have established routines that insulate us from the people. As the Brewsters (1982) point out, it is better to plunge into a new culture and experience life as the nationals see it than to first establish ourselves in a foreign enclave from which we launch out to do our work. They add, *"From the very first day* it is important to develop many meaningful relationships with local people. The newcomer should early communicate his needs and his desire to be a learner. *People help people who are in need!* Then, when potentially stressful situations come up he can, as learned, secure help, answers, or insights from these insiders" (1982:8–9).

When we enter another culture as genuine students, the people are usually anxious to teach us, for they are proud of their culture. While learning about the culture, we build relationships that make us part of the community.

Interestingly enough, learning a new culture is also an important means of evangelism. We often find more opportunities to witness to non-Christians when we enter the culture as learners than in more formal missionary roles. As we study people, they become interested in us and our beliefs. As their students we are not threatening to them.

Finally, learning the language and culture well is critical to our future missionary service. During our first years, it is important that we learn to speak the language properly, which takes a great deal of time and practice. We are usually so intent upon learning how to communicate our messages that we overlook the sounds and structures of the language. Consequently, we learn to speak, but with foreign accents and broken sentences. We must take the time at the beginning to learn the sounds correctly, for errors soon become unconscious habits that are hard to change and stay with us.

Similarly, we need to learn the local culture in our first years. During this time we are more aware of cultural differences. Later we will lose our sensitivities to strange ways, and work will occupy much of our time. If we want to know a culture well, we must begin to study it immediately and continue to do so all our lives.

Building Trust

Learning to know a new culture and appreciate its ways is not enough. We can do this and still remain outsiders whom the people view with suspicion. As Marvin Mayers (1974) points out, the most important step in entering a new culture is to build trust. Only when people trust us will they listen to what we have to say.

Trust has to do with the value we place upon a relationship, although it is something we seldom stop to consider. Since we build relationships in order to accomplish something—to carry out business, to teach or learn a lesson, or to enter a marriage—we normally focus on what we want to achieve. We stop to consider the state of the relationship only when things go wrong.

Within our own culture, there are many cues that help us evaluate our relationship with each other. They include such things as titles and roles (we would normally expect to trust a preacher or judge); social context (we do not expect a checker at a supermarket to short-change us); and social standing (we are more suspicious of a vagrant than of a well-dressed person).

In a strange culture, however, we do not recognize such cues. Consequently, we find it hard to judge when we can trust a person. Nor do we know how to convince other people that we are trustworthy. There is therefore a great deal of mutual suspicion when a stranger comes to town, particularly when she or he is a foreigner. Relationships in mission service must take priority over the task, particularly at the beginning. Trust in the message depends first upon trust in the messenger.

Trust building begins with an *interest in* and *acceptance of* those among whom we serve. We have our reasons for coming to minister, but these are of little concern to the people. They have their own motives for wanting to relate to us. Only as these are fulfilled will they have reason to continue the relationship. Much later, after a relationship has been established, the people will continue the relationship for its own sake, as friendship and companionship.

Our interest in others must be genuine. People soon detect and deeply resent our building relationships simply to carry out our own goals, for this is a subtle form of manipulation. They feel "used."

True interest expresses itself in many ways. It is seen in our desire to learn about the people, their lives, and their culture. It is reflected symbolically in our willingness to wear their type of clothes, try their food, and visit their homes. It is demonstrated in hospitality, when we invite the people into our homes and let their children play with ours. And it is shown in formal rituals, through official visits, exchanges of gifts, ceremonial banquets, and polite introductions. These formal ways need to be carefully studied and informally checked beforehand with those in the culture, for a mistake here is a public affront and hard to undo. Mayers (1974:34) tells how he invited the assistant mayor of a rural village to a banquet because the mayor was absent, only to find that he had offended the man who was hosting the occasion. The host had a higher social status in the village than the assistant mayor. When, through Mayers's error, he was forced to entertain the assistant mayor, he was publicly acknowledging the superiority of the assistant mayor.

Acceptance begins when we love people as they are, not as we hope to make them. At first this may be hard to do, in part because they are so different from us, and in part because we come with strong desires to bring about change. Unfortunately, we often unknowingly show rejection of other people as individuals. We cut them off when they are talking, laugh at their remarks, question their facts, talk down to them, and compare their culture unfavorably with our own. Or we avoid them, forget their names, or fail to trust them with money or tasks. One missionary never gave tickets to the "natives" because he was afraid they would lose them. By doing so, he expressed distrust as loudly as if he had said it in words.

Building trust requires *openness*. It is a two-way street. Before we can expect others to trust us, we must trust them. If we expect them to open up their lives to us, we must open up ours to them. We need to tear down the pretenses and masks we wear to impress others and must allow them to see who we really are, revealing our weaknesses and fears as well as our strengths. Trust also requires *consistency*. We need to be predictable so the people know what to expect, and what we say in private needs to correspond with what we say in public. It does little good to praise local customs if we make snide comments about them when alone with friends, for what we do in private reflects our true attitudes toward the people.

Finally, trust must be nurtured to maturity. At the outset it is often fragile and easily broken. Consequently, we must focus on building the relationship. We often agree with people not because we accept what they are saying, but as a sign of trust. Disagreement in the early stages of a relationship is often seen not as a difference in opinion, but as a rejection of the person. Later, as the relationship grows, it can stand arguments and dissensions. It can also serve as an effective bridge for the communication of the gospel, for the people can now trust the message because they have learned to trust the messenger. The final stage of a good relationship implies full trust and confidence in another person and a total willingness to entrust oneself into his or her hands.

No task is more important in the first years of ministry in a new culture than the building of trusting relationships with the people. Without these, the people will not listen to the gospel, nor will we ever be accepted into their lives and communities.

Dealing with Stress

Another way to deal with culture shock is to reduce stress whenever possible. When we move into new situations, we experience a great deal of tension, so we need to monitor our feelings to see if we or other members of our family are growing tense, irritable, inflexible, and ready to explode at any minute. But what can we do to reduce the stress before it becomes destructive?

Set realistic goals.   One important way to reduce stress is to set realistic goals. As Myron Loss points out (1983:67), Western Christians have come to equate spirituality with intense activity, and leisure is often seen as a waste of time. We need to recognize that we ourselves are God's first work. Only as we are physically and spiritually healthy can God use us in his work. We need to measure our progress more by who we are becoming than by what we are doing. We need to remember that we are human. We must take time for ourselves and our families—for leisure, exercise, and recreation; for reading and personal growth; and for our devotional life. We must avoid burnout in the short run and live in such a way that we have a lifelong ministry.

There is a second reason why we must set realistic goals during the first years of our ministry, namely, the fact that we simply cannot produce at the same level in foreign situations. We need more energy and time to perform even the simplest task, such as finding shops where supplies are available, papers can be duplicated, and checks cashed. Added to this is our frustration at not being able to "get to work" at what we have come to do. Most of our energy and time is spent simply on survival, and what little we have left must be given to learning the new culture.

Myron Loss charts this tension between our self-expectations and our actual performances in new cultural settings (Loss 1983:66, Figure 13). He points out that within their own culture, the self-expectation of well-adjusted people slightly exceeds their performance. In other cultures, this gap increases significantly. The only way we can deal with the stress produced by this great discrepancy between what we (and others) expect of us and what we, in fact, can do is to reduce our goals to realistic proportions.

FIGURE 13

Expectation Versus Achievement

From Myron Loss, *Culture Shock* (Middleburg, Pa.: Encouragement Ministries, 1983), p. 66.

Learn not to take ourselves too seriously.   A second way to deal with stress is to see ourselves in proper perspective. It is natural to perceive ourselves as the center of activity and the present as the most important time. This, however, places great importance on everything we do and fills each moment with high tension.

We need to see present opportunities within the perspective of our lifelong ministry. Missing tomorrow's meeting, which seems so crucial to us now, will most likely be forgotten five years from now. On the other hand, taking time to learn the language and visit with the people, which now seem to keep us from our work, may in retrospect be the most significant achievements of our early ministry.

Similarly, we need to see our work within the broader ministry of our missionary and national colleagues. No one person is called to carry the full responsibility for the work. We may be needed, but we are not indispensable. The realization of this frees us from a false sense of our importance.

Humor is a great medicine for an excessive sense of self-importance, as it is a sign of inner security and self-esteem. We need to laugh with the people at our mistakes—we make many of them learning a new culture, and they are often very funny. Remember, people are not laughing at *us*, but at our strange ways and our cultural *faux pas*. Learning to laugh with them helps us overcome the fear of failure that so often keeps us from trying something new. We learn new cultures best when we try and fail, laugh, try again, and learn from our mistakes.

Flexibility, too, is a remedy for stress. We are often cantankerous, unbending, and authoritarian when we are self-centered or uncertain. Then every change in plans and every unexpected event generate a great deal of internal stress. But it is hard to program life, particularly in cross-cultural situations and in vocations that relate to people. It is important, therefore, that we hold our plans lightly and are flexible in our lifestyles and in our dealings with human beings.

Forgiveness is a third antidote for the tension that arises from a false sense of self-importance. Ministering the gospel and serving as leader too easily infects a person with a spirit of perfectionism that can ravage his or her Christian life. In that case we begin by not forgiving ourselves and end by not forgiving our fellow missionaries, the national Christians, or the non-Christians around us. The message of God's forgiveness and salvation is blotted out, and we are destroyed by stress arising out of the deepest levels of our identity. After all, if we want to be anything, it is to be righteous!

But the heart of the gospel is forgiveness for sin and failure. So long as we remain on earth, we are not saints untouched by temptations and sins. We are saved sinners, helping one another amid our human failings to follow Jesus Christ. Like Peter, we need to cultivate a life-style of forgiveness both for others and for ourselves. We need to learn again and again that our righteousness is not of our own doing. It is a gift of God to repentant sinners.

Thankfulness is another counteragent to stress. It is easy in strange settings to notice everything that goes wrong and overlook the many things that have gone well. If we stop to think about the events of the day, we will find many moments of joy—mastering a new verb, making a new acquaintance, or watching with awe the sun's setting. Joy and thankfulness contribute a great deal to a peaceful life.

Treat ourselves.   There are times in cross-cultural situations when, no matter how hard we try, our stress levels go up. Even our efforts to reduce tension produce more of it. We are simply fed up with the whole situation and want to leave. At such times we need to treat ourselves and withdraw from our involvement in the new culture. We may read a good book, go on a family picnic, or take a few days off. Sometimes, when homesickness for our original culture becomes too strong, it helps to go to the city and eat at a restaurant in a modern hotel. We all retain identities rooted in the cultures of our childhood, and we cannot starve those identities completely. Often a brief involvement in our first culture is all we need to prepare us for re-immersing ourselves in the new society.

A word of caution is needed here. When we go overseas, there is always the temptaton to withdraw from the people and form a small ghetto of our own. While this may temporarily reduce our stress, in the long run it prevents our entry into the new culture, which would reduce in turn the stress arising from living outside the local cultural frame.

Treating ourselves also implies that we can monitor the timing of particularly stressful situations. There are times when we are prepared to venture into bold new experiences and other times when we are already under such stress that we need to avoid them. Learning a new culture always involves stress, which is essential for growth. What we need is not stress avoidance, but stress management.

Share burdens.   Paul advises us to bear one another's burdens, and this is particularly appropriate in missionary service. A missionary needs to be concerned with the burdens of others, particularly those of his or her spouse and children. This can help prevent the self-centeredness that is a by-product of high stress.

This advice, however, has two sides to it. While we are encouraged to bear the burdens of others, we must be willing to share our own with them and permit them to help carry the load. It is essential that as missionaries we find others to whom we can tell our troubles and turn for advice. Too often there is a tendency to feel that now we are leaders and therefore no longer need someone to pastor us. Nothing is farther from the truth. It is precisely as missionaries that we have the greatest need for someone to whom we can turn for spiritual and personal counsel. Like all vocations, being a missionary has its own problems and temptations. Unfortunately, mission agencies often do not arrange for someone to pastor those in the field, so missionaries are left to find someone on their own.

Beyond Culture Shock

Culture shock may dominate our attention in the first year or two of missionary service, but although at the time we may not believe it, this is a passing experience associated with entry into a new society. Not so with culture learning, which can and should continue throughout our entire ministry.

But culture shock is an important experience, for through it we develop the attitudes and types of relationships that will characterize the nature and effectiveness of our ministry in that society. It is crucial, therefore, for us to know what is happening to us when we enter a new culture, and to mold our responses accordingly.

Alicja Iwanska (1978:701–702) captured well the essence of cross-cultural attitudes and relationships, in her analysis of people living in the northwestern United States. She found that they tend to divide their world into three broad domains of experience. The first is "scenery." This includes nature, the weather, politics, sports, and other events over which they have little control. Scenery provides them with topics for most of their casual conversations. They discuss the seasons, the climate of world affairs, and the Olympics. They suffer through vacations so that they can talk about them later at work and church.

The second domain, according to Iwanska, is "machinery." This includes the "tools" people use for work and for accomplishing their goals. Tools are cared for so long as they are repairable and needed, and then they are discarded. Tools include tractors and livestock, pencils and books, chairs and beds, clothes and homes. They are anything people use to "do the job." They are possessions.

Finally, Iwanska says, these Americans have a domain for "people." These are human beings to whom they relate, who are seen as thinking, feeling, and caring people like themselves.

The significant finding of Iwanska's research is that the group she studied did not see all humans as "people." They saw strange people, such as the American Indians, as "scenery." They visited the reservations the same way they went to a zoo, to see the sights. Moreover, they saw workers, such as Mexican migrant laborers, as "machinery," valued for their productivity and discarded like an old tool when they were no longer useful. The only humans the Americans saw as real "people" tended to be relatives and friends.

The importance of this illustration for young missionaries is obvious. We all tend to treat strange people and new cultures as scenery. We also tend to see those who work for us as machines, whether they are secretaries, nurses, or servants. The most crucial change that must take place in our adjustment to a new culture is to learn to see its people as "people"—as human beings like ourselves—and their culture as our culture. We need to draw a mental circle around them and us and say "we." We need to break down the barrier that separates us into "we" and "they." But this lesson is not new. It lies at the heart of the Christian message of love.

The Incarnational Missionary

So now we have adjusted to our new culture. We have survived culture shock. We know enough of the language to begin our work and have made friends among the people. We have established a household and settled into a routine. The serious problems of dealing with cultural differences are behind us—or so we think.

In fact, our adjustment to the new culture is only beginning at this point. We know enough to carry on our work and conduct our daily lives with a minimum of stress. But we also are becoming aware that there is much more we need to learn about the culture if we truly are to understand and enter it, and we have a vague feeling that we have not yet come to grips with the profound questions raised by the fact that cultures order the world in different ways. The truth is, we are now ready to undertake the difficult task of learning to know and identify with the culture—in other words, we must become incarnational missionaries and deal with the theological issues raised by cultural differences.

Identifying with a New Culture

As we have seen, cultures have three dimensions—knowledge, feelings, and values. There are stumbling blocks along each of them as we seek to become full participants in a society. What are these, and how can we overcome them?

91

Cross-Cultural Misunderstandings

The first barrier to fully entering another culture is misunderstanding. As the term denotes, this has to do with a cognitive block—a lack of knowledge and understanding of the new culture—and that leads to confusion.

Misunderstandings are often humorous and may have little serious consequence. If we eat with our left hand in India, it is to the amusement of the people, who use that hand only for dirty work. We may extend our hand to shake another's in Japan, only to find that others are bowing graciously.

Sometimes, however, misunderstandings are more serious. To give an Indian a gift with the left hand is a serious insult, worse than slapping him in the face. Equally serious is to look at a high-caste person's food when he or she is eating. One North American couple was invited to a high-caste Brahmin wedding. After the ceremony, the foreigners were served first at the feast because they were meat eaters, and it would not do for them to eat with the ritually pure Brahmins. After the meal, the American woman went to thank the hostess for the hospitality and found her in the kitchen. The Westerner did not realize that since her presence as a polluted person in the kitchen defiled all of the food that had been prepared for the Brahmin guests, the unfortunate hostess had to cook another whole feast for them!

Eugene Nida tells of the confusion that arose in one part of Africa when the missionaries came. At first the people were friendly, but later they began to avoid the missionaries. The newcomers tried to find out why. Finally, one old man told them, "When you came, we watched your strange ways. You brought in round tins and on the outside of some were pictures of beans. You opened them and inside were beans, and you ate them. On some were pictures of corn, and inside was corn, and you ate it. On the outside of some were pictures of meat, and inside was meat, and you ate it. When you had your baby, you brought tins and on the outside were pictures of babies. You opened them and fed the meat inside to your baby!" The people's conclusion was perfectly logical—but it was a misunderstanding.

In another part of the world, the missionaries took along a cat as a pet for their children. Unknowingly, they went to a tribe where the only people to keep cats were witches. The locals believed that at night the witches left their bodies and entered the cats, in order to prowl through the huts stealing the souls of the villagers. The next morning, those whose souls had been stolen felt lethargic and weak, and if they did not go to a witch doctor who could retrieve their souls, they would grow weak and die. When the people saw the family cat, they concluded that the missionaries were witches. It did not help when the missionary man got up to preach and said that they had come to gather souls! Nor did it help when the missionary woman washed her hair in the river, and the villagers saw the foam from her shampoo bubble out of her head. Since they had never seen soap, they were certain the bubbles were the souls that the missionaries had stolen.

Unfortunately misunderstandings arise not only in relationships but also with regard to the gospel. For example, young Christians in the highlands of New Guinea came to one missionary and asked him to teach them powerful prayer. Although he told them he had taught them all he knew about prayer, they persisted. They said that they had talked and talked into their boxes, but nothing happened. When the missionary asked what they meant, they brought a small hand-made bamboo box with knobs on the front. They said, "We talk into the box and turn the knobs but nothing happens." Suddenly the missionary realized what had gone wrong. They had often seen him go into his office and turn on the shortwave radio to ask for sugar, meat, tinned goods, and the mail. The next day, out of the sky, came the Missionary Aviation Fellowship plane with the sugar, meat, tinned goods, and mail that he had requested. The people, who knew nothing of shortwave radios, were certain that the missionary had taught them weak prayers, but had kept the strong prayers for himself!

Overcoming misunderstandings. There are two types of misunderstanding that we need to overcome: our misunderstanding of the people and their culture, and their misunderstanding of us. To overcome the first of these, we must enter the new culture as learners. We must make the study of the culture one of our central concerns throughout our missionary ministry, for only then will we be able to communicate the gospel in ways the people understand.

Our temptation here is to think that because we are bearers of the Good News, we have come as teachers. But as teachers we often close the door to our learning to know the people and their customs and beliefs. Through our attitudes of superiority, we also make it difficult for the people to accept us and the message we bring.

Strangely enough we usually have more opportunity to share the gospel meaningfully when we enter a people's society as students rather than teachers. People are proud of their culture, and if we are genuine students, many of them are all too happy to teach us their ways and take us into their lives. When trust has been built, they will become interested in us and our beliefs. We then can share with them the gospel in nonthreatening ways, as friends and participants in their society.

One common and pernicious temptation we face after we have studied a culture for a time is to think that now we really understand it. But this is rarely the case. Years of study only make us aware of how far we are from seeing a cultural world as an insider. One clue that we do not understand some part of a culture is that it seems to make no sense to us. We need always to remember that a culture makes sense to its people. If it does not seem clear to us, we are the ones who misunderstand, and we must study it further.

To overcome the people's misunderstanding of us and our customs, we need to be open and explicit in explaining our ways to them. Once a measure of trust has been built, their questions will be many: "Why do you sleep on beds?" "Do you really eat meat?" "Why haven't you married off your daughter yet; she is already six!" "How much does this cost, and that and this?" "How much money do you make? What do you do with so much?"

People stop by to see our strange ways—how we eat and get ready for bed, how we brush our teeth and write our letters. They want to try our strange machines—the radio, tape recorder, camera, stove, and flashlight. Our children's dolls are passed from hand to hand, and the children themselves are often the objects of careful examination and discussion. And when they are through, they talk about us at the village well and under a tree. For many missionaries, this loss of privacy is hard. They do not realize that such investigations are important in developing trust. Even when they know this, their patience may wear thin after explaining twenty times the way a tape recorder works.

Inside and outside views.   In learning another culture and sharing our own, we soon become aware that there is more than one way to look at a culture. First, we all learn to see our own culture from the inside. We are raised within it and assume it is the only and right way to view reality. Anthropologists refer to this insider's perspective as an "emic" view of a culture.

When we encounter another culture, however, we soon realize that we are looking at it as outsiders. We examine its cultural knowledge by using the categories of our own. Later we discover that the people of the other culture are looking at our ways through their own cultural assumptions. Does this mean we are condemned forever to look at other cultures only from the perspective of our own? If so, is cross-cultural understanding ever possible?

Cross-cultural understanding is possible, and we see it happening all the time. People migrate to new cultures, and people with different backgrounds interact in many settings. Their understandings of one another are never perfect, but they often are pretty good. At first we may think that people must discard their own culture and convert to another one to understand it. For example, we may argue that missionaries must reject their own cultures to become members of another. But this is impossible, since we can never fully erase the imprint of our original culture on the deepest levels of our thoughts, feelings, and values. Even if we could, it would not always be good to do so. As Jacob and Ann Loewen point out (1975:428–443), much of our value to the people we serve is our knowledge of the outside world. In a sense we are culture brokers who live between two worlds and transmit information from one to the other. This does not mean that we should live detached from the culture in which we serve. It does mean that even after we have identified with it as closely as we can, we recognize that in some sense we are still outsiders.

The exception to this may be "migrant" missions. For the most part, Western missionaries have identified with their first culture. They speak of it as "home" and hope to retire there someday. Migrant missionaries, such as the Spanish and Portuguese of the eighteenth and nineteenth century, settle down in a new area and become local citizens. Their offspring marry local people and in time are absorbed into the society. Even here, however, the first-generation migrants are not free from their first culture. It takes several generations for a migrant group and their offspring to be fully assimilated into a society.

Even if the missionary identifies with a new culture, the gospel in one sense always comes from without. It is divine revelation, given in one cultural context to modern recipients.

How, then, is cross-cultural understanding and communication possible? When we participate deeply in another culture, we discover that there are different views of reality. We are forced by this to step outside the thought system of our own culture and think in new ways.

At first we learn, however imperfectly, to see the world through the eyes of our hosts. We then develop higher levels of analysis—metacultural conceptual frameworks—that enable us to stand above both our own and other cultures and compare and translate between them. In the process we become more aware of our own fundamental cultural assumptions, which until now we have taken for granted. For example, we become conscious that in our culture people think of time as an ever-flowing river, moving along in one direction. In another culture it is an ever-circling merry-go-round, always returning to the same place and never going anywhere. When we realize this, we begin to contrast the two systems of time and, in so doing, develop a way of comparing their similarities and dissimilarities.

It is the development of this metacultural framework that characterizes what we call bicultural people—those who have participated deeply in more than one culture. Their broader vision enables them to detach themselves in some measure from their first culture and translate beliefs and practices from one culture to another. They have, in fact, become culture brokers, traders who move between cultures and bring ideas and products from one to the other.

Such an outsider's perspective, not tied to any one culture, is an "etic" view of culture. Anthropology has specialized in developing etic models for the study and comparison of cultures, but in a sense all bicultural people create them, for communication between and understanding of different cultures would be impossible without such a view.

Edward Hall (1959) provides us with an excellent example of how an etic comparison of cultures can help us to understand and communicate with people in another culture. He points out that space, like time, is a silent language and one that is commonly misunderstood in cross-cultural situations because it deals largely with implicit communication. We North Americans, for example, normally stand about four or five feet apart during casual conversations. The topics we discuss at this distance are politics, local matters. recent vacations, the weather, or any public topics in which anyone can take part. Hall calls this our Social Zone (from three to twelve feet away from us). We often feel obliged to relate to people within this zone, to talk to those who sit next to us in a plane or at a ball game.

Outside this Social Zone is our Public Zone. People in this zone can be ignored, for they are too far away for normal conversation.

When we want to communicate more intimately, we drop our voices and move closer together, from one to three feet away. Hall calls this our Personal Zone.

Finally, Hall notes, we have an Intimate Zone that extends from physical contact to within a foot. We use this distance for the most personal communication.

Latin Americans have a similar spatial language, but their zones are smaller. They stand closer to one another when they converse, and they often embrace as a sign of greeting. So long as North and Latin Americans stay within their own cultures, there is no confusion. When they meet, however, there are misunderstandings. In casual conversations we North Americans are uneasy if the Latin Americans are in our Personal Zones, yet are discussing general things that we assign to the Social Zone. So we step back until they are at a comfortable distance. Now the Latin Americans are uneasy—we are in their Public Zones and out of reach. So they step closer until we are in their Social Zone. Again we are uneasy and step back, and again they feel distant and step forward. Neither of us is aware that our cultures use space in different ways. We end up feeling that the Latin Americans are pushy. They, in turn, feel that we are cold and distant. By providing us with a theoretical framework in which both cultures can be compared, Hall helps us to understand the differences between them, so that we can move from one to the other more comfortably.

Emic and etic understandings of a culture complement each other. The former is needed to understand how the people see the world and why they respond to it as they do. The latter is needed to compare one culture with other cultures and test its understandings of the world against reality.

Both approaches are important for us in missions. We need to understand the people and their thinking to translate the gospel into their thought patterns. We need also to understand the Scriptures within their cultural contexts, so that we can translate them into the local culture without losing their divine message. In this sense both the missionary and the message are "incarnational." They must become insiders in a culture to present the gospel in ways the people understand. At the same time, they will remain outsiders—the missionaries as members of other cultures, and the gospel as God's revelation.

Ethnocentrism

Cross-cultural confusion on the cognitive level leads to misunderstandings, but on the affective level it leads to "ethnocentrism," the normal emotional response people have when they confront other cultures for the first time. They have the feeling that their culture is civilized and that others are primitive and backward. This response has to do with attitudes, not with understandings.

The root of ethnocentrism is our human tendency to respond to other people's ways by using our own affective assumptions, and to reinforce these responses with deep feelings of approval or disapproval. When we are confronted by another culture, our own is called into question. Our defense is to avoid the issue by concluding that our culture is better and other people are less civilized (Figure 14).

But ethnocentrism is a two-way street. We feel that people in other cultures are primitive, and they judge us to be uncivilized. This can best be seen by way of an illustration. Some North Americans were hosting a visiting Indian scholar at a restaurant, when one of them who had never been abroad asked the inevitable question, "Do you really eat with your fingers in India?" Implicit in his question, of course, was his cultural attitude that eating with one's fingers is crude and dirty. North Americans may use fingers for carrot sticks, potato chips, and sandwiches, but never for mashed potatoes and gravy, or

FIGURE 14

Ethnocentrism Is a Feeling of Cultural Superiority

Remember: people love their cultures. We need to learn to appreciate another culture and learn not to complain about areas we do not like.

From Paul G. Hiebert, "Anthropological Tools for Missionaries" (Singapore: Haggai Institute, 1983), p. 13.

T-bone steaks. The Indian scholar replied, "You know, in India we look at it differently than you do. I always wash my hands carefully before I eat, and I only use my right hand. And besides, my fingers have never been in anyone else's mouth. When I look at a fork or spoon, I often wonder how many other strangers have already had them in their mouths!"

Ethnocentrism occurs wherever cultural differences are found. North Americans are shocked when they see the poor of other cultures living in the streets. People in those societies are appalled when we surrender our aged and sick and the bodies of our departed to strangers for care.

Ethnocentrism can also be found within a society. Parents and children can be critical of one another because the cultural frames in which they were raised are different. People from one ethnic group see themselves as better than those in another; urban folk look down on their country cousins; and upper-class persons are critical of the poor.

The solution to ethnocentrism is empathy. We need to appreciate other cultures and their ways. But our feelings of superiority and our negative attitudes toward strange customs run deep and are not easily rooted out. One way to overcome enthnocentrism is to be learners in the culture to which we go, for our self-centeredness is often rooted in our ignorance of others. Another is to deal with the philosophical questions raised by cultural pluralism. If we do not examine them, we will be unconsciously threatened by accepting another culture, for to do so calls into question our implicit belief that our own culture is right and others are wrong. A third way to overcome ethnocentrism is to

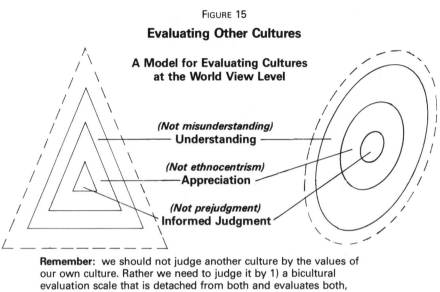

FIGURE 15

Evaluating Other Cultures

**A Model for Evaluating Cultures
at the World View Level**

(Not misunderstanding)
Understanding

(Not ethnocentrism)
Appreciation

(Not prejudgment)
Informed Judgment

Remember: we should not judge another culture by the values of
our own culture. Rather we need to judge it by 1) a bicultural
evaluation scale that is detached from both and evaluates both,
and by 2) the Scriptures and God's revelation.

From Paul G. Hiebert, "Anthropological Tools for Missionaries" (Singapore: Haggai Institute,
1983), p. 13.

avoid stereotyping people in other cultures, but rather to see them as
human beings like ourselves. The recognition of our common humanity bridges the differences that divide us. Finally, we need to remember
that people love their own cultures, and if we wish to reach them, we
must do so within the context of those cultures.

Premature Judgments

We have misunderstandings on the cognitive level and ethnocentrism on the affective level, but what can go wrong on the evaluative
level? The answer lies in premature judgments (see Figure 15). When
we relate to other cultures we tend to judge them before we have
learned to understand or appreciate them. In so doing, we use the
values of our own culture, not of some metacultural framework. Consequently, other cultures look less civilized.

The Viable Missionary: Learner, Trader, Story Teller

Donald N. Larson

As I see it, there are three roles that the missionary can develop in order
to establish viability in the eyes of the national non-Christian: learner, trader
and story teller. I would first become a learner. After three months I would add

another: trader. After three more months, I would add a third: story teller. After three more months, while continuing to be learner, trader and story teller, I would begin to develop other roles specified in my job description.

Let me elaborate. From his position as an outsider, the missionary must find a way to move toward the center if he hopes to influence people. Some roles will help him to make this move. Others will not. His first task is to identify those which are most appropriate and effective. Then he can begin to develop ways and means of communicating his Christian experience through these roles in which he has found acceptance.

Learner

More specifically, as learner, my major emphasis is on language, the primary symbol of identification in my host community. When I try to learn it, they know that I mean business—that they are worth something to me because I make an effort to communicate on their terms. I learn a little each day and put it to use. I talk to a new person every day. I say something new every day. I gradually reach the point where I understand and am understood a little. I can learn much in three months.

I spend my mornings with a language helper (in a structured program or one that I design on my own) from whom I elicit the kinds of materials that I need to talk to people in the afternoons. I show him how to drill me on these materials and then spend a good portion of the morning in practice. Then in the afternoon I go out into public places and make whatever contacts are natural with local residents, talking to them as best I can with my limited proficiency—starting the very first day. I initiate one conversation after another, each of which says both verbally and non-verbally, "I am a learner. Please talk with me and help me." With each conversation partner, I get a little more practice and a little more proficiency, from the first day on.

At the end of my first three months, I have established myself with potentially dozens of people and reached the point where I can make simple statements, ask and answer simple questions, find my way around, learning the meaning of new words on the spot, and most importantly, experience some measure of "at-homeness" in my adopted community. I cannot learn the "whole language" in three months, but I *can* learn to initiate conversations, control them in a limited way and learn a little more about the language from everyone whom I meet.

Trader

When my fourth month begins, I add a role—that of trader, trading experience and insight with people of my adopted community—seeing ourselves more clearly as part of mankind, not just members of different communities or nations. I prepare for this role by periods of residence in as many other places as I can, or vicariously, through course work in anthropology and related fields. I also come equipped with a set of 8 × 10 photos illustrating a wide range of ways to be human.

During the second three months I spend mornings with my language helper learning to talk about the photos in my collection. Thus I build on the language proficiency developed in the first month. I practice my description of these pictures and prepare myself as best I can to answer questions about them. Then in the afternoon I visit casually in the community, using the photos as part of my "show and tell" demonstration. I tell as much as I can about the way others live, how they make their livings, what they do for enjoyment, how they hurt, and how they struggle for survival and satisfaction.

At the end of this second phase, I establish myself not only as a learner but as one who is interested in other people and seeks to trade one bit of information for another. My language proficiency is still developing. I meet many people. Depending upon the size and complexity of the community, I establish myself as a well-known figure by this time. I become a bridge between the people of the local community and a larger world—at least symbolically.

Story Teller

When I begin my seventh month, I shift emphasis again to a new role. Now I become a story teller. I spend mornings with my language helper. Now it is to learn to tell a very simple story to the people whom I meet and respond to their inquiries as best I can. The stories that I tell are based on the wanderings of the people of Israel, the coming of Christ, the formation of God's new people, the movement of the Church into all the world and ultimately into this very community, and finally, my own story of my encounter with Christ and my walk as a Christian. During the mornings I develop these stories and practice them intensively. Then in the afternoon I go into the community, as I have been doing for months, but now to encounter people as story teller. I am still language learner and trader, but I have added the role of story teller. I share as much of the story with as many people as I can each day.

At the end of this third phase, I have made acquaintances and friends. I have had countless experiences that I will never forget. I have left positive impressions as learner, trader and story teller. I am ready for another role, and another and another.

From *Missiology* 6 (April 1978): 158–161.

Cultural relativism.   Premature judgments are usually wrong. Moreover, they close the door to further understanding and communication. What then is the answer?

As anthropologists learned to understand and appreciate other cultures, they came to respect their integrity as viable ways of organizing human life. Some were stronger in one area such as technology, and others in another area such as family ties. But all "do the job," that is, they all make life possible and more or less meaningful. Out of this recognition of the integrity of all cultures emerged the concept of cultural relativism: the belief that all cultures are equally good—that no culture has the right to stand in judgment over the others.

The position of cultural relativism is very attractive. It shows high respect for other people and their cultures and avoids the errors of ethnocentrism and premature judgments. It also deals with the difficult philosophical questions of truth and morality by withholding judgment and affirming the right of each culture to reach its own answers. The price we pay, however, in adopting total cultural relativism is the loss of such things as truth and righteousness. If all explanations of reality are equally valid, we can no longer speak of error, and if all behavior is justified according to its cultural context, we can no longer speak of sin. There is then no need for the gospel and no reason for missions.

What other alternative do we have? How can we avoid the errors of premature and ethnocentric judgments and still affirm truth and righteousness?

Beyond relativism.   There is a growing awareness that no human thought is free from value judgments. Scientists expect one another to be honest and open in the reporting of their findings and careful in the topics of their research. Social scientists must respect the rights of their clients and the people being studied. Businessmen, government officials, and others also have values by which they live. We cannot avoid making judgments, nor can a society exist without them.

On what basis, then, can we judge other cultures without being ethnocentric? We have a right as individuals to make judgments with regard to ourselves, and this includes judging other cultures. But these judgments should be well informed. We need to understand and appreciate other cultures *before* we judge them. Our tendency is to make premature judgments based on ignorance and ethnocentrism.

As Christians we claim another basis for evaluation, namely, biblical norms. As divine revelation they stand in judgment on all cultures, affirming the good in human creativity and condemning the evil. To be sure, non-Christians may reject these biblical norms and use their own. We can only present the gospel in a spirit of redemptive love and let it speak for itself. Truth, in the end, does not depend on what we think or say, but on reality itself. When we bear witness to the truth, we do not claim a superiority for ourselves, but affirm the truth of the gospel.

But what is to keep us from interpreting the Scripture from our own cultural point of view, and so imposing many of our own cultural norms on the people? First, we need to recognize that we have biases when we interpret the Scriptures, and thus be open to correction. We also need to let the gospel work in the lives of new Christians and through them in their culture, recognizing that the same Holy Spirit who leads us is at work in them and leading them to the truth.

Second, we need to study both the values of the culture in which we minister and those of our own. By this approach, we can develop a metacultural framework that enables us to compare and evaluate the two. The process of genuinely seeking to understand another system of values goes a long way in breaking down our monocultural perspectives. It enables us to appreciate the good in other systems and be more critical of our own.

Since even in the formulation of a metacultural system of values our own cultural biases come into play, we need to involve Christian leaders from other cultures in the process. They can detect our cultural blind spots better than we can, just as we often see their cultural prejudgments better than they.

The critical hermeneutics that involve a dialogue between Christians of different cultures can help us all to develop a more culture-free understanding of God's moral standards as revealed in the Bible. On the one hand, it keeps us from the legalism of imposing foreign norms upon a society without taking into account its specific situations. On the other, it keeps us from a situational ethics that is purely relativistic in nature.

Interestingly enough, we cannot reach such a transcultural understanding of the Bible without first experiencing the shattering of our monocultural perspectives of truth and righteousness. Our temptation, when we first realize that other cultures have different norms, is to reject them without examination and to justify our own as biblical. But this only closes the door for us to deal biblically with the problems of another culture. Moreover, it makes the gospel seem foreign to other cultures.

In a sense, to free ourselves from our monocultural biases, we need to face the relativism that comes when we realize that our cultural values are not absolute and then we begin to view all cultures with greater appreciation. But we can develop such a perspective only if we avoid premature judgments and seek to understand and appreciate another culture deeply before we evaluate it. As we enter into another culture, the control our own has on us is weakened. Interestingly enough, when we become bicultural people, we are more appreciative of other cultures and more critical of our own.

Having experienced the shattering of our own cultural absolutes and faced the abyss of relativism, we can move beyond monoculturalism and relativism to an affirmation of cultures and of the transcultural norms of the Scriptures. A truly metacultural perspective can also help us to be more biblical in our understanding of reality.

Evaluation in the three dimensions. As humans we pass judgment on beliefs to determine whether they are true or false, on feelings to decide likes and dislikes, and on values to differentiate right from wrong. As missionaries we are faced with evaluating other cultures and our own along each of these dimensions.

On the cognitive level, we must deal with different perceptions of reality, including diverse ideas about hunting, farming, building houses, human procreation, and diseases. For example, in South India, villagers believe illnesses are caused by local goddesses when they become angry. Consequently, sacrifices must be made to them to stop the plague. We must understand the people's beliefs in order to understand their behavior, but if we want to stop illness, we may decide that modern theories of disease are better. On the other hand, after examining their knowledge of hunting wild game, we may conclude that it is better than our own.

We need to evaluate not only the people's folk sciences but their religious beliefs, for these affect their understanding of Scripture. Although they already have such concepts as God, ancestors, sin, and salvation, these may or may not be adequate for an understanding of the gospel.

On the affective level, we may find that much is a matter of "taste." People in some cultures like their food hot, in other cultures sweet or salty. In one culture they prefer red clothes, houses with steep roofs, eating with their fingers, and entertaining themselves with dramas. In another they choose dark clothes, flat-roofed houses, eating with spoons, and entertaining themselves with mournful songs. Even on this level, however, cultures that prefer peace and compassion may be better than those that emphasize hatred and revenge.

On the evaluative level, a great many of the norms in other cultures are "good." A high value is often placed on loving children, caring for the aged, and sharing with the needy. On the other hand, there may be norms that conflict with biblical values, such as slavery, head-hunting, burning of widows on the funeral pyres of their husbands, or oppression of the poor.

We will find that there is much in every culture that is worthwhile and should not only be retained but encouraged. For instance, most cultures are much better than ours in human relationships and social concern, and we can learn much from them. Much, too, is "neutral" and need not be changed. In most settings wood houses serve as well as mud or brick ones, and a dress is no better than a sari or sarong. Some things in all cultures, however, are false and evil. Since all people are sinners, we should not be surprised that the social structures and cultures they create are affected by sin. It is our corporate sins, not only our individual sins, that God seeks to change.

Living in Two Worlds

When we become bicultural people, we live with two worlds within us. How can we reconcile them?

Rejection

One solution to living in two worlds is to reject one of them. This is most easily done by rejecting the culture in which we are ministering. Obviously, we cannot do this by leaving the society—after all, we are here to be missionaries. But we can do it in more subtle ways. We can brand the culture "primitive," in which case we need not take it seriously. We can reconstruct our own culture within our homes and compounds, creating islands of security in an alien sea. Both of these approaches close the door for us to communicate the gospel meaningfully to the people. On the one hand, the people soon know that we really do not love them. On the other, the gospel comes clothed in a foreign dress.

A second solution is to reject our own culture and "go native." In one sense this seems ideal. Are we not called to identify fully with the people for the sake of the gospel? This approach usually fails for a number of reasons. First, our motives for rejecting our first culture may be wrong. We may have a deep sense of guilt because we belong to an affluent society, yet we know that the gospel has called us to a simple lifestyle and to sharing with a needy world. This, however, is a spiritual problem we must face within ourselves before we enter mission work. We cannot run away from it by simply going abroad. Or we may be cultural misfits in our own society, estranged from our own people. Running away to another society does not solve the psychological problems that give rise to such alienation.

Second, there is a sense in which, no matter how hard we try, we can never truly "go native." We do not come as blank pages on which the new culture can be written. Our lives are already fully scrawled with the writings of our childhood and youth. To deny our early life is to suppress much of who we are. In time this suppression leads to illness, to anger and hatred, and to mental explosions. Identification with another culture cannot come through a denial of some part of ourselves.

Third, try as we may, the people will always know we are foreigners. William Reyburn (1978:746–760) discovered this. After living with the Quechuas—dressing as they dressed, eating as they ate, and walking as they walked—they still referred to him as *patroncito*. No matter what he did to identify with them they considered him an outsider. Finally, in desperation he asked why they did so. A leader stepped up and put his arm around Reyburn's shoulder and whispered, "We call you *patroncito* because you weren't born of an Indian mother."

Fourth, to reject our first culture reduces our usefulness to the church as outside contacts. As insiders of the new culture, we are rivals for resources and positions of leadership. But as outsiders who identify with the local people, we are sources of new ideas, and advocates who can defend their interests in the world at large.

Once-isolated societies can no longer live in detachment. They are being caught, whether they like it or not, in the economic and political webs that encircle the earth. Having little knowledge of how the outside world operates, they are often victims of exploitation—driven from their lands because they have no deeds registered with the government, reduced to field labor because they need money to pay taxes, and robbed of their culture as they are absorbed into towns and cities. One dual role the missionary can play in such situations is to defend the people and their culture against outside invasions and to prepare them to face the modern world into which they will inevitably be absorbed.

An incarnational approach to missions calls for us to affirm both cultures within us—and to build a bridge between them.

Compartmentalization

Another solution to the problem of living in two worlds is compartmentalization. In choosing this option, we adapt ourselves to whatever culture we are in, but we separate the different cultures in our mind. For example, in Africa we act and think African. In the United States we act and think American. And we keep those two worlds apart.

All bicultural people use compartmentalization, and it often provides the simplest and most immediate solution to living in different cultural worlds. Colin Turnbull (1968) describes some modern African leaders born and raised in tribal villages who today live in modern houses in the city. Their city wives dress in Western high fashion and send their children to English schools. They drive cars, drink whiskey, travel the world in jets, and stay in international hotels. But when they visit their relatives in the village, they dress in *dashikis*, speak their native language, eat their tribal food and, in some cases, have a second and third wife who raise their village children according to traditional customs. Turnbull describes one leader who lived in the city in a two-story house: the upstairs was modern, and the downstairs was tribal!

Missionaries, too, compartmentalize cultural worlds. We often move from one culture to another, and from one context to another within a culture. We visit with Brahmin leaders in an Indian village in the morning, with untouchables in the afternoon, and with government officials the next day. This requires "shifting gears" mentally. We learn to live in many different settings and cope with the mental stress created by moving from one to the other.

If carried too far, however, compartmentalization can have serious consequences. First, a particular missionary may be accused of hypocrisy and duplicity. So long as the people in one culture do not see us in another setting, this danger is slight. But eventually this barrier breaks down. The nationals read the reports and articles we write for our home churches, and they see us in the company of foreign visitors and government officials. If they notice too great a change in us, they suspect us of playing games and of identifying with them not because we love them but to achieve our own goals.

Second, compartmentalization does not deal with the inner tensions we face when we live in two worlds. Not only is there the inevitable stress of moving from one context to another, there is also the mental conflict of living in two cultures that have contradictory beliefs, feelings, and values. For example, we are raised in the West to respect individual ownership, but we may serve in a society in which everything—food, clothing, and tools—belongs to the group and can be used by all. The constant shift from one culture to the other can lead to confusion and insecurity and, in the extreme, to an identity crisis and cultural schizophrenia.

Compartmentalization is a tactic all bicultural people must use in certain areas of their lives, but it does not resolve the deep problems raised by living in two or more cultures.

Integration

In the long run and at the deepest levels, we need to work toward an integration between the two cultures within us. To do so we need a well-developed metacultural framework that enables us to accept what is true and good in all cultures and to critique what is false and evil in each of them. Besides a healthy acceptance of cultural variance, it must also provide us with a clear understanding of who we are as bicultural people.

For Christians, this metacultural perspective must be deeply rooted in biblical truth. God's revelation must provide the ultimate assumptions that underlie our beliefs, affections, and norms. And God's redemptive history must provide the greater saga within which we understand all human stories.

Having laid these foundations, we must deal with questions raised by cultural differences as these relate not only to the task of missions but also to the unity of the church. In one sense, the church is a human, multicultural institution; in another, it is one spiritual body. Christ has broken down the walls that divide us, so that we can be united in spite of our differences. Christ is the relativizer of all cultures, for his kingdom stands in judgment of them all.

Levels of Identification

Christ provides us with God's model for ministry. In Christ, God became fully human to save us. But, in doing so, he remained fully God (Phil. 2:5–8). We, too, must identify ourselves as closely as we can with the people without compromising our Christian identity.

Lifestyles

At first we think of "identification" in terms of lifestyle. Naturally, we need to learn the language well, for nowhere is our foreignness more obvious than when we speak with Western accents and broken sentences. For the most part, we can also dress like the people, eat their food in the ways they do, and practice their courtesy. We can even learn to live according to their concepts of time and space.

Many missionaries find it more difficult to adjust to local transportation and housing. Since Westerners find it hard to break their addiction for cars, mission administration meetings are full of discussions regarding automobiles. We argue that they make us more efficient, that we can preach at more meetings and do more work and that we can do so without wearing down our bodies. This may be the case. But we must weigh these arguments against the fact that owning a car in many countries identifies us with the government, with the rich, or with the "foreigners." We must also be careful not to measure our success as missionaries by the number of times we preach or the meetings we attend.

Housing, too, presents problems in identification. We are used to certain types of houses and often find local ones ill-arranged for our purposes. The bathrooms are different, the kitchen is outside, the laundry is a set of tubs, and the living room and bedroom are combined. Even more difficult is a loss of privacy. In the West a person's home is a private sanctuary in which he or she can take refuge when the pressures of the outside world are too great. But in many other societies homes are open to friends and relatives who can drop by unannounced and stay uninvited for a meal or two. Moreover, there may be servants wandering around the house at any time.

Here, too, we must recognize that there are limits to our abilities to identify with another culture—limits determined by the differences between the cultures, by our own personalities, and by the local people. It is easier to identify closely with another culture for a short time—for a year or two—than for a lifetime, particularly if one's family is involved. It is also easier for some to adjust than for others who are less flexible. We must identify as closely as we can with a culture, but not at the expense of our sanity and ministry. We must also keep in mind that people are not always satisfied with everything in their culture and may be looking for better ways of life. Missionary lifestyles should reflect not only the local culture, but also improvements that are within the reach of its people.

No area of identification is more difficult to deal with than our children. We can choose to make sacrifices for ourselves, but can we impose them upon our offspring? Obviously, we should let our children play with the local children, but what about their schooling or dating or even marriage? We will look at these questions in greater detail in chapter 9. Here, it may suffice for us to remember that since our children will never belong fully to our original culture, giving them the opportunity to become aware of the world may be among the greatest gifts we can give them.

Roles

Less obvious is the need for us to work with and even under native leaders as the occasion demands. No matter how much we seek to identify with people, if we are in social positions that place us above them, there will be barriers that divide us. Too often we assume that a missionary is automatically in charge of an institution in which she or he serves. Or that what the missionary says has greater weight than what others say.

It is important, where churches already exist, that missionaries be willing to serve alongside and eventually subordinate to local leaders. For instance, missionary nurses must show respect when they work under national doctors, as must missionary evangelists when they serve under local church leaders.

Problems arise in such situations. The national church leaders may have no vision for evangelism or church planting, and the doctors may be more interested in building their own reputations than in the welfare of their patients. But these problems are found in churches in all parts of the world. In such situations we need—as much as possible but without compromising our own personal calling—to work within the existing structures to bring about change. We will look further at these problems in chapter 10.

Attitudes

Ultimately identification does not take place just because we live like the host people or even if we become part of their social structures. It begins with our attitudes toward them. We can live in their houses, work under their authority, and even marry our children to theirs, but if we have a sense of distance and superiority, they will soon know it. On the other hand, if we live in foreign houses and eat foreign foods, but truly love the people, they will know that, too.

A genuine love for the people will lead us to treat them with dignity and respect and to trust them not only with our goods but also with power and positions of leadership. It will prevent us from treating them with condescension as "children," or with disdain as "uncivilized." It will also give us a deeper desire to share with them the Good News of the gospel that has been given to us.

Identification on the level of attitudes is the basis for all other identifications. Strangely enough, when we truly love people and see them as humans like ourselves, differences in lifestyle and roles seem less significant. There is an underlying bond that unites us with them. On the other hand, this love enables us to go much further in identifying with people in our roles and lifestyles than we can out of duty alone. But this is nothing new for the Christian. The apostle Paul wrote, "Though I give away all that I possess, and even give my body to be burnt, if I have no love, it goes for nothing" (1 Cor. 13:3).

5

Cultural Assumptions of Western Missionaries

As we have seen, two of the greatest problems faced by missionaries entering new cultures are misunderstandings and premature judgments. These are particularly damaging because we are generally unaware of them. As individuals we have strong convictions about reality. Rarely do we stop to ask whether others see it as we do, since it seems so obvious that things are as we see them.

But other people see the world differently. The assumptions they make about reality are different from ours. Consequently their world view—the ways they look at the world—is different.

How, then, can we uncover the misunderstandings and false judgments we make when we enter another culture? Obviously, we must study the other culture to understand it as those within it see it. This, in fact, should be our lifelong endeavor.

Less obvious is our need to understand our own world view. After all, don't we already know about our own culture and its beliefs? The answer to this is no, as we have already seen. We know much about our culture, but we are largely unaware of the deep assumptions we make about the nature of reality. We must therefore also study our own world view if we wish to uncover the misunderstandings and ethnocentrism that arise when we serve in another culture. Only then can we build bridges of understanding and acceptance with the local people.

Studying World Views

If world views are largely implicit, how can we study them? There is no easy answer to this question, nor are our conclusions always certain. As we study a people's culture, we must infer their basic assumptions from their beliefs and practices. We need to look for similarities that seem to run like a thread through a wide range of cultural beliefs and behavior and that make sense out of them. We need to examine the language in order to discover the categories the people use in their thinking. And we need to study their symbols and their rituals, such as festivals and rites of birth, marriage, and death. These often reveal their deepest beliefs. We often see the basic assumptions underlying another culture better than we recognize our own. We learn our primary culture as children and now take its assumptions for granted. Other cultures, however, are strange to us, so we look for their foundations in order to understand them. Similarly, foreigners often see our assumptions more clearly than we do, and we need to listen to what they say about us. Our initial reaction is often to reject their observations as overly critical. On further reflection, however, we often find them to be true.

We also see our own culture more clearly when we come back from living in another setting. As we have seen, entering another culture forces us to develop a measure of detachment from our own. When we return "home," we see it through new eyes.

There are several ways we can go about studying a world view. The easiest, and the one we will use here, is to look for common themes that run throughout a culture. These may be expressed in different ways in different areas of life. For example, after studying North American culture, we may conclude that its people desire material comfort and possessions. This is seen in the houses they build, the cars they drive, and the goods in their shops. It is also seen in the fact that they evaluate one another's status by their material possessions, or that they find it hard to adjust to the living conditions in other parts of the world.

North American and Other World Views

What, then, are some themes in a North American world view, and how do these contrast with themes in other parts of the world? To make our study manageable, we must oversimplify our analysis. There are many cultures in North America, and their world-view themes differ markedly. At best we can suggest some themes that characterize mainstream North American culture, particularly middle-class life, keeping in mind that there are a great many exceptions to each.

To understand them more clearly by way of comparison, we will refer occasionally to themes found in other parts of the world. Obviously, such comparisons are gross generalizations, but they can help us begin thinking about our own world view and its differences from other ones. Later, each of us must examine in more detail our own personal assumptions and those of the people among whom we work if we want to build bridges of mutual understanding and appreciation.

A Real and Rational World

One assumption most Americans make is that we live in a real world that exists outside ourselves. We see this world as rational and orderly and operating according to natural laws that can be discovered and understood by human reason. Matter obeys the laws of physics and chemistry, and animals reflect the laws of biology, psychology, and sociology. The importance of the sciences in our society is one evidence of this conviction.

Because the world is real, we take history seriously. We make a sharp distinction between actual events and myth, facts and fiction, reality and dreams or illusions.

This perception of reality is rooted in a Judeo-Christian belief that God created a universe that exists outside of but dependent upon himself. It stands in stark contrast to the world views of South and Southeast Asia, where the outside world is thought to be an illusion, a dream in the mind of a god. People exist only as projections of that dreamer. To discover reality, they must look within themselves by meditation and realize that they are but a part of one universal spirit. Clearly in such a world people can learn little about ultimate truth through science and the systematic examination of the external world.

Obviously our Christian appeal to history as proof of the gospel makes little sense to those who see all history as merely a figment of their imaginations. To them the biblical stories are myths, not records of facts.

Cartesian dualism. As we have seen, a basic shift took place when the gospel was translated into the neo-Platonic world view of the Greeks. The biblical dualism that differentiates between God and creation (which included spirits, humans, and nature) was replaced by a dualism between spirit and matter, soul and body. This Greek dualism has dominated Western thought since the seventeenth century and has led to a sharp distinction between science and religion.

At first, science was seen as the servant to Christian faith. In time, however, it gained its independence and began to dominate the modern scene. Many Westerners today use science to explain the natural world and limit religion to miracles and visions and to such matters of ultimate concern as creation and spiritual destiny.

This dualism has led Western missionaries to make a distinction between "spiritual ministries," such as evangelism and pastoral work, and the "social gospel" that deals with the material problems of this world. Consequently, although they preached the gospel, they introduced science in schools and hospitals. The result, too often, has been a spread of secularism, as people accepted the sciences the missionaries brought but rejected their religious teachings.

Most cultures do not make a sharp distinction between the natural and the supernatural. For them, the supernatural pervades the natural. It should not surprise us, therefore, that Christians in these cultures in some ways understand the biblical message better than we do, or that they do not separate the spiritual and human dimensions of the gospel.

Humans versus nature. As North Americans we draw a sharp line between humans and other forms of life. We see humans as having a unique value.

This view is partly a Christian legacy. It arose from the Christian view that humans have eternal souls. Such a view stands in sharp contrast to that of many cultures in which humans are seen as one kind of life among many. Nature itself is thought to be alive. Animals and even inanimate objects have their own spirits, and no dividing line separates humans from plants, mountains, rocks, and rivers.

Because most North Americans think of humans as unique, they see them in charge of the natural world. Humans must tame it and make it serve them. Edward Stewart (1972:62) comments:

> The American's formidable and sometimes reckless drive to control the physical world is perhaps unmatched as a dominant assumption in any other major society. It is best expressed by the engineer's approach to the world based on technology and applied to social spheres as "social and human engineering." . . . The natural laws assumed to underlie the physical world seem to be harnessed for producing material welfare and hence are at the service of man.

This view has led Americans to study the world and develop their sciences and technology. It has also led to a combat mentality in which humans must "beat the heat," "fight diseases," and "conquer space." The result has been a destructive exploitation of nature, with little concern for the ecological system.

Other societies make alternative assumptions about the relationship between humans and nature. In much of the Far East, humans are considered to be part of nature and the physical world, instead of opposed to it. For example, in contrast to North American buildings, which are often built to dominate their surroundings, the forms and lines of those in Japan stress a unity between the natural environment and man-made structures.

The Jews in the Old Testament saw themselves as the gardeners of nature. For them, nature was basically good and kind, and God's command to "subdue" the earth did not mean to fight it. Rather, humans were meant to care for nature. Western Christians owe their view of a hostile nature more to the Greeks than to the Bible.

People in other cultures see themselves not as controlling or integrating with the natural world, but as overwhelmed by it. The Colombian mestizos, for instance, consider nature dangerous and animated by the presence of spirits.

> Sun, moon and stars, wind and rain, heat and cold, light and shadow—all are believed to have occasionally harmful powers over the body and the mind. The cool air near the river, or the reflected heat from rocks or trails, are thought to be dangerous, the same as the shadow of certain trees or the damp of the forest. Dangers are seen everywhere in nature and to try to understand them or to overcome them would be considered foolishness [Reichel-Dolmatoff 1961:440].

The people's attitude, therefore, is one of helplessness and distrust, which are confined not only to the physical environment but extend also to social and political life.

Materialism and property. Given our dualism between spiritual and material realities and our growing emphasis since the sixteenth century on the material world and the sciences, it should not surprise us that we North Americans tend to judge humans by what they own. We measure achievement and success primarily by the quantity of material goods a person possesses. Moreover, we tend to equate happiness more with material wealth and physical well-being than with intellectual or spiritual gains. Condon and Yousef (1975:114) write, " 'The pursuit of happiness' means, for many Americans, the opportunity to secure property and material comforts."

This emphasis on material gain can be seen in North American business practices. A higher priority is normally placed on profit than on the well-being of the workers. There is little place for the aged, the disabled, and the slow. In times of company crisis, low-level workers are laid off long before the salaries of high-level administrators are cut.

Abroad North Americans tend to judge other cultures by their technological development. Stewart (1972:61) notes that "guided by his stress on material things, the American overseas almost invariably judges the local society by his standards of material welfare defined in the broad sense of including physical comfort and health." As missionaries we compare our culture with the cultures in which we serve: cars versus oxcarts and cycles, electricity versus oil lamps, gas stoves and refrigerators versus campfires and dried foods, and sanitary toilets versus the bush. And we conclude that we are more civilized.

Stewart (1972:64) points out that Americans consider it almost a right to be materially well off and physically comfortable. We expect swift and convenient transportation, clean and healthful foods, and comfortable homes equipped with numerous labor-saving devices, certainly including central heating and hot water.

The right of private ownership.   This emphasis on material things is associated with a deep belief that property can be privately owned. We buy land, houses, cars, and other goods outright, and no one can use them without our permission. We can sell them without getting the approval of our relatives or neighbors.

The concept of private ownership stands in sharp contrast to much of the tribal world, where land, boats, houses, and even food belong to larger groups such as family lineages, associations, or the tribe as a whole. Individuals can use, but not sell, such property. An example of this is the recent decision by an American Indian tribe not to sell its tribal lands. The elders said that the ancestors did not object, nor did the living; but the unborn children objected, because they would lose if the land was sold.

Missionaries often misunderstand this joint ownership of property. They try to buy land, and later they try to sell the houses they build. In many tribes these always belong to the group. Or missionaries refuse to let the people use their material goods freely, or take food from their store, and the people see them as stingy.

Progress.   For the most part, North Americans believe in progress. We look for a better way of life and think of this largely in material terms. We tend to believe that the basic problems of the world are technological and can be solved by more scientific research and more money. "Progress" means physical comfort, good health, a high standard of living for everyone, and an avoidance of hardship and danger. We assume that there are enough resources in the world for all people to have such a life.

George Foster (1965) has found that people in peasant societies believe that basic resources—land, wealth, health, friendships, power, status, and security—are limited and in short supply. There is not enough for everyone. Consequently, people must compete for them. The result is a suspicion of others and the belief that if one person is getting ahead the others must be losing out. People in such societies are not encouraged to work hard to advance, and those who do are often boycotted by the group. Rather, they are encouraged to keep their place and fit into the society as it already exists.

Analytical Approach

North Americans love to analyze situations. We believe not only that the world is real, but also that it is orderly. We believe that with careful study we can understand why things happen and remedy whatever goes wrong.

One basic way we analyze things is through science. We use it to break down the world into neat categories and discover causes and consequences. We use that knowledge to control the world around us. When problems arise, we assume they can be solved if we have enough time and money.

This problem-solving approach extends to most areas of Western life. When an accident happens, we want to know what went wrong and who is at fault. At home we want to know who left the lights on or the door open, so that we can fix the blame. If human organizations experience difficulties or do not achieve their goals, we assume there is a "problem" that we can solve. All this assumes that the world is orderly, that humans can understand this order, and that they have the power to change things.

Peoples in many cultures see the world as basically incomprehensible or, if it can be understood, as beyond human control. We see this as "fatalism," for the people seem to make no effort to change their conditions. But many see this as the way things really are. Others see the world as having many interlinked causes and effects. Consequently, planning is difficult and blame cannot be fixed on any one cause, person, or action.

Either-or thinking. In their analysis of situations North Americans tend to sort reality into opposing categories which are often assigned moral values. Arensberg and Niehoff (1964:214) state:

> A special characteristic of Western thinking ... is that of making twofold judgments based on principles. ... A situation or action is assigned to a category held high, thus providing a justification for positive effort, or to one held low, with justification for rejection, avoidance, or other negative action. Twofold judgments seem to be the rule in Western and American life: moral-immoral, legal-illegal, right-wrong, sin-virtue, success-failure, clean-dirty, civilized-primitive, practical-impractical, introvert-extrovert, secular-religious, Christian-pagan.

For example, many North Americans believe that other countries must be on the side of either the United States or the Soviet Union. There is no allowance made for politically neutral countries that want to go their own ways and be friends with both.

North Americans also make a sharp distinction between work and play. Work is what people do for a living, and at work they must obey the boss and keep busy. Play, on the other hand, is a time for relaxation and enjoyment when people may do as they please.

North Americans place a great emphasis on work. To be without it is to be a social leper. This is what one Indian anthropologist found when he tried to study an American village. As long as he just sat around, trying to talk with the men, no one spoke to him. But when he got a part-time job with a local farmer, he was accepted by all.

But work is not all there is to American life. There is also play, an activity that is sharply distinguished from work. Arensberg and Niehoff (1964:161–162) write:

> To most persons brought up in the present-day American environment of farming, business, or industry, work is what they do regularly, grimly, purposefully (for the money, or to do a good job, or to make a success), whether they enjoy it or not. It is a necessity, perhaps even more importantly, a duty, a "good thing in itself since one ought to keep occupied." A man is judged by his work. It is serious adult business, for a man is supposed "to get ahead" or "make a contribution" to the community or mankind.
>
> Play is different. It is fun, an outlet from work, without serious purpose except to make work more efficient. It is the lesser category ... [so] when it is time for work, then play and the lighter pursuits must be put aside.

Work is serious business; play is fun. At work we are machines: at play we can be intensely personal.

This dichotomy between work and play is incomprehensible to societies where work and play are interwoven in everyday life. In these societies building a new house or netting a school of fish may provide the occasion for a whole community to work, dance, and sing together. And planting crops is a social activity characterized by singing and visiting.

Another North American dichotomy is the separation of public from private. We carry on business, politics, and religion in public. Here we are expected to conform to the norms of the society and be on our best behavior. By contrast our home is our private refuge where we can express ourselves as we wish. Until recent times, only men were allowed to compete in the public domain. Women were supposed to maintain the private domain so that men would have a place to recover after a hard day at work.

Planning. In a rational orderly world it is possible to plan for the future—to set goals and achieve them, to see problems and forestall them. It is important, therefore, to plan ahead.

We also believe that people have the power of choice. We have control of our lives, and we can do something if we really want to. Choice carries with it a sense of responsibility. Those who succeed are applauded, and those who fail are blamed. A great deal of time in North American life is spent on fixing blame.

Given our penchant for planning, it should not surprise us that we are often frustrated when we go to societies where people do not plan ahead. Even more frustrating is the fact that in many cultures people not only do not plan, they think it is wrong to do so. Some anthropologists argue that even more than technology, Westerners today are exporting to the world high management skills that are based on planning and organizational leadership.

Pragmatism. When we take a problem-solving approach to life, we generally examine several solutions. In choosing between them, we usually want to know which one of them works, not which is true or right. In other words, we are pragmatists. We seldom stop to ask whether the goals we pursue are themselves worthwhile. We want to know how to get things done, and we rarely examine the means we use to see if they are "good." We assume they must be if they do the job.

In much of the world this attitude is seen as bad. People in other countries feel that being a good person and building relationships is more important than getting a job done and that using evil methods to achieve good goals is wrong. Consequently, they judge us by looking at what kinds of lives we live and how we relate to others. We may do great work, but if our daily living does not reflect our message, the people will reject what we say. Regarding the planting of the church in New Guinea, G. F. Vicedom (1961:16–17) writes:

> God comes to the people through His messengers. It is by their behavior that God is judged. If the missionaries succeed in entering into the life of the people, in adapting themselves to their way of living, if they learn the language and become in many ways the advisers, friends and helpers of the Papuans, gradually confidence in the missionaries is established. This confidence is at once transferred to God. God is always judged in the light of what the missionaries are.

Stewart (1972:36) points out that "the means-orientation or operationalism of the American from the point of view of the non-Westerner often appears to sacrifice the end for the means."

A Mechanistic World View

We Americans tend to think of nature as if it were a machine in which the actions of the various parts are determined by external forces. This mechanistic view of reality emerged during the sixteenth century as part of the physical sciences (Burtt 1954). In fact, the first science was "mechanics." Later, social scientists, seeing the success of the natural sciences, adopted mechanistic models of humans and societies.

According to Peter Berger (1974), this mechanistic way of looking at things has come to dominate our thinking and is reflected in the two hallmarks of society in the United States, the factory and the bureaucracy. In the former we treat nature as if it were a machine and mold it to fit our purposes. We think of it as composed of lifeless atoms and chemicals controlled by impersonal forces. In the latter we organize people as if they were cogs in a machine. A bureaucratic approach tends to standardize roles, such as secretaries or miners or nurses, so that they are interchangeable like bolts in a car. We do not want people to bring their personal problems to work because then we must begin treating them as human beings.

In a mechanistic world we can control both nature and humans if we know the right formulas. We can be in charge in our assigned areas and pursue our goals without constantly having to negotiate them with others. At work, completing tasks takes priority over building relationships.

This mechanistic view stands in sharp contrast to most other world views, which treat nature and humans as living beings. In these worlds life is full of negotiations over which an individual has only limited control. Relationships take precedence over completing tasks. It is no wonder, then, that people in these cultures see North Americans as impersonal and rude. When they come to visit the missionaries, they are so busy that they have little time for socializing. According to the local people, such missionaries have their priorities wrong. They should leave their work and take time for visiting. After all, the people say, are not relationships more important than getting work done?

Production and profit.   Here are the central values in factories and bureaucracies, the criteria by which the success of these institutions is measured. Work and "doing" are therefore important. We must keep busy. To be idle is laziness—one of the key sins of our culture. In fact, as Warner, Meeker, and Eells (1960) point out, we measure a person's status in the society chiefly in terms of his or her occupation and income.

In most of the non-Western world, *being* and *becoming* take priority over *doing* (Kluckhohn and Strodtbeck 1961:15–17). The contemplative person is revered. The intellectual, mystic, or guru are highly respected, rather than the North American cultural heroes who perform great deeds—the sportsman, rock star, and corporate executive. When Americans go abroad, this difference creates a great deal of confusion, particularly in the area of leadership. We look for young influential persons motivated toward action. Orientals and South Asians, however, listen to wise old leaders who take time to think.

Quantification.   Another basic characteristic of a mechanistic world view is measurability. Without quantified measurements, it is hard to assess production and profits. Stewart (1972:68) points out:

> Success and failure are measured by statistics; so is amount of work, ability, intelligence and performance. The quantification of the world and experience is deeply ingrained in the American. It is only with difficulty that he can understand the reactions of others to his practices. Yet, to some foreigners the description of, say, the Washington Monument in terms of statistics, devitalizes the experience of seeing it.

Along with quantification goes an emphasis on scale—the more or bigger, the better. Greatness is attributed to those who can accumulate the most money, win the most games, or fight the biggest battles. This emphasis on bigness appears grandiose in those cultures that emphasize simplicity and balance, or that measure greatness by qualities that cannot be measured.

Assembly-line mentality.   An important ingredient in a mechanistic approach to production is an assembly-line mentality. Peter Berger

(1974) observes that in bureaucracies as well as in factories, jobs are broken down into small tasks that are arranged sequentially and are done by different people. By doing this, we can standardize the procedure and get the same results every time.

Breaking down jobs into little parts leads to specialization. One person in a factory puts the tires on an automobile, another the bumper. One doctor in a hospital fixes the feet, another the eyes or the nose and throat.

This fragmentation and specialization of work is totally foreign to societies in which craftsmanship plays a central role. In these a workman produces an object as a whole. He first has a vision of a mask or canoe. Then he works to make that vision a reality. What he produces is a part of himself. He is an artist.

Individualism

One of the most fundamental themes in the world view of the United States is that the individual is the basic building block of society. Each human should be an autonomous person with his or her own separate identity. We learn this from childhood. At an early age we are taught to think and choose for ourselves, given our own personal property, and encouraged to stand up for our rights. Edward Stewart (1972:32) writes:

> The self-centeredness of the child is seldom questioned. It is implicitly accepted that each child or person should be encouraged to decide for himself, develop his own opinions, solve his own problems, have his own things and, in general, learn to view the world from the point of view of the self.

Even in our groups everyone is expected to retain his or her individuality.

Closely related to this individualism is our belief that each person has worth and that all people have inalienable rights to life, liberty, and the pursuit of happiness. Freedom is an unquestioned value.

In many tribes and in the Orient, the basic building block of the society is not an individual person but a group. People do not see themselves as autonomous, but as members of the groups to which they belong. The individual is not highly differentiated from the social nexus. In Japan, for instance, people get their identity from their groups (cf. Nakamura 1964). Because they are involved in different groups, they have different "faces." In such situations maintaining "dignity," "respect," "honor," and harmonious relationships is of highest importance. The most valued human qualities are those that help preserve group loyalties and maintain congenial social relationships. Qualities needed to achieve certain individual goals are secondary. This, of course, is very confusing to a North American who may suggest an objective and practical course of action in order to complete a task, only to find it rejected to preserve someone's "face."

Search for identity. One thing outsiders frequently note is that we Americans seem to be searching for an identity. If we are autonomous persons, that identity is tied primarily to who we are as individuals. Consequently there is a great need to achieve—to become somebody. Those who lack this motivation are not rewarded in our society.

This emphasis on personal achievement is closely tied to our notion of competition between individuals, whether for material goods, status, or power, and to our concepts of free enterprise. In a world in which it is thought there are ever more goods to be had, one person's gain does not necessarily mean another person's loss. Consequently, competition is not often seen as destructive to those who lose. We believe all can win if they have a strong motivation to achieve and if they strive hard enough.

The search for personal identity is largely foreign in societies where the basic reference point is the group, not the individual. A person is born into a group and therefore has an identity within the society. For example, a woman knows who she is because she belongs to a family, lineage, and clan that have certain statuses in the tribe. She knows that all important decisions concerning her life, such as marriage, place of residence, and work, will be decided by her groups. Although this may restrict her personal freedom, she is taught that self-actualization and personal growth must always give way to the best interests of her groups. This, of course, frustrates North Americans, and they may try to get her to assert herself.

Self-reliance. At the heart of a North American's identity is self-reliance. Francis Hsu, a Chinese anthropologist, points out (1961:248) that the greatest fears Americans have are to be dependent on others and to be without money. When our car breaks down, we hesitate to call friends for help. And when we need money, we would rather borrow from a bank than beg a loan from a brother or cousin. On the other hand, when others ask us for help, we take the request seriously, just because we know it is not made lightly. But we resent it when people constantly ask for loans, for help in baby-sitting, and for transportation. We expect people to take care of themselves.

Self-reliance belongs to a cluster of North American values: autonomy, self-actualization, and personal growth. Even in the United States, however, we gain much of our identity and self-realization within the context of other people. How can we organize groups when we place so much emphasis on individuals? The answer lies partly in voluntary associations of people who get together on the basis of common goals or shared interests. In these, membership is gained not by rights of birth or power but by personal conformity to the group. It should not surprise us, therefore, that while most Americans stress their rights as autonomous persons, in practice they choose to conform to the groups of which they are a part. Few of us dare to be different. Eccentricity is reserved for those who have a clear sense of identity and an established place in society.

Self-reliance is not necessarily a positive value in much of the world. In the Orient and Latin America, where there are strong attachments to family and immediate groups, it marks a loner—someone who is antisocial.

In South Asia the ideal relationships are ones of dependency. One such relationship is that of *patron* and *client*. The patron, like a parent, is totally responsible for the welfare of his clients. He not only provides them with basic foodstuffs and a small income, he must also give them blankets when their old ones are in tatters, extra rice when a festival comes, and straw for their cattle when the supply runs out. Clients, in fact, can ask a patron for whatever they think he may grant, but this is not considered begging—no more than Christians think they are begging when they ask God for help.

Clients, for their part, must be totally loyal to their patron. They must work for him whenever he has work to be done, and for no additional wage. They must vote for him and, if necessary, fight for him. On the other hand, they are assured work, for they cannot be fired. Many inherit their right to serve a particular patron from their parents. Both patrons and clients gain in the relationship. The patron gains power and prestige within the society, and the client gains security.

This difference in view about what constitutes a good relationship has led to a great deal of confusion between North Americans and South Asians. Americans are upset when they find themselves totally responsible for those who work for them. They misinterpret the requests of their workers as begging. South Asians, on the other hand, see us as cold and impersonal when we are not willing to build deep, lasting relationships that involve total commitment to one another. American relationships are seen as superficial because they are limited merely to friendships.

Contractual groups.   In a society that emphasizes individualism and achievement, relationships are often weakly bonded. We tend to participate in group activities as separate individuals united in a common activity, rather than as a corporate body in which our personal rights and interests are subordinate to those of the group. Stewart (1972:56) writes:

> [North Americans] do not commit themselves wholeheartedly to a group or organization. They pursue their own personal goals while co-operating with others who, likewise, pursue their own. They accept the goals of the group, but if their expectations are unfulfilled they then feel free to leave and join another group.

This commitment to our own self-interests can be seen in our re-lationships to our kinsmen and local community. When a better job appears elsewhere, we are ready to leave relatives and friends for the sake of advancement and higher incomes. The results are high mobil-ity and a tendency to limit our group activities to superficial relation-ships in voluntary associations that we can leave when we want. We join because they meet our needs and are free to leave when they do not. As Francis Hsu (1963) points out, the basic form of social organ-ization in North America is the club. We organize clubs to serve almost any purpose. There are sports clubs, business and neighborhood as-sociations, friendship cliques, common-interest groups, professional societies, and special task forces such as the American Cancer Society. We even think of our churches as voluntary associations rather than groups based on kinship and birth.

Relationships are casual in many voluntary associations, and the associations themselves are often short-lived. Other groups such as schools, hospitals, and businesses become formal institutions with clearly organized roles and property, and they endure over time. Even in these, however, relationships are often superficial and confined to such specific areas of life as work, sports, and politics, and individuals have a right to leave if they wish.

This emphasis on voluntarism seems strange in societies where the strongest relationships are inherited and one's strongest ties are to kinsmen and the local community. These are the basis for enduring groups that meet all of a person's essential needs and, in return, de-mand his or her greatest loyalties. A person does not form casual associations with virtual strangers, for they may be enemies, although often they are permitted to enter the community after they have been adopted by one of the kinship groups. For example, missionaries are often considered outsiders until they are made members of a local tribe.

Need to be liked.   North Americans place a high value on being liked and see it as a sign of success in social relationships. Since we worry over how others feel about us, we read acceptance or rejection into every comment and gesture they make. The glad handshake, the ready smile, the slap on the back, and the word of praise have all become our normal behavior. Without such expressions of friendship and popularity, we are confused and unsure of ourselves because we are denied one of the requirements for personal assurance in a highly individualistic society. Social success is an important measure of achievement. Stewart (1972:58) notes, "Americans tend to judge their personal and social success by popularity—almost literally by the number of people who like them." To be liked means we are worthy of love. It does not necessarily mean we need to like others in return or that our relationships with them will result in friendships.

This need for acceptance is especially strong when we go overseas. North Americans expect common folk throughout the world to like them, and we are deeply hurt when we are rejected. We therefore hate to be involved in tasks that are "unpopular," even though we know they need to be done. Our need to be liked often frustrates our European missionary colleagues, who feel that popular approval is a poor measure of success and that doing one's task well is its own reward.

Private ownership.   One particularly important expression of American individualism is private ownership of property. At an early age, children have their own toys and rooms. They may be encouraged to share what they have, but the fact that they own these things is not questioned. Later, ownership is extended to most things—land, cars, trees, pens, and books. There are exceptions. Fish and birds are public property until caught. Air and ocean, too, can be used by everyone. Private ownership carries with it the exclusive right to use and dispose of property. A buyer becomes an outright owner of a house or car and can destroy either if he or she wishes.

The American concept of ownership is not shared in many cultures, where ownership lies with the tribe or a kinship group. For example, the land of the American Indians belonged to clans and lineages. A young son needing land would ask his elders, and they would give him a piece that he could keep as long as he cultivated it. When he stopped, the land reverted back to the kinship group. When foreigners such as the pilgrims came, they were allowed the use of land that was not already being used. The Indians assumed that the gifts the newcomers gave in exchange were normal tokens of appreciation for the temporary use of the land. Later, when the tribe needed the land for its own people, they asked the foreigners to leave. In their eyes, Indian land could never be alienated from its tribal owners, for it belonged not only to the living but also to the ancestors and the unborn. The pilgrims, on the other hand, thought they had bought the land with their small gifts and called the natives "Indian givers" for wanting back what they had apparently sold.

Humanitarianism.   One expression of the North American emphasis on the worth of every individual is humanitarianism. We often respond promptly to calls for help and give liberally to others when disaster strikes. American aid for victims of famines or earthquakes, or when wars leave children orphans and nations destroyed, is well known.

Concern for human suffering is one of the finest heritages of our culture. Unfortunately, it is too often highly institutionalized and impersonal. In many parts of the world humanitarianism means hospitality, which is highly personal. It means taking the victim into one's home and social life. As Mortimer Arias (1982) points out, this was one of the recommended ways by which the Old Testament Israelites were encouraged to evangelize their neighbors.

We must recognize that the people of poorer countries usually do not share with everyone; they cannot. However, they do have their own patterns of sharing that are selective and personal. For example, in the Middle East the halt, lame, and blind line up at the mosque or church door where they are given alms. The naive American reaction is too often condemnatory: "All these poor people! This community must be very cruel or backward not to take care of these people!" (Arensberg and Niehoff 1964:183).

Equality

The American concept of the dignity of each individual is closely tied to another of its fundamental assumptions, namely, the equality of all human beings. Interpersonal relationships are typically horizontal, conducted between autonomous individuals who are presumed to be equals.

For us, equality means equal opportunity, not the automatic leveling of everyone to a common social and economic standard of living. We have rejected socialistic forms of government. Rather, we idealize a democracy where everyone has a say in decision making, but in which the majority does not violate the rights of the minority.

To say that equality is a fundamental assumption in the United States does not mean that society always puts it into practice. Our culture's treatment of blacks and women is evidence of this. But it does mean that when blacks and women call for equality in opportunity, few Americans argue publicly that these groups are inferior and should be content with lower positions.

This emphasis on equality seems absurd to the majority of the world's cultures, in which hierarchy is seen as the reality and the norm for all forms of life. Just as humans are higher than animals and some kinds of animals higher than others, so some kinds of humans are higher than other kinds of humans. For instance, in South Asia, people born into different castes are seen as intrinsically different and do not have the same rights or responsibilities within a society. Those who are born low are impure because of sins in their previous lives. Only through suffering and acceptance of their lot in life will these sins be consumed. Then they will be reborn as high-caste people or as gods. Consequently, to say that all people are born the same is to say that sins go unpunished and righteousness is destroyed.

Informality. Because of our emphasis on equality, Americans are uneasy in hierarchical relationships. Consequently, even in these we tend to establish an informal atmosphere of equality. For example, a boss may kid around with his or her workers, or a commanding officer may ask a subordinate a personal question or offer a cup of coffee before beginning a conversation. Underlying this superficial egalitarian ethos, however, there is usually an unspoken yet well-defined hierarchy based on class, wealth, education, and/or authority.

This informality, at times, is an asset when North Americans are abroad. However, it is more often misunderstood, particularly in parts of the world where proper formalities are emphasized. Arensberg and Niehoff (1964:180) point out;

> To neglect giving a man his due deference in countries where rank is important is to insult him. The American tendency of trying to make a foreigner into a regular or average guy by an informal, breezy, and "kidding" approach is dangerous. The informality of genuine kindness, courtesy, and unostentatious living is worth retaining. But when informality means belittling or disparaging a person whom his own society ranks high, then it is not advisable. American "kidding" and humor are very special products of an egalitarian culture. They are best kept at home.

Until we are thoroughly familiar with a culture and its people's ways of thinking it is best to be respectful and retain a measure of reserve.

Competition and free enterprise. North Americans place high value on competition; winning is encouraged from early childhood on. Schoolchildren are taught to compete for grades, and learn that hero worship goes with success in sports. Parker Palmer (1977:9) points out that the American schooling system has become a training ground for competition and self-reliance. And "more than a training ground, education itself has become a competitive arena where winners and losers are determined even before the contest is scheduled to begin."

Later in life North Americans compete for status, power, fame, and fortune. There is little place for the losers, the weak, the failures, the slow, and the retarded. The prevailing attitude often is that anyone could win if he or she tried hard enough.

Closely tied to competition is the idea of free enterprise. Everyone should have an equal chance to achieve, and competition guarantees that the best person wins. Underlying this is the notion of "fair play." All must compete by the same rules. In sports there are umpires, who act like miniature gods and make sure that all play fairly. In life there is the government, which is expected to mete out equal justice to all.

This emphasis on competition and personal achievement is foreign to many societies, such as the Hopi Indians of North America, the Kikuyu of Kenya, and the Thai, who are taught at an early age not to compete or take issue with others, especially those of their own age or older. Consequently, in school they help each other complete their homework and do not try to be the first to complete their lessons. Nor do they disagree with their teachers, who are their elders. And in sports they do not like to keep score because they do not want to win over others in their group. This type of attitude is almost incomprehensible to many Americans.

Direct and confrontational. Because of our emphasis on completing tasks and on informality, we tend to be direct, even confrontational, in our relationships. When faced with a problem, we want immediately to get to its source. As Stewart (1972:52) explains, "This means facing the facts, meeting the problem head on, putting the cards on the table, and getting information 'straight from the horse's mouth.' It is also desirable to face people directly, to confront them intentionally." There is little time for politeness and etiquette or for building relationships.

In contrast to this, Japanese culture places a high premium on manners and on working indirectly to achieve one's purposes. Skill in social maneuvers is esteemed. Bluntness or open confrontation embarrasses friends and is ridiculed by others. Unlike North Americans, who want to lay out the matters and reach decisions in business meetings, the Japanese prefer to reach decisions in personal negotiations behind the scene. Meetings are used to confirm decisions already reached and to make them known to the public.

Another contrast to the American idea of confrontation is found in many societies, such as Thailand, that use a third party to reach agreements. Important business is often conducted by means of an emissary and not by the direct face-to-face negotiations of the principals involved. This includes even such personal decisions as choosing a mate or buying a house.

Cooperation. It may seem contradictory, but a little reflection shows that competition among North Americans occurs within the context of cooperation, for competition requires a considerable amount of coordination among individuals and groups (Stewart 1972:56). For example, in football, players must compete as teams, even though honor in the end is often given to individuals. It should not surprise us, therefore, that Americans are known for their ability to work together, even as they pursue their personal goals.

This ability to combine competition and cooperation rests in the fact that Americans do not commit themselves wholeheartedly to a group or organization, but cooperate so long as they see some personal gain in doing so. They accept the goals of a group and play by its rules, but if their expectations are not fulfilled, they feel free to leave it and join another group.

The facility to cooperate with others who strongly disagree with them is an asset when North Americans go overseas, for it enables them to act as catalysts to bring others to work together. It is also misunderstood. People in other cultures often feel that we are opportunists, willing to give up our principles to get a job done.

Priority of Time over Space

North Americans place high value on time. It is scarce and should be saved, for it can be wasted and lost. Above all, time is money, for work and wages are tied to it. Employers buy the time of their workers. They assign work, set deadlines, and pay wages on the basis of time. Airlines set tight schedules, and travelers fret if they have to wait. Schools and offices order their activities by the clock. Time is one of the major means by which the complex activities of American society are organized.

This emphasis on time is quite foreign to peoples of nonindustrial cultures. In most peasant societies work is not tied to time, but to the immediate task to be done; to seasonal emergencies and fluctuations in temperature and rain; and to ceremonial cycles. Rituals, dramas, and church services begin when the people have gathered and continue until the performance is finished. Friends and relatives visit without watching the clock. North Americans run into trouble in such societies if they expect people to show up for meetings "on time" or to attend regularly.

Linear time. For Americans, time is linear. It has a beginning and an end. It flows by at a steady rate without repeating itself and can therefore be measured and planned.

With a linear time reference, two questions are of vital importance: How did things begin, and how will they end? These have played an important part in Western thought, both religious and secular. In Christianity we have both theologies of creation and eschatology that deal with the world and teachings on salvation and eternal destiny that deal with the individual.

Time in many parts of the world is not a commodity nor is it linear. In much of Africa, for instance, it is episodic and discontinuous. There is no absolute "clock" or single time scale. Rather, there are many kinds of time—mythical time, historical time, ritual time, agricultural time, seasonal time, solar time, lunar time, and so on. Each of these has a different duration and quality. Farming takes place in agricultural time, but births, marriages, deaths, and festivals occur in ritual time. In a way, North Americans handle time this way when they speak of a calendar year, which begins January 1; a business year, which may begin July 1; and a school year, which begins in the fall. But in Africa there is no one fundamental system of time to which all the others relate. They all relate to one another in complex ways. Moreover, in all these times the focus is on the event at hand rather than on time itself.

In some tribes time is almost like a pendulum, going back and forth. People in these cultures speak of going back in time, or of time "stopping."

In South Asia time is both cyclical and linear. Thus, humans are born and reborn in an endless series of lives, but these cycles are part of the greater life of a god, which has a beginning and an end.

Future-oriented. Linear time points to a future, and for North Americans it is the future rather than the past that is important. This leads us to plan for the future as if we can control it, and to look forward to good times ahead. We place little emphasis on learning about our ancestors and maintaining our family and national traditions. Old ways are readily rejected in favor of something new. Mottos like "Today is the first day of the rest of your life" and "Plan ahead" are our designs for living. This notion of time is closely tied to our faith in progress and action.

In the West, time is seen as a commodity that can be planned and controlled. J. C. Condon (1976:345) writes that "middle class Americans are obsessed with the elusive quality of time. Consequently, they attempt to control its passage with innumerable schedules. In so doing, they translate their action-orientation into a drive towards the future." We keep datebooks and plan our schedule often weeks and months ahead. This is often frustrating to foreigners from cultures where people stop to see each other without appointments. Our factories, airlines, and schools program their activities to the minute, a practice incomprehensible to people raised in cultures where activities begin when everyone is ready.

Traditional African thought focuses on the past, not the future. As John Mbiti (1969:15–28) points out, there are three divisions of time: (1) the mythical past, a long period during which the great tribal events took place; (2) the recent past, a relatively short period during which those ancestors who are still remembered lived; and (3) the present, which includes the immediate past and the immediate future. What is important is the great events that took place in the past, not events that may take place in the future.

Traditional Chinese thought, on the other hand, places the greatest emphasis on the present, which includes both the immediate past and the immediate future. Stewart (1972:67) writes:

> In effect, time does not provide the Chinese with the same rational means of explanation and prediction which the American and Western concept yields in material cause and effect. The Chinese demonstrates a much greater situation-centeredness and seeks an explanation for a specific happening in terms of other factors occurring at the same time as the event in question. . . . This view of time inclines the Chinese to integrate with the environment rather than master it and to adapt to a situation rather than change it.

Emphasis on youth. Closely related to the North American orientation toward the future is a strong emphasis on youth. This can be seen in commercial advertising and entertainment—the old are rarely represented. At work the young are often thought to be more active and productive, and to hold more promise than do the elderly, despite their experience and sense of responsibility.

There are few attempts to involve the aged in the mainstream of the society. Once they retire, they are viewed as having little to contribute. And when they can no longer care for themselves, they are often placed in nursing homes, isolated from their offspring and cared for by nonrelatives.

This emphasis on youth is the exception rather than the rule around the world. In most societies old people are viewed positively as wise and experienced. They are shown respect, given places of honor and consulted about family and community decisions. There is no retirement from public life. In fact, retirement as we conceive of it now is a twentieth-century phenomenon found mainly in the West.

Time over space. One of the more fundamental misunderstandings North Americans have of traditional peasant and tribal societies has to do with their ideas of land and its relationship to time. For us, time is more important than space. Land is a secular commodity and can be bought and sold like anything else. Time, on the other hand, is precious because once we live our lives, it is gone.

The priority that North Americans place on time as against space is seen in our emphasis on history. We put dates on our checks and applications. We keep track of birthdays, anniversaries, and other important events in our lives. It is hard, therefore, for us to understand people who see land and space as more important than time.

In many cultures, however, land is sacred and more important than time. It ties people to their ancestors, culture heroes, and gods in a way that time never can. Although the people realize that they cannot go back into the past and live in the days these great ones performed their great works, they can go to the *places* where these great events took place. Here, for instance, is the tree planted by our great forefather. There is the hill on which our founders drove out the enemy and established our tribe. Raja Rao (1967:vii) captures this view of space when he writes:

> There is no village in India, however mean, that has not a rich *sthalapurana* or legendary history, of its own. Some god or godlike hero has passed by the village—Rama might have rested under this pipal-tree, Sita might have dried her clothes, after her bath, on this yellow stone, or the Mahatma himself, on one of his many pilgrimages through the country, might have slept in this hut, the low one, by the village gate. In this way the past mingles with the present, and the gods mingle with men. . . .

Probably North American Christians come closest to understanding this view of reality when we visit Palestine and see the land God gave to Abraham, walk the streets of the city David built, and stand on the hill where Jesus died. Somehow, space makes the past real and significant by bridging the gulf of time that separates us from biblical events.

Daniel Kelly (1982) believes that it is the insensitivity of missionaries to the American Indians' views of land and relationships, and our emphasis on time and achievements, that have been the greatest obstacles in our ministry to the Indians. We have not understood the importance of space and ancestors in the lives of the people among whom we minister.

Emphasis on Sight

Another fundamental theme in the North American world view is our emphasis on sight rather than sound, touch, taste, or smell. This is seen in our choice of such phrases as "world view," "I see," and "Let's look at the situation."

This Western emphasis on a visual world had its roots in Greek philosophy. Walter Ong (1969:642) writes:

> Plato's ideas launched the new world, the opposite of the old, which his attacks on the poets proscribed. The old [oral] world had made much of man's activities and of human struggle as the focus or axis of all reality. Where the old world had been warm and human, Plato's "ideas" or "forms" . . . were cold and abstract. The old world had been mobile, [and] event-full, [and its] [oral] narrative was a swirl of exciting activity. In contrast, Plato's new ideas were motionless, ahistorical; where the old view had held all knowledge in a concrete human setting, the new traced everything to the abstract, the other-worldly, the totally objective, the fixed, modeled on an immobile figure visualized on a motionless field.

The crowning achievement of this view was literacy and the printed word.

Most of the world's people, however, continue to live in oral societies where their primary experiences are passing events and memories of these events. Since ideas are not frozen in writing, recollections are reinterpreted over time. There is less a sense of a fixed, unchanging reality and more a feeling that the world is a dynamic interaction of people and other beings.

Thought and expression in oral cultures are often highly organized, but in ways that are unfamiliar and often uncongenial to the literate mind. This organization is based on formulas, proverbs, riddles, myths, and other set expressions. For the most part, these deal with concrete human experiences rather than abstract thought, and they involve an interaction between the teller and the listener rather than a one-way communication.

As Western missionaries we need to realize how deeply literacy has molded our thinking, producing patterns of thought that seem perfectly natural to us, but which are strange to those in nonliterate societies.

Abstract knowledge. Writing divorces a message from the messenger. We read books and test their ideas not so much on the trustworthiness of the writer, whom we often do not know, as on the merit of the ideas themselves. Our tendency, therefore, is to build abstract systems of ideas that are not directly related to the experiences of everyday life.

Missionaries are often guilty of this divorce between systems of ideas and everyday life. In our sermons and books we present abstract ideas and try to set straight the cognitive structures of our listeners. In our classroom lectures we give more attention to stating right theologies than to their application to the problems young Christians face in their lives.

Developing abstract systems of thought is an important task in the church, particularly for its leaders. In a sense they are responsible for defining the meaning of the gospel within a particular cultural setting, and for defending it against the intellectual attacks of other systems of belief. But we must not forget that oral people think in terms of stories, concrete examples, and specific human problems. They speak of what they have experienced. Thus, when Jesus used parables in talking to the crowds, he was using methods of thought and communication that they readily understood. In dealing with the ordinary people in oral societies, we too must emphasize the personal and the concrete message of the gospel.

For oral people communication is always tied to a person. They hear a preacher in a particular setting and judge the message by his or her life. For this reason, we must be careful to live out what we preach, or we will not be heard.

Storage of information in writing. North Americans place a great value on written information and trust a message more if it is in print. Since they assume that literacy is the highest form of communication, they invest heavily in schools, books, magazines, and written records. Unwittingly, they often look down on nonliterate people as ignorant and without knowledge.

This bias toward literacy is common in missions, where great effort has been expended on making people literate and on producing printed Bibles, tracts, correspondence courses, and books. Little thought is given to the traditional nonliterate forms of communication found in oral societies.

But much of the world depends on the oral information stored in songs, proverbs, riddles, stories, dramas, dance, rituals, and oratory— and we can use these to store and communicate the gospel. People do not first have to become literate before they can hear and understand its message. Although literacy plays an important role in the modern world and will spread to many contemporary oral cultures, we do not have to wait until then before we bring people the Good News.

Emphasis on knowledge.   Given an efficient writing system to store and retrieve information, it is not surprising that North Americans highly value knowledge. Books, encyclopedias, and now computers make vast amounts of information available to a literate person. Emphasis is placed in schools on the acquisition of knowledge for its own sake, and those who acquire it are given high status. Science itself would be impossible without writing.

Often, however, this knowledge is divorced from life. University professors do not always live the best of lives. And in the church, faith is generally defined in terms of knowledge, not discipleship. To many of us, the lordship of Christ usually means giving mental and verbal assent to his deity, rather than living our lives in obedience to his commandments.

Oral cultures, on the other hand, prize wisdom—the ability to deal with everyday issues for the good of the society and the individuals involved, the skill of making knowledge relevant to life. Consequently, the wisdom of a teacher is tested against his or her life.

It is important for us as missionaries to realize that many national leaders with whom we work may appear to be "ignorant," or lacking large amounts of knowledge, but in fact they may be wise in their handling of church situations. They often know how to deal effectively with people and how to apply Scripture to everyday living.

Systematic.   Writing allows us to organize vast amounts of information into coherent systems of knowledge of great precision by allowing us to go back to ideas and rework them. It also fosters rational thought by divorcing ideas from feelings. No printed page carries the emotional impact that an oral presentation can.

As Western missionaries we bring along this drive to systematize and rationalize our activities. We stress long-range planning, logical development of educational programs, and well-defined institutional structures. We are upset when people are late or do not keep their appointments. In our schools we teach systems of knowledge, and in our churches we are concerned about abstract theologies.

We need to understand that in oral societies life is experienced for what it really is, as a series of rich but chaotic events often detached from one another. Life is a series of interruptions. A farmer may want to plow his field, but he must wait for rain. And when he starts, some distant relatives may drop by for a few days. At the same time, a child gets sick and needs attention, or a raiding party from up the valley steals some cattle. Given the cultural demands placed upon him, it is no wonder he finds little place for planning and punctuality.

Systems of thought are needed, particularly by the leaders who must lay the foundations for young churches and help such churches face the modern world that is increasingly encroaching them. But even they must keep in mind that communication among the common people is most effective when it draws upon the concrete experiences of life.

Our Missionary Biases

We have looked briefly at some of the major themes in the North American world view. Obviously, there are many more, and those we have considered need to be examined in far more detail with regard both to their content and to the ways in which they influence our everyday lives.

Not all Western missionaries share all these assumptions, for we are influenced by the particular cultures in which we grew up. But before we reject them, we need to take a careful look, for world-view assumptions are largely implicit, and the North American world view is far more deeply rooted in our thinking than we often want to acknowledge.

It is important to recognize the quality and extent of our cultural biases when we work in cross-cultural settings, for then we can work to reduce our ethnocentrism and mutual misunderstandings. This does not mean, however, that we must give up our basic assumptions. We must have some assumptions, for there is no way to organize a culture or our thoughts without them.

Another reason we need to examine our cultural assumptions carefully is that many of them run counter to Christian thought. True, North American culture has been deeply molded by Christianity, but it is not intrinsically a Christian culture. We must critically examine it in the light of Scripture. If we do not, we are likely to confuse it with the gospel and introduce a culture-bound gospel to others.

PART

Cultural Differences and the Message

6

Cultural Differences and the Message

Cultural differences affect the messengers, but they also affect the message. Each society looks at the world in its own way, and that way is encoded in its language and culture. No language is unbiased, no culture theologically neutral. Consequently, cross-cultural translation and communication are no easy tasks. If we do not understand this, we are in danger of being ineffective messengers at best, and at worst of communicating a gospel that is misunderstood and distorted.

Cultural differences can affect a message in several ways. First, unless the messengers themselves use forms of communication the people understand, they will not receive the message. It does no good to speak Swahili to Indian villagers, or put on a ritual dance, if the people reject or are unfamiliar with that form of communication. Second, the message itself must be translated so that the people understand it with a minimum of distortion. This involves not only putting it in local words that have similar meanings to the original, but also checking that the meanings of those words in the broader context of that culture do not introduce distortion. Third, the message must be contextualized into local cultural forms. Church buildings, forms of worship, and leadership styles should be adapted to fit the cultural patterns. Birth rites, weddings, funerals, and other rituals must be made indigenous, yet truly Christian. Finally, the people must develop a theology in which Scripture speaks to them in their particular historical and cultural setting.

We will deal in this chapter with the first of these: How can we translate the gospel into new cultural forms and communicate it effectively?

Symbols and Communication

Communication is the transmission of information from a "sender" to a "receiver." It may occur between humans, animals, and even machines. Bees communicate to each other the direction in which honey is found. Humans turn keys to start their cars and feed information and directions into calculators; time clocks ring school bells; signal lights regulate traffic; dogs warn of burglars; conductors direct orchestras; and computers fly planes. In all these cases information is transmitted to bring about change. This is one of the major purposes of all communication.

Here we are concerned not with communication in a general sense, but with interpersonal communication—between God and humans, and between humans and other humans—for this is at the heart of the missionary task. Interpersonal communication is distinct, for both the "sender" and the "receiver" are intelligent beings, and their messages include not only statements about concrete realities but also expressions of abstract thoughts and feelings.

Ideas and emotions cannot be communicated directly from mind to mind. They must first be expressed in forms that others can receive through their senses (Figure 16). It is this linkage of meanings and feelings to forms that lies at the heart of what we call "symbols."

The Nature of Symbols

Symbols are complex things. They are the linkage of meanings with forms in the minds of certain people, who use them to achieve particular goals in specific situations. In other words, symbols link together

FIGURE 16

Ideas Must Be Expressed in Concrete Forms to Be Received

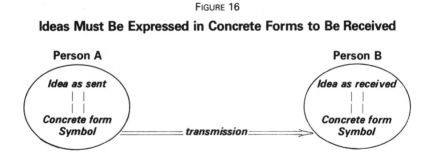

(1) meanings, (2) forms, (3) persons, (4) functions, and (5) contexts. (See Figure 17.)

For instance, North Americans in certain situations will say the word *tree*, meaning a certain type of plant ("Cut down that *tree!*"). In another context they use the word to mean genealogical descent ("This is a chart of my family *tree*"), a certain kind of animal ("Did you see that *tree* toad?"), or a wooden peg ("He used a *tree*nail to fasten the planks").

People in other cultures use different forms to express similar meanings. Indians speak of *chetlu* when referring to trees (plants), but *santhanamu* when talking of their lineages.

Culture makes communication possible. Symbols must be shared by a group of people for communication to take place. The people must associate the same forms and meanings in similar contexts and for similar purposes. Conversely, communication creates social groups that share the same cultures.

Types of symbols.   Symbols do not stand alone. They are parts of larger systems within which individual symbols find their meaning and use. For example, we have spoken language made up of thousands of words, written language composed of letters, color codes such as stop-and-go lights, designated shapes for street signs, and even smells that communicate messages (Table 2). As we have already seen, our use of time and space has meaning. So, often, does our use of silence.

Each of these systems of symbols is used to communicate certain types of information. For example, we normally use words to convey cognitive messages but gestures and tones of voice to communicate feelings. In fact, much of the time, particularly in face-to-face communication, we use several systems simultaneously—spoken language, paralanguage, kinesics or body language, and temporal and spatial symbols. Mehrabian (1979:173) estimates that in an average

FIGURE 17

Symbols Are a Complex Set of Relationships

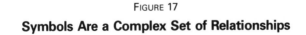
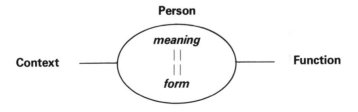

conversation between two people in North America 38 percent of what is communicated is verbal. More than 60 percent is nonverbal!

Meaning of symbols.   Through symbols we communicate ideas, feelings, and values. They acquire these meanings in two different ways. First, many symbols refer to events in everyday life. They point to trees, birds, green, happiness, jealousy, stealing, and a thousand other specific experiences people have, lumping these into categories. But in pointing to some things, they do not point to other related things. For example, in English when we say "red" we think of it as a certain color. But we are also saying "not purple," "not orange," and so on. Symbols, therefore, gain meanings partly from their relationships to other symbols that belong to their same domain or field. These meanings in which symbols point to some things and not to others are sometimes called *denotative* meanings.

Second, symbols have *connotative* meanings. These are meanings that we give to symbols that come from other domains of thought and feeling. For instance, when we speak of "red neck," "Reds," "red-eye special," and "to be in the red," the word no longer means the color red, but has taken on other meanings in the realm of politics, travel, or economics.

While it is easy to learn the denotative meanings of symbols in other cultures, it is often hard to discover their connotative meanings, in part because we are often unaware that they even exist, and also because we must look at the many ways symbols are used in different contexts to learn these meanings. It is important that we learn both sets of meanings for the symbols we use. If we do not, our messages, which may be denotatively correct, will be misunderstood because of their connotations—like the banker who said, when he heard that Jesus saves, "That's nothing. I do too."

So far we have looked at the explicit meanings of symbols. But symbols refer not only to the conscious world of human thoughts and feelings. They also reflect the implicit assumptions people make about reality—in other words, their world view. This is particularly true of words, for language is the most powerful of symbol systems. These hidden meanings often create the greatest problems in cross-cultural communication, because we and the people themselves are often unaware of them. The people take them for granted, since that is the way the world is for them, and we find it hard to discover them if the people cannot articulate them. Often we learn of them only by observing how the people use these symbols in relationship to one another in many different contexts (Table 3).

Implicit meanings can best be seen by way of an illustration. When

TABLE 2

There Are Many Different Systems of Symbols

1 Spoken Language	Speech, radio broadcasting
2 Paralanguage	Rhythm, pitch, resonance, articulation, inflection, speaking rates and pauses, emotional tones
3 Written Language	Writing, inscriptions, billboards
4 Pictorial	Road signs, street maps, magical drawings, astrological charts, diagrams, graphs, military insignias, college decals, logos
5 Kinesics	Body gestures, movements of hands and feet, facial expressions, eye contact, postures
6 Audio	Music (rock, jazz, waltz, etc.), bells, gongs, drums, firecrackers, gun salutes, temple horns
7 Spatial	Standing distances, crowding, closeness or intimacy, separation between speaker and audience, marching in rank order (sometimes referred to as "proxemics")
8 Temporal	Meaning of "on time" and "late," importance placed on time, New Year festivals, relative ages of communicators, sequence of events in rituals
9 Touch	Embraces, shaking hands, guiding the blind, touching one another's feet, placing hands on one's head, physical torture, religious flagellation
10 Taste	Cakes and sweets for celebrations, prestige foods, ethnic and cultural foods, peace pipes, "hot" and "cold" foods in South Asia, vegetarianism, sacramental foods
11 Smell	Perfume, incense, shaman's smoke-filled hut, body odors, smell of flowers
12 Ecological Features	Holy mountains, sacred trees, tabooed territories, hallowed rivers, historical sites
13 Silence	Pauses in sentences, blank page, silence in court or temple, empty space in Japanese art, lack of response
14 Rituals	(Rituals use many of the systems above but add another dimension of symbols, namely reenactment or symbolic performance.) Weddings, funerals, ritual sacrifices, church services, Lord's Supper
15 Human artifacts	Architecture, furniture, decor, clothes, cosmetics, symbols of wealth such as watches, cars, houses, hats.

Adapted in part from a list suggested by Donald Smith, Daystar Communications, Nairobi.

missionaries went to South India, they wondered what word they should use for "God." There were several words in Telugu from which they could choose: *parameshwara* (Ruler of All), *bhagavanthudu* (One

Worthy of Worship), *ishvarudu* (The Supreme Siva), and *devudu* (God). The first three had problems, for they were commonly associated with specific gods in the Hindu pantheon, so the translators chose to use the last word.

TABLE 3

Words Have Implicit As Well As Explicit Meanings

	Denotative Meanings	Connotative Meanings
Explicit Meanings	The meanings of words, which the people give to us	Ideas, feelings, and values consciously associated with the words
Implicit Meanings	Basic structure of the words as categories systems	Deep beliefs, feelings, and judgments unconsciously associated with the words

An analysis of the implicit meanings of these words, however, shows us some of the problems in using any of these terms to translate the biblical concept of God. If we ask English speakers to organize a list of categories related to nature, they tend to do so in certain ways (see Figure 18). Most of them put *woman, man*, and *girl* together and call them "humans." They put *tree* and *bush* together and label them "plants." They put *lion, dog*, and *cow* together and refer to them as "animals." They classify *sand* and *rock* as "inanimate objects," and they put *God, angels*, and *demons* together and designate them "supernatural beings." Since many are not sure what to do with *bacteria, virus, fly*, and *bug*, they often create still other categories for them. They reject putting *Mickey Mouse* into any of these groupings, claiming that he belongs to another domain of categories altogether, namely "fictional characters" as against "real things."

There are fundamental philosophical and theological assumptions implicit within this classification. First, it makes a sharp distinction between supernatural beings and natural ones. Most Westerners think of the former in religious terms and mentally place them in some other world, whether heaven or hell. The rest they think of in scientific terms and locate them on earth.

Second, living beings are divided into distinct categories that are thought to have different kinds of life. For example, we can eat animals but not humans, because the life of the latter is somehow different from that of the former. Similarly, we worship God, but to worship a human is sacrilegious, because the worship is given to beings that are not gods. Finally, a sharp distinction is drawn between "living" and "nonliving" things, between organic and inorganic, or animate and inanimate.

If we asked Telugu speakers to organize the same words or their connotative equivalents in Telugu, they do so differently (see Figure 19).

The fundamental assumptions underlying this Telugu classification are obviously different from those in English. First, there is no sharp distinction between kinds of life. In fact, *all life is considered to be the same*. This is a cardinal belief in Hinduism *(eka jivam)*. Consequently, since there is no real difference between gods and humans, one can worship a saint or guru. On the other hand, since there is no real distinction between the life in an animal and that in a human, killing a cow or, for some, even a dog or a bug is murder!

Second, all living beings, including the gods, are part of the "created" world. The word *creation* in fact is misleading, for this universe and its gods, spirits, humans, animals, and plants are all dreams in the mind of the great god Brahma, who himself is an emanation of Brahman. Hence they are *maya*, or transient and illusory. Brahman, however, is not a living being, but an ultimate impersonal force. Finally, the earth itself is not totally inanimate. There is a sense in which it too is alive and therefore must be respected.

Cultural Differences in Symbol Systems

Different cultures have different symbols. We know that languages are different, but we may not realize that so are body motions, tones of voice, tastes, and even the use of silence. Samarin points out (Smalley 1978:673–677) that the Blackfoot Indians of the United States often did not talk for five minutes, even when they were making social calls, while the Gbeya of the Central African Republic engage in conversation after a meal rather than during it. And, when visiting the sick, the Gbeya assume a mournful expression and sit in silence to show their solidarity with the patient. Samarin adds, "A minimal amount of chitchat may go on between the visitors, but it does not involve the patient. For a Westerner these comforters can be extremely disquieting as they stare into space."

There are also cultural variations in the symbol systems people use for different types of communication. Protestant Americans, for instance, communicate religious messages primarily by song and spoken word. Many tribal cultures do so through dance, drums, drama, bardic chants, and primarily rituals in which the messages are enacted. For them, the preaching method may have little religious meaning. It is important, therefore, for the missionary to use cultural systems of symbols that are appropriate for the communication of the gospel.

Translation

If symbols, particularly words, had only explicit, denotative meanings, the translation of a message from one culture to another would not be too difficult. We could, for example, point to a tree and ask the people what they call it. Then we would use that term in referring to trees. We would, of course, need to rearrange the words to fit their

FIGURE 18

Categories of Living and Nonliving Things in English

1. Organize the following terms into a few basic categories

tree	dog	woman	fly	lion
man	sand	God	virus	demons
bush	girl	rock	cow	flower
bug	angels	bacteria	ant	Mickey Mouse

2. Categories commonly used by English speakers to classify these words

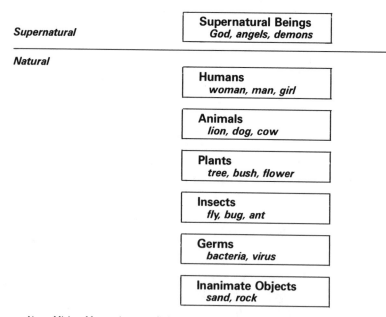

Supernatural

> **Supernatural Beings**
> *God, angels, demons*

Natural

> **Humans**
> *woman, man, girl*

> **Animals**
> *lion, dog, cow*

> **Plants**
> *tree, bush, flower*

> **Insects**
> *fly, bug, ant*

> **Germs**
> *bacteria, virus*

> **Inanimate Objects**
> *sand, rock*

Note: Mickey Mouse does not fit into this domain of classification. He belongs to the domain of "fiction."

rules of grammar. But words also have connotative meanings, many of which are implicit. This is what makes translation so difficult.

Form and Meaning

We need here to go back to the distinction we made earlier between form and meaning in symbols and in culture. Initially we tend to equate the two. We do not stop to distinguish between the sounds for "tree" and the meanings we associate with these sounds. This is because we have grown up in a single culture, and the distinction need not be made in our conversations with others within that culture. Moreover, we need not differentiate between the connotative and denotative meanings of words, again because this is not necessary in discussions with others in our own culture.

When, however, we translate a message into a new culture, we are forced to deal with the relationship between forms and meanings and between connotative and denotative meanings. In speaking, we soon realize that other people call trees *chetlu* or *baum* or something else

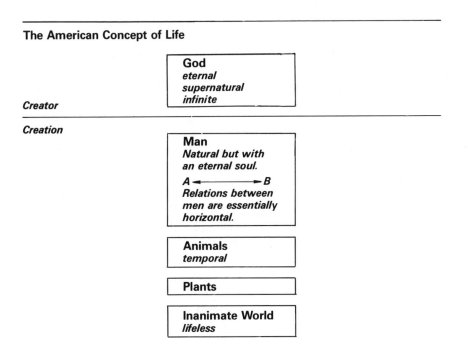

The American Concept of Life

Creator

God
eternal
supernatural
infinite

Creation

Man
Natural but with an eternal soul.

A ◄────────► B
Relations between men are essentially horizontal.

Animals
temporal

Plants

Inanimate World
lifeless

From Paul G. Hiebert, "Missions and the Understanding of Culture," in *The Church in Mission*, ed. A. J. Klassen (Fresno: Board of Christian Literature, Mennonite Brethren Church, 1967), p. 254.

FIGURE 19

Categories of Living and Nonliving Things in Telugu

Brahman *(the ultimate cosmic force)*

Maya *(transient world of illusions)*	gods *(devas, parameshwara,* etc.)
	angels
	demons *(rakshasas, apsaras,* etc.)
	humans (high caste, then middle caste and low caste)
	animals (cows, then lions, dogs, etc.)
	plants
	inanimate objects

to denote the same things, and if we want to communicate with them, we must use their words. We often overlook the fact that the same is true in other areas of communication as well, such as gestures, architecture, worship forms, and dress. For example, in some cultures people show reverence by taking off their hats, in other cultures by removing their shoes. Similarly, we need songs written in the melodies and rhythms native to the culture so that the people can understand them. Even though we translate the words into the local langauge, if the music remains foreign, the message coming through is that this religion is for strangers.

We face a more difficult question with regard to connotative meanings. How important are they for translation? Many early missionaries emphasized denotative meanings in their communication. Consequently, their translations were "literal" or formal. When they thought of "shepherd," they chose a native term that pointed to people who cared for sheep. Or when they translated "door," they used the local term with the closest denotative meaning. Often they were unaware that the connotative meanings of these words were quite different in the new language. In Telugu, for example, "shepherds" care for sheep (denotative meaning), but they are seen as debauched drunkards (connotative meaning). Consequently, the message the people heard was often quite different from the message the missionaries thought they were communicating.

In statements of facts, denotative meanings are usually most important. We say, for example, "Mary went to town." The translation of this into another language is generally straightforward. But in much of our communication, particularly that having to do with analogies,

The Indian Concept of Life

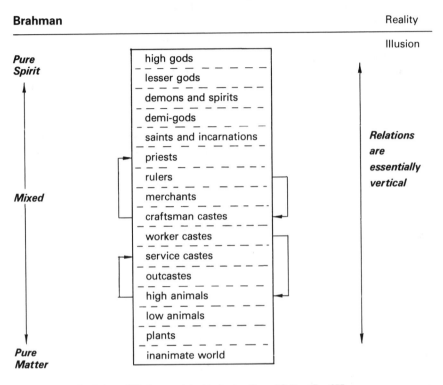

From Paul G. Hiebert, "Missions and the Understanding of Culture," p. 255.

allegories, metaphors, humor, idioms, and the like, connotative meanings are of equal if not greater importance. And since these various forms play an important part in religious thought, we cannot ignore them. For example, in parts of Latin America, "fathers" are seen as often unfaithful, distant, and authoritarian (Nida 1978:46–54). "Mothers" on the other hand are faithful, loving, and benevolent. In such situations it is easy to see the misunderstandings that arise when we speak of God as our Father, for when we say this we are not thinking of God as our biological progenitor, but as acting like a "father," a word that has more positive connotations for us.

To minimize misunderstandings, recent translators have emphasized dynamic interpretations in which an emphasis is placed on retaining connotative meanings. In some cases this may mean changing the symbol or word. The Bible speaks of the tax collector "beating his breast" as a sign of repentance. As Nida (1981:2) points out, this may seem strange to West Africans, in whose language the idiom "to beat the breast" can only mean to take pride in one's accomplishments. When speaking of repentance, they would say, "He beat his head."

So far we have been speaking of translation in general. In preaching, teaching, writing music, and translating Christian books, we have a great deal of flexibility in choosing words and symbols that best convey the meanings (whether connotative or denotative) that we wish to communicate. But what about the Bible? We dare not take undue liberties when we translate it, yet we want it to be clearly understood by its readers.

Here Eugene Nida and William Reyburn (1981) provide some guidance on how far we can change forms and denotative meanings in order to retain connotative meanings and still remain true to the text. They point out, for example, that the translator should not alter the original text when it refers to historical events. We cannot change the fact that Jesus was circumcised on the eighth day, even though some societies consider this a cruel way to treat a newborn baby. In such cases we need to provide the people with additional information through notes and teaching so that they will understand the Jewish customs of that day. Similarly, the casting of lots, frequently referred to in the Scriptures, is entirely unknown in some cultures and needs some kind of further explanation so that the people will understand the passages. But we are not free to add such information in the text.

The question of idioms and figures of speech is more difficult. How, for example, should we translate the phrases "white as snow," "millstones," or "camel" for people who know nothing about them? We may have to use terms like "very, very white," "a heavy stone," and "an animal called camel." Similarly, in parts of West Africa the "royal stool" is equivalent to a "throne," and elsewhere "wolf" may have to be translated as "jackal" or "hyena-like animal." Nida and Reyburn (1981:54) point out:

> In certain cases a literal translation is impossible because of special symbolic values associated with certain cultural objects. For example, in Balinese, the viper is regarded as a snake of paradise, and hence "generation of vipers" (Matt. 3:7, 12:34, 23:33; Luke 3:7) would scarcely be a denunciation. However, it is possible to communicate the meaning of this phrase by substituting a more generic term—for example, "vermin."

Meaning Across Cultures

Eugene A. Nida and William D. Reyburn

. . . The presuppositions and values of a culture [are] spoken of as though they [constitute] a single consistent whole. This is, however, by no means the case. Within the Bible itself there are quite different presuppositions. The henotheism (that is, one God superior to all others) of certain parts of the Old Testament gives place to monotheism, which denies the very existence of other gods. The sacrificial system of the Old Testament is completely rejected in the New Testament. The polygamy of the Old Testament is set aside in the New Testament. Jesus himself referred to certain aspects of the law as "you have heard it was said," and then proceeded to give the law a quite different interpretation and relevance. It was precisely the differences in presuppositions that gave rise to the first conflict within the church—namely, the manner in which Gentiles were to be admitted to the fellowship.

Not only does the Bible reflect different sets of presuppositions of ancient Palestinian life, it also contains references to certain Greco-Roman presuppositions of the ancient world. The Johannine writings clearly indicate the struggle of the early church against the beliefs of Gnosticism, which were based on a primordial dualism of spirit and matter and which sought to interpret the incarnation and the resurrection in dualistic terms, thus allowing for the death of Jesus and the resurrection of Christ.

If one is prepared to recognize differences of presuppositions in the Bible, it is even more necessary to realize that there are quite different sets of cultural assumptions in most present-day societies. Within the western world, for example, the "scientific viewpoint" is supposed to represent the thinking of "modern man," but this is far from being generally true. Perhaps most intellectuals possess a "scientific secular view of the world," which might be characterized roughly as (1) an explanation of life on the basis of biological evolution, (2) a mechanistic interpretation of the universe, requiring no "supreme intelligence," (3) an interpretation of history based essentially on purely human forces operating within certain ecological limits, and (4) a set of ethical values that are derived from human nature and are essentially humanistic. Along with such views of the world go a rejection of supernatural beings, a repudiation of magic, and lack of interest in religious activities.

But for a majority of persons in the modern world, this scientific view of life is quite foreign. They may have rejected established religions, but they have certainly not given up clairvoyance, astrology, mediums, witches, and amulets (such as rabbits' feet, lucky pennies, and images). Some may even claim a "scientific view" in certain contexts of life, but they fear a curse from a good person and they seek healing from those claiming "miracle cures." In fact, many persons, despite their formal adherence to one or another system of thought, have strange mixtures of belief, and rarely if ever do they attempt to resolve the underlying contradictions: they believe what they want to believe. In a sense they are "spreading their risks," and they seem to be as content with second-hand doubts as with second-hand faith.

In view of the important differences of presuppositions that may exist within a single society, it is not surprising that there are vast differences between the biblical culture and other cultures in the world. One might assume that the differences would be particularly striking if one compared the culture of the Bible with that of some present-day society in Central Africa. In reality, however, they have much in common: polygamy, belief in miracles, the practice of blessing and cursing, slavery, systems for revenge, sacrifice, and communications through dreams and visions. The pastoral Navajos see much in the Bible that is parallel to their own way of life: tending sheep, casting out evil spirits, corporate responsibility, discerning the weather by the sky, fortelling events, and the expectation of the end of this world (after which great changes will be instituted).

In a sense the Bible is the most translatable religious book that has ever been written, for it comes from a particular time and place (the western end of the Fertile Crescent) through which passed more cultural patterns and out from which radiated more distinctive features and values than has been the case with any other place in the history of the world. If one were to make a comparison of the culture traits of the Bible with those of all the existing cultures of today (one would have to reckon with some two thousand significantly different groups of persons), one would find that in certain respects the Bible is surprisingly closer to many of them than to the technological culture of the western world. It is this "western" culture that is the aberrant one in the world. And it is precisely in the western world, and in the growing number of persons in other parts of the world who share its worldview, that the Scriptures have seemingly the least ready acceptance.

One of the important developments in Christianity that relfects this difference in cultural outlook is the rapidly growing number of "indigenous churches." It is estimated that in Africa alone, within the last twenty years more than fifteen million persons have become related to the "independent" or "separatist" churches, which for the most part find themselves at home with the Bible but alienated from the traditional institutions of western Christianity. Instinctively these persons feel an identity with the Bible, but they feel out of place in traditional western churches, which in so many ways no longer reflect "the life and faith of the Bible."

Though one cannot face fairly the problems of the translator without reckoning with the many and often striking differences between the culture of the Bible and that of other societies, it would be quite wrong to exaggerate the diversities, as some persons have done. As anthropologists have frequently pointed out, there is far more that unites different peoples in a common humanity than that which separates them into distinct groups. Such cultural universals as the recognition of reciprocity and equity in interpersonal relations, response to human kindness and love, the desire for meaning in life, the acknowledgment of human nature's inordinate capacity for evil and self-deception (or rationalization of sin), and its need for something greater and more important than itself—all these universals are constantly recurring themes in the Bible. These are the elements in the Scripture that have appealed to numberless persons through the centuries and across cultural frontiers.

What is important about recent interest in the Bible in the western world is the very fact that the Scriptures come from another age and from a distant culture. For a long while modern persons have been told that their problems are the direct result of their technologically based life characterized by urbanization and industrialization, but now many are discovering that persons portrayed in the Bible had precisely the same problems and needs as persons today—the proclivity to sin even when they want to do right, the feeling of guilt, a need for forgiveness, power to resist temptation, and the desire to love and to be loved. The fact that these universal needs are exemplified within the context of concrete historical events involving real life is what makes the Bible so much alive and appealing to persons in so many societies.

As compared with the basic documents or verbal traditions of other religions, the Bible is unique in its portrayal of actual events involving specific human beings. Whereas the religious documents of Hinduism concern primarily the exploits of the gods, the Bible is concerned essentially with the activity of God in human history. And in contrast with the religious treatises of Buddhism (which contain primarily philosophically derived ethical principles) and with the Koran (which focuses upon the exhortations and warnings of the prophet), the Bible is rooted in history and consists primarily in recounting how God has entered history to reveal the divine power, will, and person. Biblical faith is thus firmly rooted in events—in a God who acts.

Moreover, the God of the Bible is portrayed as acting in specific instances and not merely in generalized ways. Thus the specific historical context of the biblical account acquires very important theological implications, and Christians have almost instinctively reacted against any attempts to transpose the cultural and historical context of the biblical accounts. In reaction to one attempt to transpose the biblical message into an African setting, a chief remarked, "If that was what really happened, then why did not our grandfathers tell us about it?" Making the biblical account too contemporary can, in fact, destroy some of its very credibility.

From the standpoint of Judeo-Christian biblical theology, the entrance of God into history at specific times and places is both relevant and crucial. It is obvious, therefore, that the events recorded in the Bible cannot be altered. If, however, a certain event depends for its meaning upon a set of presuppositions that are conspicuously different from those of the receptor culture, what is the translator to do to prevent serious misunderstanding? In the first place, the translator cannot hope to make the message so clear that any reader can fully understand it without any reference whatsoever to the presuppositions that underlie the biblical account. That is to say, the translator cannot be expected to so transpose the message linguistically and culturally that it will fit completely within the interpretive frame of the receptor culture. To do this would mean to rob the message of its distinctive time-space setting. Furthermore, the translator's purpose is not to make the message sound as though the events took place in a nearby town only a few years ago. Rather, the objective should be to so translate (and with the translation to provide such background data) as to prevent receptors from misunderstanding what the original receptors understood when they first received the message.

Exegesis may be described as the process of reconstructing the communication event by determining its meaning (or meanings) for the participants in the communication. Hermeneutics, on the other hand, may be described as pointing out parallels between the biblical message and present-day events and determining the extent of relevance and the appropriate response for the believer. Both exegesis and hermeneutics are included within the larger category of interpretation.

It is the task of the biblical scholar to provide insight into the problems of exegesis, and it is primarily the task of the preacher to help persons understand the relevance of the biblical message for the quite different language-culture settings of today.

From Eugene A. Nida and William D. Reyburn, *Meaning Across Cultures* (Maryknoll, N.Y.:, Orbis, 1981), pp. 26–30.

Translating Implicit Meanings

The most fundamental problem we face, however, is the fact that the words in any culture have implicit meanings that reflect the world view of that culture. As we have seen, there are no words in Telugu that have exactly the same meanings as the biblical words for "God," "humans," "sin," "salvation," and the like. What, then, can we do to preserve the message of divine revelation?

Take, for example, the word *devudu*, used by the early missionaries for "God" in their translation of the Telugu Bible. As we have seen, this word does mean supreme being, but not ultimate reality. There are many *devas*, and all belong to this passing world of illusion. Moreover, there is no real difference between them and humans. Consequently, if we use the word *devudu*, we lose many of the biblical meanings associated with God. He no longer is the ultimate Creator, and his incarnation simply connotes a higher creature helping a lower one. Obviously, the word *devudu* has problems for our purposes. What about the words *parameshwara*, *bhagavanthudu*, and *ishvarudu*? These, too, belong to this universe and, like the *devas*, will cease to exist in the end of time and merge back into Brahman, the source. What about Brahman? It is not a personal being to whom we can relate; it is a supreme force.

What, then, should translators do? They can use words that speak of gods as persons, like *devudu*, but these are not eternal and omnipotent; they can use *Brahman*, but this is not a person; or they can bring in a foreign term like "God" or "Theos," but then no one will understand them. This is often the dilemma of translation.

The fact is, there is no simple correspondence between words in different languages. Consequently in translation there is always some distortion of the message. First, there is some loss of the meanings found in the first language; second, there is the addition of meanings not found in the original (Figure 20).

How do we avoid the loss of meanings or the addition of unintended

FIGURE 20

Categories in Different Languages Are Not the Same

**Meaning of a Word
in Language A**

**Meaning of a Cognate
Word in Language B**

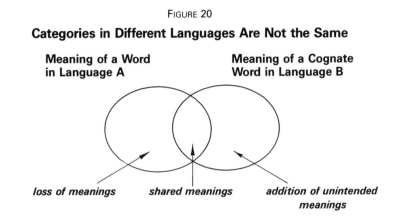

loss of meanings   *shared meanings*   *addition of unintended
meanings*

meanings in Bible translation—or, for that matter, in preaching and teaching? In a few cases we may need to create new words or import them from another source. For instance, in the English Bible we use the Hebrew word *shekel* and the Latin word *cubit*. But these have little meaning to most readers, particularly non-Christians.

Generally we must choose the most suitable word from those in the local language and then make explicit through teaching and preaching where the biblical meaning of the word is different from its ordinary meaning in the culture. In the case of translating "God" into Telugu, we may choose to use *devudu* because it speaks of a personal god, but then we must make clear that the God of the Bible is the ultimate reality, not simply the highest being in the universe, and that humans are separate creations, not simply fragments of God's spirit. We must continue to clarify the differences, for *devudu* will continue to be used by the majority of Telugu people with Hindu meanings.

The distortions that occur when Christians do not deal with the implicit meanings of their cultural symbols can readily be illustrated from Western Christianity. We have already seen that most Christians in the West tend to lump together "God," "angels," and "demons" as supernatural beings and distinguish them from natural beings such as humans and animals. But this is a cardinal Christian heresy. If there is one fundamental distinction in the Bible, it is between God as Creator and all the rest as creation. We should never put God in the same category with anything else.

Then how have we come to think of God, angels, and demons as belonging together? The answer is the spread of a Greek world view in the West during the Renaissance (Figure 21). In the Hebrew world view, God is by himself. All else is dependent upon his ongoing act of

FIGURE 21

Hebrew, Greek, and Modern World Views

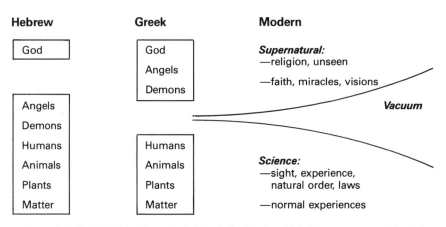

From Paul G. Hiebert, "Anthropological Tools for Missionaries" (Singapore: Haggai Institute, 1983), p. 22.

creation. There is, in fact, no word in Hebrew for "nature" as a self-sustained cosmic order. In the Greek world view, however, the gods *(theoi)* are part of a supernatural realm inhabited by spirits of many kinds. The natural world, on the other hand, includes humans, animals, plants, and matter. As the West adopted this Greek world view, Western Christians absorbed its implicit meanings into their theologies. The result is a two-tier universe in which we use religion to describe supernatural realities and a secularized science to explain the natural order.

Bible translation is obviously a complex task, and those who undertake it need specialized training. But since all missionaries are involved in translating biblical ideas into local cultures, they need to be aware of the many facets involved.

Cross-Cultural Communication

We spend most of our time in communication—talking, reading, listening to the radio, watching television, dressing ourselves up, and (as some psychologists remind us) talking to ourselves. Rarely do we give much thought to the processes involved, for our attention is on the messages being sent and received. Only when communication breaks down do we normally stop to look at what has been going on and what has gone wrong.

In communication many things happen at the same time (Figure 22). A sender wishing to communicate a message for whatever reason encodes it into symbols and transmits them to a receiver, who receives the symbols, decodes them to learn the message, and responds. All this takes place within specific contexts that affect the end result. As we shall see, many things can go wrong in the process, thus hindering communication, particularly in cross-cultural settings.

Messages and Paramessages

Communication takes place along each of the three dimensions of culture we have already examined. Cognitively, it is the transmission of information and meaning; affectively, the sharing of feelings; and evaluatively, the conveyance of judgments such as acceptance and censure. In most communication all three occur simultaneously, even though one or another of them is in focus.

There are many ways of transmitting information. People use rituals and dramas to communicate ideas by enacting them. They also use signs such as stoplights, turn signals, and bells to transmit knowledge. But the method they use most to communicate cognitive messages is language, whether spoken or written, for it is through words that abstract human thoughts are most easily expressed. Consequently a mastery of the local language is crucial for missionary service. There is little use in crossing cultural boundaries if we cannot communicate the gospel effectively by what we say.

Along with cognitive messages, we communicate feelings and sentiments and even whether we like the person we are talking to. We indicate anger over the subject under discussion, or we are joking,

FIGURE 22

Communication Involves Sending and Receiving Messages

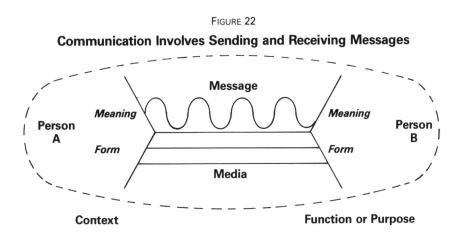

serious, sad, sarcastic, reserved, or critical. And poetry, ironic comments, tongue-in-cheek statements, sermons, and marriage proposals can be used to communicate our feelings.

We communicate our judgments as well. We show by our words and actions whether or not we think others are telling the truth, whether we like or dislike what they say, and whether we judge them to be upright or crooked.

During normal communication, one of these three types of message is "in focus." In other words, it is the main message we are trying to convey. For example, Western-style teaching concentrates on transmitting ideas, while in music, poetry, art, and drama we are often trying to communicate moods and feelings. Preaching, on the other hand, is used to teach ideas and, to a lesser extent, express feelings, but its main purpose often has to do with values and decisions.

While we focus on transmitting one message, we unconsciously communicate a great many more. For example, in ordinary conversation we concentrate on expressing ideas, but by our facial expressions, gestures, tones of voice, body postures, standing distances, and use of time we communicate feelings and values such as distrust, concern, disdain, inattention, agreement, and love. And often we are unaware of these secondary messages.

Secondary or paramessages provide the immediate context within which communication takes place and determine the way in which the primary message is to be understood. They tell us, for instance, whether we should interpret the meanings of the words as irony, sarcasm, humor or double entendre, or whether we should take them straight. Paramessages tell us what the speaker thinks of the receiver.

Normally we are less conscious of paramessages because they are out of focus. But they are no less real. In fact, in retrospect, we often recall the communicated feelings more vividly than the ideas. We also trust paramessages more than primary messages. It is harder to tell a lie in a secondary message because we are not aware of what we are saying on this level. For instance, a child denies stealing a cookie from the cookie jar, but we see guilt written all over his face. This is why we like to see people when we converse.

Paramessages play an important part in missions. In communicating the gospel, we may *say* that we love the people, but our paramessages may proclaim loudly that we cannot stand them. We may feel righteous in visiting their homes, but refuse to invite them into ours. Our most fundamental messages are our paramessages, and when these are not congruent with our explicit message, the people will come to distrust us.

Media and Paramedia

As we have seen, we can use many different media or symbol systems to communicate our messages—words, tones, gestures, space, time, and the like. Our choice depends upon the occasion, our personal preferences, and our culture. Touching is a common way of showing affection in some cultures; in others, it is taboo. In some, rituals and dance are important; in others, not.

Normally we use several media at the same time—one to communicate the message, others to convey paramessages. In some situations, however, we use several media to reinforce the same message. This multimedia approach is particularly powerful in helping us to remember messages (Table 4). After three days we remember twice as much of what we see as what we hear. But when the two media of sight and sound are used together, we remember more than six times as much. This has great significance for how we communicate the gospel.

TABLE 4

Percent of Things We Remember

	After Three Hours	After Three Days
What we hear	70%	10%
What we see	72%	20%
What we see and hear	86%	65%

From Jack Dabner, "Notes on Communication" (Singapore: Haggai Institute, 1983), p. 4.

Symbol systems serve a second important function, namely, to store information. All societies store their knowledge in different ways. Those who are literate depend heavily on the written page, almost to the exclusion of other methods for storing information. We make notes to ourselves, write down our thoughts, and read books, magazines, signs, and skywriting. We build libraries and file endless piles of paper. When in church we sing by memory but may know only the first verses of most hymns. Without writing, most of us would be lost.

People in oral societies depend on memory and reinforce it with various media. They store information in songs, poems, proverbs, riddles, chants, and stories, all of which aid recall. They use repetition and multiple media to retain their knowledge, singing the same songs over and over again and reenacting their stories in dramas, dances, and rituals. They use cultural objects such as houses, temples, images, and paintings to recall religious beliefs. And, as we have seen, they associate their cultural knowledge with the natural world around them.

There are many implications in this for the communication of the gospel. First, we must choose media that are appropriate to the message we are communicating and to the culture in which we are located. We who are literate tend to think only in terms of storing and communicating the gospel in spoken and written forms. We fail to realize that oral societies are not "illiterate." They have, in fact, a rich supply of cultural knowledge and many different ways of storing it. In such societies we must use these media to present the gospel in concrete ways that the people will recall. Although we should not ignore literacy altogether, we need to use the media that already exist within the society if we want to reach the people now in ways they understand.

P. Y. Luke and John Carman (1968) point out the importance of singing for the communication and retention of the gospel in oral societies. During their research on village churches in India, they found that most Christians there are nonliterate and cannot read the Scriptures. But they do have a theology that they store in songs—what the authors call a "lyric theology." The people gather at night and sing ten or twelve verses of one song after another from memory. Fortunately most of their songs have more solid theological content than many in the West.

Senders and Receivers

Communication involves a sender and a receiver. In missions both of these are people.

Senders initiate the process by selecting a medium and encoding their message into symbolic forms such as speech, gesture, or writing. The process is so nearly automatic when we are in our own culture that we rarely give it conscious thought. Most of our attention is focused on formulating the message. Only when the mechanism falters—for example, when we are trying to speak in another language—do we become conscious of encoding the message.

Encoding depends on many factors. Obviously senders use cultural symbols to communicate messages. These include not only words but gestures, use of time and space, and so on. Less obvious is the fact that we encode our messages in terms of our own experiences. Our choice of words and pronunciation, the feelings we assign to symbols, and even the messages we communicate are determined by such factors as our age, sex, position in society, geographic location, past experiences, and present attitudes. It is important to remember that not all communication is determined by culture. There is a highly personal dimension to it.

Encoding also takes into account the context. Each of us shifts smoothly in the course of a single day from one set of symbols to another, from one type of message to another, depending on where we are and whom we are addressing. We communicate one way with our friends, another with our spouses, and still another with teachers, preachers, policemen, or presidents. We have special languages for courts, politics, trade, each of the sciences, entertainment, and religion.

Finally, encoding is multilayered. For example, in a simple conversation we choose a message and put it into words, taking care to modify them according to tense, gender, number, and other rules of the language; to arrange them in the proper order; and to produce the spoken sounds with sufficient accuracy so that the listener understands them. At the same time, almost unconsciously, we encode the paramessages that communicate attitudes and values through tone of voice, gestures, and other paramedia.

Receivers must reverse the process and decode the symbolic forms they receive into meanings. Like senders, they filter the message through the beliefs and values of their culture and their own personal experiences. If they belong to a culture in which Christianity is seen as an enemy, they may find it difficult to give the gospel a fair hearing. Or they may have had a bad experience with a Christian that colors their response to the gospel.

Receivers also decode the paramessages and use them to evaluate the primary message. What we say may be true, but others may not believe it if we transmit attitudes of superiority and disdain. No matter how hard we try to cover them, these feelings will be communicated.

How do we measure successful communication? Ordinarily we think we have communicated when we send a message. For example, as missionaries we measure our communication by the number of sermons we preach, classes we teach, or times we witness. And when the people misunderstand us, we say, "But I said ..." or "You weren't listening." In all these cases we are assuming that communication implies only the *sending* of messages.

A little thought, however, shows us the fallacy of this approach. There is more to communication than sending a message. Communication occurs only when the sender and the receiver have something in common, and both understand what the communicator intends to say. As Charles Kraft (1979) points out, communication must be measured not by the messages we send but by the messages the people receive. In other words, *our communication must be receptor-oriented.* It must be understood by the people and meet their needs. There is little use in preaching if the people misunderstand the message, just as there is little use in broadcasting evangelistic messages when all the listeners are Christians already.

In receptor-oriented communication the sender, not the audience, must take the responsibility to make the message understood. There are times when listeners deliberately distort its meaning, but in most cases it is the senders who must make the message clear. As communicators we must test to see whether the people understand us, and if they do not, we must take the blame and go back to our drawing boards.

Filters and Feedback

There can be a big difference between the message we send and the way other people receive and interpret it. James Engel (1984) points out that people tend to see and hear what they want to see and hear. Their deeper beliefs, feelings, and values act as filters that open when they want to hear the message, and close when they do not. People can avoid the message if they know it is coming, or not listen to it when it does come. They can also reinterpret its meaning to fit their purposes, or fail to change in response to it. On the other hand, they tend to listen when they believe the message to be relevant and helpful to themselves. As Engel reminds us, our audience is sovereign. They decide to a great extent whether or not our message gets through. It is important, therefore, that we make our message clear, credible, and relevant to those with whom we are communicating.

How do we know when our messages are misunderstood? The answer, in part, is feedback—listening to those receiving the message. We are usually so intent upon sending the message that we do not hear the responses of our listeners. As Stephen Neill (1961) points out, good communication begins with the art of listening.

Listening includes tuning in to paramessages. We need to be sensitive to people's facial expressions, gestures, tones of voice, and body postures, which say much about their attitudes and responses to the message.

In many types of communication, such as preaching, teaching, radio broadcasting, and literature distribution, we need more formal methods for getting feedback. A teacher can encourage discussion and listen to it carefully. A missionary can ask the people how they understood the message. Those in media can use such formal research methods as questionnaires and interviews to determine who is listening or reading and what they understand from the message. In all of these situations we must accept the audience as judge. If they have not understood the message, it is we senders who have not communicated it clearly.

Feedback should modify our communication, immediately and continually. If we see that people do not understand the message on the cognitive level, we need to slow down, simplify the material, go over it again, illustrate it with concrete examples, or stop and let them ask questions. If they are hostile, dubious, or rejecting, we must stop to build trust and examine our own paramessages for possible sources of misunderstandings on the affective level.

Static and Incongruity

Another barrier to communication is "static," anything that might distract people from receiving the message. If there is too much frequency noise when we listen to the radio, we turn to another station. Similarly, students lose interest if the classroom is too hot or cold, if the fan is too loud, or if the teacher has distracting mannerisms or a heavy accent. Likewise, people may be diverted from listening to the gospel by a missionary's foreign clothing and behavior, by the apparent magic of his or her technology, or by poor mastery of the local language.

Incongruity is static of another kind. When a preacher speaks about sacrifice and simple Christian living, but drives an expensive car and dresses in hand-tailored suits—or a missionary talks about loving the people, but will not let them into his house—the paramessage is not congruent to the message. In such cases the people usually believe the paramessage.

Foreignness is a type of incongruity particular to cross-cultural situations. Our messages may be understood, but our ways are strange and distracting. For example, missionary women in India wore knee-length skirts, not realizing that in these villages baring the calves of the leg is seen as indecent. And in New Guinea some missionaries did not freely share their personal property such as food, lamps, typewriters, and guns with the people in the same way the people shared with one another.

Two-Way Communication

Rarely is personal communication a one-way process. In a conversation, as soon as someone begins to talk, we begin to think of things to say. And when we speak, the other person is waiting to cut in. This is good, for other than the transmission of information, communication should be a dialogue in which both parties listen and learn (Figure 23). But there is also the danger that neither side really listens to the other. In good communication we must give as much attention to listening as to speaking.

Two-way communication is particularly important in missions. We do have a gospel to share, but we also have much to learn. It is in this learning that we come to identify with the people and their ways and build trust.

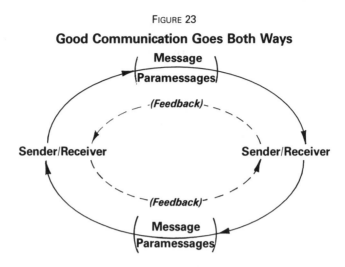

FIGURE 23

Good Communication Goes Both Ways

Reinterpretation and Response

The result of the give-and-take of communication is a response of some sort. Receivers interpret messages within their cultural and personal contexts. They discard what they dislike or do not understand, often without giving it a fair hearing. They add what makes sense to their knowledge, changing its meaning to fit their beliefs. In the process they often distort the message to hear what they want to hear. It is estimated that in normal communication within the same culture, people understand only about 70 percent of what is said. In cross-cultural situations the level is probably not above 50 percent. So we need feedback, and we must be clear, explicit, concrete, and even redundant if we wish to be understood.

New information often leads to decisions. As people gain accurate information about the gospel, they are able to make meaningful responses to it. But information is not the only factor involved in decision making. Feelings play an equally important part for most people. Like most educated people, missionaries are taught to make decisions on the basis of information and reason. In their everyday lives, however, like buying new clothes or a car, they are highly influenced by their likes and dislikes of styles and colors. The same is true of those who hear the gospel. Their feelings play as important a part in their response to the gospel as their knowledge of its content.

The feelings people have toward the gospel are often influenced by the manner and context within which the message is transmitted. Newly literate people, for example, often place a high trust in the printed page. Experienced television watchers, on the other hand, tend to develop a cynicism toward that medium, even though they continue to use it to acquire information.

People's feelings are also influenced by their degree of trust in the communicator. If the messenger lacks credibility in their eyes, the message itself is generally rejected. On the other hand, if they sense that the missionary truly loves them, they are more open to the gospel.

The deepest decisions people make are those that change their lives. These are evaluative determinations, and they form the core of conversion. Changes in knowledge and feelings are not enough. Only when these lead to shifts in allegiances and behavior can we speak of the lordship of Christ and of Christian discipleship.

After decisions are made, however, they are usually reevaluated in the light of subsequent events. People who decide to become Christians may find the pressures of their communities too great. Or they may assess their response in the light of new information. This is particularly true of new converts who receive little support for their faith from the local Christian community. They, like us, constantly reexamine their beliefs within the belief framework of those closest to them, and if there is little reinforcement from their peers, their faith weakens. It is important, therefore, that we understand communication and decision making not only from a personal point of view, but also with the social dynamics in mind.

We communicate for many reasons. For example, in a classroom our chief goal is to transmit and evaluate information. We add jokes to make the job more enjoyable, but they are not central to our purposes. Concerts, on the other hand, are held to entertain and to express feelings. Churches are for worship and fellowship, courts for enforcement of social norms (see Table 5).

It is important to remember that specific media are used for certain

TABLE 5

Communication Serves Different Functions

Function	Communication
Cognitive	—to ask and receive information —to coordinate activities —to pass on a cultural heritage
Affective	—to entertain —to express feelings and moods —to worship
Evaluative	—to make and enforce social rules —to show status and prestige —to allocate social positions and resources

functions, and these differ from culture to culture. For example, in tribal societies religious worship and instruction are communicated primarily through rituals. To worship services, African villagers add dances, and Indian villagers add dramas and bardic performances. Preaching, as we know it, is rare in these societies, and the people are often confused and bored with evangelistic sermons. On the other hand, when the gospel is presented in India in dramatic form, most of the villagers show up, and they stay until the end of the story. It is important, therefore, to use media that are appropriate to the purposes of our communication in that culture.

Context

One final element of communication that needs to be mentioned is that of context. Communication always takes place within a setting and an occasion, both of which shape the nature and interpretation of the message. The same words said in a drama have different meanings when they are said in real life, just as gestures we use in church may be made in jest in a comedian's routine. Words said by a judge in court carry different weight than those he or she says in conversation to a friend. Similarly, what missionaries say in private will be understood differently than what they say in the pulpit.

One important part of many contexts is the audience. So far we have looked at communication as it takes place between two individuals. In real life, however, there are other parties directly or indiretly involved in the process. This can best be seen by way of illustration. Two college students may be engaged in casual conversation when a female professor walks by. They immediately raise the level of discussion to impress her. Although on the surface the two continue to talk to each other, they have actually directed their conversation to an audience.

Audiences play an important role, particularly in public communications. Missionaries abroad must keep in mind their sending boards and churches when speaking to the people. And when reporting in their home churches, they must be sensitive to how their reports might look to the people among whom they work. Formerly churches overseas were largely unaware of what missionaries said about them on furlough. Today with travel and the wide dissemination of published materials, this is no longer the case.

Communication and the Missionary

What implications does all this have for missionaries and their work? First, we need to recognize that effective communication is central to our task. There is little point in giving our lives or in going ten thousand miles if we cannot bridge the final five feet. Communication is a complex process, and we need continually to be studying its effectiveness. Careful reflection on the ways we are or are not communicating the gospel can help us greatly in our task.

Second, we need to be more aware of the implicit elements of communication. We study the language and maybe the culture, but we are seldom taught the more implicit dimensions of communication. Nor do we generally give thought to media foreign to our own culture and training or to the question of what media are most appropriate for the communication of the gospel in another culture. Consequently, we too often overlook the most effective ways of reaching the people.

Third, we must become receptor-oriented in our thinking. It is natural to think of communication in terms of what we do. We must learn to measure by what people hear. If they do not hear or if they misunderstand us, it is we who must change our methods. The gospel is God's message of salvation, but the people must understand it within their own cultural and personal contexts if they are to respond.

Finally, as we communicate the gospel, we must never overlook the fact that God is at work through his Spirit in the hearts of the listeners, preparing them for the Good News. Without this, true conversion is impossible. God uses the imperfect means of human communication to make his message known to us and then through us to others. And even when we are unskilled in transmitting the message, he often uses it to transform the lives of people. This is not to justify our neglect of good communication, but to say that in the end the communication of the gospel depends on the work of God in the hearts of people whom he has prepared, and that Christian communication must always be accompanied by prayer and obedience to the guidance of the Holy Spirit.

Critical Contextualization

$\mathbf{W}$hat should people do with their old cultural ways when they become Christians, and how should the missionary respond to these traditional beliefs and practices?

When missionaries arrive in a new region, they do not enter a religious and cultural vacuum. They find societies with well-developed cultures that provide for essential needs and make human life possible. They also find religious and philosophical beliefs that provide the people with answers to many of their deepest questions. How, then, should they relate to the existing cultural beliefs and practices? Are they all evil? Or are they good?

Traditional Cultures

As we have seen, cultures are made up of systems of beliefs and practices that are built upon the implicit assumptions that people make about themselves, about the world around them, and about ultimate realities. What are some of these beliefs and practices to which Christians must respond?

Material Culture

People create objects for use and entertainment. They construct houses out of branches, mud, stones, or cement. They make dugouts, outriggers, yachts, and steamboats; dog sleds, ox carts, and horseless carriages; digging sticks, hoes, plows, and harrows; leather pouches, baskets, pots, and bins. They domesticate dogs, pigs, chickens, buffalo, llamas, elephants, and monkeys; raise wheat, rice, yams, chilies, chicory, plums, coffee, alfalfa, larkspurs, motherworts, bluegrass, and a thousand other plants; and they catch fish and birds and trap crabs and lobsters.

People make medicines for the sick. South Indian villagers grind up the leaves of indigo trees, the dried fruit of cherry plums, and powdered iron with the juice from the roots of a tree and sheep urine, and put it on their hair to turn it from gray to black. Their cure for "cold diseases" includes eating hot, salty, chile-spiced foods, spitting often, massaging, taking snuff, and abstaining from sleep.

People also use magic as cures and protective charms. The Burmese cure the sick by burying small images of them in tiny coffins. Siamese magicians make effigies of people who are dangerously ill and recite chants over them in solitary places. Muslims make miniature Qurans that they hang around their necks. And Indian villagers chant sacred *mantras* or inscribe magical drawings on sheets of copper that they tie to their wrists or waists (Figure 24).

Other objects are used for religious purposes. Among the Yorubas of West Africa, when a twin dies, the people make a roughly fashioned human shape, which the mother carries with her. This not only keeps the living child from missing its lost twin, but also gives the spirit of the dead child something to enter so that it will not disturb the living child. The Haida of the northwestern coast of North America carved totem poles in memory of their ancestors. Other peoples make fetishes, icons, and idols, and build temples, mosques, high places, and other sacred shrines.

These and many more are the material objects of a culture to which Christians must respond. What should they do with all of them?

Expressive Culture

All cultures provide ways for people to express their feelings, whether these be the joy and excitement of entertainment, the sorrow of partings and death, the creative exhibitions of tribal artists or philosophers, or the awe and fear of gods and spirits.

One of the most common of human expressions is music. In Central Africa this centers around rituals and entertainment and is closely associated with drums and dancing. In Tibet the people use long horns to announce the beginning of services. South Indian women sing work songs as they transplant rice. American Indians sing to their guardian spirits as they await death. North Americans listen to classical music, Country and Western, jazz, or rock.

FIGURE 24

Magical Charms from South India

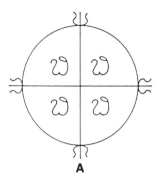
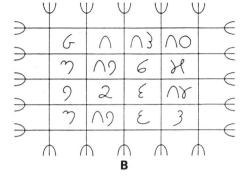

A

B

C

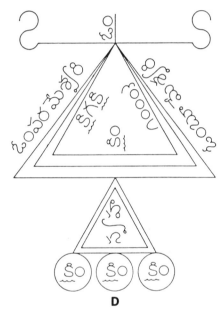

D

E

Magical charms, when properly used in a South Indian village, will automatically bring about the desired results. These charms combine powerful figures, sounds, and words. A: Yantra for a headache, including writing it on a brass plate, lighting a candle before it after it is wrapped in string, covering it with red and yellow powders, and tying it to the head. B: Yantra for assuring conception, involving inscribing it on a piece of paper or copper sheeting and tying it to the arm of the barren woman. C: Used for malaria. D: To the god Narasimha, for power and general protection. E: (For use by young men), when written on paper and tied to the arm, it will cause the woman of a man's choice to fall in love with him. (There are other charms to protect women from lecherous men who use this charm.)

From *Konduru* by Paul G. Hiebert. Reprinted by permission of the Publisher, University of Minnesota Press. Copyright © University of Minnesota.

People sing about many things. Balengi mothers of central Africa sing lullabies to their children such as this (adapted from Radin 1957:140):

> Why do you cry, my child?
> The sky is bright; the sun is shining.
> Why do you cry?
> Go to your father: he loves you,
> Go tell him why you cry.
> What! You cry still?
> Your father loves you, I caress you:
> Yet still you are sad.
> Tell me, then, my child, why do you cry?

Hindu mothers sing to their daughters:

> Blessing on you, daughter of the mountain king,
> Maidens will sing of your beauty in a cradle of gold,
> Sleep, oh lily-eyed one, sleep peacefully,
> You are the chosen of Siva, play with your toys.

People also recite proverbs and riddles. One South Indian village aphorism is: "Flies, wind, prostitutes, beggars, rats, village headmen, tax collectors; these seven always pester others."

Another goes:

A wife who refuses to eat the leavings on her husband's plate
  will be reborn a buffalo,
A wife who adorns herself when her husband is away
  will be reborn a pig,
A wife who eats before her husband returns
  will be reborn a dog,
A wife who sleeps on the bed and makes her husband sleep on the floor
  will be reborn a snake.

And another:

> The saint who says the sound *om*
> Will become one with you,
> Oh great god Rama.

In all cultures people also pray. Villagers in Ghana pray to their ancestors at the burial ceremony (Taylor 1977:153):

You are leaving us today; we have performed your funeral. Do not let any of us fall ill. Let us get money to pay the expenses of your funeral. Let the women bear children. Life to all of us. Life to the chief.

On the other hand the Pawnee Indians of North America prayed to the high but unknown God (Radin 1957:361):

> Father, unto thee we cry!
> Father thou of gods and men;
> Father thou of all we hear;
> Father thou of all we see—
> Father, unto thee we cry!

Folk poets and philosophers also reflect upon the realities of life and human destinies. Often they provide down-to-earth answers with sharp insights into reality. One ancient Indian sage captured human avarice in the following ditty (Ryder 1956:374):

> A beggar to the graveyard hied,
> And there "Friend corpse, arise," he cried;
> "One moment lift my heavy weight
> Of poverty; for I of late
> Grow weary, and desire instead
> Your comfort: you are good and dead."
> The corpse was silent. He was sure
> 'Twas better to be dead than poor.

One of the most widespread forms of folk literature is the story. People in all cultures tell anecdotes about the incongruities of life and the strange ways of others. They tell children's stories and stories for women and for men. They also tell tales about the origins of the world and of their tribes. Such stories, commonly known as myths, express their fundamental beliefs about the nature of things, especially about the nature of human beings and their relationships to their ancestors, the spirits, and the gods.

The Demon Who Destroyed Himself

Once upon a time Basma, the demon, was learning arts and sciences from Ishvara the god. Parvati, Ishvara's wife, was impressed with the student and begged Ishvara to give him a special boon. Finally, because of Parvati's intercession, Ishvara gave the demon a secret mantra known as the "essence of fire spell," which gave him the power to convert everything he touched to fire and ash.

In time Basma fell in love with Parvati and secretly thought of seducing her. He decided to touch Ishvara and burn him up, but when Ishvara saw him coming, he ran away.

Maha Vishnu, the great god, saw this and decided to put an end to the demon. He took on the guise of an even more beautiful woman and created a golden swing. When Basma saw the woman swinging and singing love songs, he was immediately infatuated with "her" and asked her who she was. "Can't you see I am a female," Vishnu said.

"Are you married?" Basma asked?

"No," said Vishnu.

"Will you marry me?" the demon begged.

"Yes, but I do not trust men. So place your hand on your head and swear that you will be faithful to me and never leave me," said Vishnu.

Basma was so infatuated that he forgot his hand was charmed. He touched his head and swore fidelity to the beautiful woman and thus was consumed into ashes.

Adapted from Gananath Obeyesekere, *The Cult of the Goddess Pattini* (Chicago: University of Chicago Press, 1984), pp. 113–114. © 1984 by the University of Chicago Press.

In the case of universalistic religions such as Buddhism, Islam, and Hinduism, such stories and the religious theologies related to them are codified in sacred scriptures such as the Tripitaka (Buddhism), the Quran (Islam), and the Vedas and Puranas (Hinduism).

Ritual Culture

Missionaries find it particularly difficult to deal with rituals in the new culture, since these often speak of the most profound experiences of human life and reflect the deepest beliefs of the people. How should Christians respond to them?

Life-cycle rites. All people face the question of the meaning of human life. And all of them do so, in part, by marking the important transitions in life with rituals for such events as birth, initiation into adulthood, marriage, and death. These rites often show us the people's most significant assumptions about the nature and destiny of human beings and their place in the world.

A child does not become a human being merely by biological birth. He or she must be transformed into a social being, a member of the society. This is often done by mystically creative rites in which a baby is made human. Among the Chagga of Africa, for example, the baby is formally presented to the mother's relatives on the fourth day after birth. A week later it is made a member of the father's clan with elaborate ceremony. After another month it is taken outside and lifted toward the snowy summit of Kilimanjaro with the prayer, "God and Guide, lead this child, guard it and let it grow up and arise like smoke!" (Taylor 1977:94–95).

After a birth the Gikuyu of East Africa bury the placenta in an uncultivated field and cover it with grain and grass to ensure the strength of the child and the continued fertility of the mother. The father cuts four sugar canes if the child is a girl or five if it is a boy, gives the juice to the mother and child, and buries the scraps on the right side of the house if the child is a boy and on the left if it is a girl. He sacrifices a goat to celebrate, and the medicine man is called to purify the house. The mother and child are kept in seclusion for four or five days, and the husband sacrifices sheep of thanksgiving to God and the living-dead.

Omodo

Walter A. Trobisch

On one of my trips I worshipped in an African church where nobody knew me. After the service I talked to two boys who had also attended.

"How many brothers and sisters do you have?" I asked the first one.

"Three."

"Are they all from the same stomach?"

"Yes, my father is a Christian."

"How about you?" I addressed the other boy.

He hesitated. In his mind he was adding up. I knew immediately that he came from a polygamous family.

"We are nine," he finally said.

"Is your father a Christian?"

"No," was the typical answer, "he is a polygamist."

"Are you baptised?"

"Yes, and my brothers and sister too," he added proudly.

"And their mothers?"

"They are all three baptised, but only the first wife takes communion."

"Take me to your father."

The boy led me to a compound with many individual houses. It breathed an atmosphere of cleanliness, order and wealth. Each wife had her own house and her own kitchen. The father, a middle-aged, good-looking man, tall, fat and impressive, received me without embarrassment and with apparent joy. I found Omodo, as we shall call him, a well-educated person, wide awake and intelligent, with a sharp wit and a rare sense of humor. From the outset he made no apologies for being a polygamist, he was proud of it. Let me try to put down here the essential content of our conversation that day which lasted for several hours.

"Welcome to the hut of a poor sinner!" The words were accompanied by good-hearted laughter.

"It looks like a rich sinner," I retorted.

"The saints come very seldom to this place," he said, "they don't want to be contaminated with sin."

"But they are not afraid to receive your wives and children. I just met them in church."

"I know. I give everyone a coin for the collection plate. I guess I finance half of the church's budget. They are glad to take my money, but they don't want me."

I sat in thoughtful silence. After a while he continued, "I feel sorry for the pastor. By refusing to accept all the polygamous men in town as church members he has made his flock poor and they shall always be dependent upon subsidies from America. He has created a church of women whom he tells every Sunday that polygamy is wrong."

"Wasn't your first wife heart-broken when you took a second one?"

Omodo looked at me almost with pity. "It was her happiest day," he said finally.

"Tell me how it happened."

"Well, one day after she had come home from the garden and had fetched wood and water, she was preparing the evening meal, while I sat in front of my house and watched her. Suddenly she turned to me and mocked me. She called me a 'poor man,' because I had only one wife. She pointed to our neighbor's wife who could care for her children while the other wife prepared the food."

"Poor man," Omodo repeated. "I can take much, but not that. I had to admit that she was right. She needed help. She had already picked out a second wife for me and they get along fine."

I glanced around the courtyard and saw a beautiful young woman, about 19 or 20, come out of one of the huts.

"It was a sacrifice for me," Omodo commented. "Her father demanded a very high bride price."

"Do you mean that the wife, who caused you to become a polygamist is the only one of your family who receives communion?"

"Yes, she told the missionary how hard it was for her to share her love for me with another woman. According to the church my wives are considered sinless because each of them has only one husband. I, the father, am the only sinner in our family. Since the Lord's supper is not given to sinners, I am excluded from it. Do you understand that, pastor?"

I was entirely confused.

"And you see," Omodo continued, "they are all praying for me that I might be saved from sin, but they don't agree from which sin I must be saved."

"What do you mean?"

"Well, the pastor prays that I may not continue to commit the sin of polygamy. My wives pray that I may not commit the sin of divorce. I wonder whose prayers are heard first."

"So your wives are afraid that you become a Christian?"

"They are afraid that I become a church member. Let's put it that way. For me there is a difference. You see they can only have intimate relations with me as long as I do not belong to the church. In the moment I would become a church member their marriage relations with me would become sinful."

"Wouldn't you like to become a church member?"

"Pastor, don't lead me into temptation! How can I become a church member, if it means to disobey Christ? Christ forbade divorce, but not polygamy. The church forbids polygamy but demands divorce. How can I become a church member, if I want to be a Christian? For me there is only one way, to be a Christian without the church."

"Have you ever talked to your pastor about that?"

"He does not dare to talk to me, because he knows as well as I do that some of his elders have a second wife secretly. The only difference between them and me is that I am honest and they are hypocrites."

"Did a missionary every talk to you?"

"Yes, once. I told him that with the high divorce rate in Europe, they have only a successive form of polygamy while we have a simultaneous polygamy. That did it. He never came back."

I was speechless. Omodo accompanied me back to the village. He evidently enjoyed to be seen with a pastor.

"But tell me, why did you take a third wife?" I asked him.

"I did not take her. I inherited her from my late brother, including her children. Actually my older brother would have been next in line. But he is an elder. He is not allowed to sin by giving security to a widow."

I looked in his eyes. "Do you want to become a Christian?"

"I *am* a Christian." Omodo said without smiling.

As I walked slowly down the path, the verse came to my mind: "You blind guides, straining out a gnat and swallowing a camel."

What does it mean to take responsibility as a congregation for Omodo? I am sorry that I was not able to see Omodo again, because I had met him while I was on a trip. I just report to you the essence of our conversation because it contains in a nutshell the main attitudes of polygamists toward the church. It is always healthy to see ourselves with the eyes of an outsider.

I asked myself: What would I have done if I were pastor in Omodo's town?

From Walter A. Trobisch, "Congregational Responsibility for the Christian Individual," in *Readings in Missionary Anthropology II*, ed. William A. Smalley (South Pasadena: William Carey Library, 1978), pp. 233–235. Used by permission.

In most societies marriage is the central ritual of life. It rearranges the social order by taking one or both partners from the parental home. Marriage establishes a family and speaks of fertility and children, and it often is associated with deep religious meanings. Among the Bhotiya of Tibet, the process lasts at least three years! Some of the important steps along the way are (1) astrologers determine whether the marriage will be favorable; (2) uncles of the girl and boy act as go-betweens and carry gifts back and forth as the promises are made;

(3) the intermediaries give a feast and invoke the blessings of the gods upon the couple; (4) a year later all the relatives on both sides attend a great feast and the bride price is paid; (5) another year later the astrologer determines the auspicious time for the bride to join her husband, the lamas or priests come to celebrate, two "thieves" try to steal the girl and are driven away, guests give presents to the bride, and the girl returns home; and (6) after one more year the parents give the bride her dowry and she is escorted to the boy's home. The marriage ceremonies are now completed.

Among the most feared rituals are funerals. The spirit of the deceased is widely believed to join the ancestors or remain around the house for some years, influencing the affairs of the living. Funerals may also attract evil spirits who plague close relatives.

Such beliefs are found among the Kols of India (Van Gennep 1960:151). The corpse is placed on the ground immediately after death so that the soul can find its way to the home of the dead beneath the earth. The body is washed and painted yellow to chase away the evil spirits who try to stop the soul on its journey. It is then placed on a pyre, together with rice and the tools of the deceased. Rice cakes and silver coins for the journey to the nether world are placed in the mouth of the corpse. After cremation the men gather the bones and take them to hang in a pot in the house of the dead. Rice is thrown along the way that the deceased, should he or she return in spite of all precautions, will have something to eat and will not harm anyone. After a time the deceased is "married" to the spirits in the lower world with singing, dancing, and feasting. Finally, the bones are buried in a field.

The life-cycle rite least understood by Western missionaries is that of initiation. In most parts of the world, children are transformed into adults through a ritual that often involves tests of suffering, separation from parents and village, and initiation into adult gender roles. Those who do not go through these rites are considered to be children or incomplete humans, no matter how old they are.

The Chagga of East Africa, for example, have several rituals that mark entry into adulthood. When children approach puberty, their ears are pierced. This ceremony links them in a special way to their paternal grandfathers on the one hand and their maternal uncles on the other. They are then ceremonially introduced to domestic and agricultural work and, as a recognition of their new status, are allowed for the first time to taste game and beer. From this time onward, the young adults are taught about their ancestors through the recitation of stories and songs. Then, when they are about twelve, their two lower front teeth are removed and offered to the first ancestor. Finally they are circumcised, a ritual that transforms boys and girls into full manhood and womanhood within the family.

In such rites the initiates are often seen as dying to their childhood world and being reborn in the adult world. The Kore of West Africa, for instance, take the young boys into the forest for fifteen days. The initiation grove is situated to the west of the village, symbolic of the death they must experience. Inside, the elders whip them with thorn branches and burning torches. The former signify the pain of leaving their former life and the difficulties of acquiring new knowledge. The latter represent divine enlightenment.

The initiates are now regarded as "dead," entombed in the grove and surrounded by thorn hedges. But they are also embryos about to be reborn as adults. Mothers bring food to the grove but do not see their sons, who remain completely passive and helpless and must be fed by the elders.

Finally, the novices are covered with a large blanket of animal skins, and a leader chants a prayer of resurrection and fertility: "If the sky is curved, then it will rain. Let the millet be abundant, let births multiply, let sickness go, let the 'dead' [the initiates] return to life, forever, forever, forever" (Ray 1976:93). When the blanket is removed, the novices are reborn as adults.

Some initiation rites involve an introduction to sexual behavior. About the elaborate female initiation rituals of the Banaro of New Guinea, Richard Thurnwald writes:

> [For nine months] the girls are confined to a cell in the family house, getting sago soup instead of water. . . . At last their cell is broken up by the women, the girls released and allowed to leave the house. The women get coconuts laid ready beforehand, and throw them at the girls, whom they finally push into the water, again pelting them with coconuts. The girls crawl out of the water on the bank, receive portions of sago and pork, and are now dressed, and adorned with earrings, nose sticks, necklaces, bracelets and aromatic herbs. After this a dance of the women takes place.
>
> That same evening . . . the men assemble on the streets of the village. The old men consult with each other, agreeing to distribute the girls according to their custom. This custom was explained to me in the following way. The father of the chosen bridegroom really ought to take possession of the girl, but he is "ashamed" and asks his sib friend, his *mundu*, to initiate her into the mysteries of married life in his place. This man agrees to do so. The mother of the girl hands her over to the bridegroom's father, telling her that he will lead her to meet the goblin. . . .
>
> The bridegroom is not allowed to touch her until she gives birth to a child. This child is called the goblin's child. When the goblin-child is born, the mother says, 'Where is thy father? Who had to do with me?"

The bridegroom responds, "I am not his father; he is a goblin-child"; and she replies, "I did not see that I had intercourse with a goblin." [Reprinted from American Anthropological Association Memoir No. 3, "Bánaro Society: Social Organization and Kinship System of a Tribe in the Interior of New Guinea," 260–262, 1916. Not for further reproduction without permission of the publisher.]

The Banaro bridegroom, for his part, is initiated into sexual activity by the wife of his grandfather's friend.

Healing and prosperity rites. All societies seek prosperity, whether in the form of offspring, good crops, success in love, or special power. And all face crises of illness, death, droughts, floods, earthquakes, and the like. Every society also has common folk knowledge to deal with these problems. But what happens when human knowledge fails? At that time many people turn to religious or magical rites for answers.

In Guinea in West Africa, for example, young women offer carved dolls of women suckling children to a fetish in order to assure pregnancy, while young men fire guns and brandish swords to drive away the demons. Among the Chukchee the shaman becomes possessed by a spirit of healing, speaks in strange tongues, and goes to the spirit world to bring back the soul of the patient who has gone astray. The Greeks in New Testament times went to oracles who prophesied the future and helped their clients avoid danger.

Many people are afraid of evil spirits and have ways to exorcise the demons from individuals or from whole towns. In Bali the people make a feast for the devils, which they place at a crossroad outside the village. They then drive the spirits out to the banquet by waving torches lit from the holy temple lamp and making a great noise. Then suddenly all is silent as the people steal home, leaving the spirits to feast. The silence continues the whole next day and no work is done. After the feast the demons want to return home, but hearing no sounds, they believe the village is some deserted island and leave.

Annual Cycles

Many rituals are corporate in nature and are celebrated by the society as a whole. Among these are the annual cycles that mark transitions in time, such as the beginning of the year, the cycles of the week or of the moon, the planting and harvesting of the crops and other fertility rites, and the changes in the seasons.

The Chinese, for example, used to close the gate between the Mongol and Chinese sections of the city of Peking for a half hour at midnight on New Year's Eve. Pieces of red paper and similar items were fastened to house doors and cupboards. After this, sacrifices were made to the ancestors and deities, and a meal was eaten by all the relatives who gathered to celebrate the New Year. Many Chinese still observe the Feast of the Hungry Ghosts, in which the spirits of wandering ancestors are fed in order to satisfy them and keep them from harming the living.

Similarly, Hindus, Muslims, and Buddhists have a great many annual rituals that mark important points in their religious calendars. To these we must add the many national and secular rites such as independence days, memorial days, and birthdays of great heroes.

Feasts, Festivals, Fairs, and Pilgrimages

People love celebrations. It should not surprise us, therefore, that they take any possible occasion to sing, dance, play, and eat together.

There are festivals of all kinds: secular and religious, joyful and sad, local and national. All Muslims, for example, celebrate Ramadan and Id Al-Kabir, and many observe the festivals of the *wali* or saints. Chinese Buddhists set aside the eleven days following New Year's Day as a festival of supplication and honor various Bodhisattvas or lesser gods throughout the year. Hindus celebrate Holi, Divali, Ugadi, Shivaratri, and a great many other festivals. One study of an Indian village showed that there was some festival or other, whether Hindu, Muslim, Christian, or caste celebration, on more than three hundred days in a year!

Christians, too, have their religious celebrations, including Saint Thomas à Becket's Day (December 29), Epiphany (January 6), Ash Wednesday (first day of Lent), Easter, Ascension Day, Pentecost, and, of course, Christmas.

Most cultures have many other rituals, such as religious fairs with markets and sideshows, drama or music performances, and religious processions; public feasts and celebrations; sports events; and pilgrimages to distant shrines.

Dealing with Tradition

How should Christians respond to all this? How should new converts relate to their cultural past—to the food, dress, medicines, songs, dances, myths, rituals, and all the other things that were so much a part of their lives before they heard the gospel? What responsibility do missionaries have to young churches regarding all this? How far can the gospel be adapted to fit into a culture without losing its essential message? And who should make the decisions about the old culture? These are crucial questions we face constantly in our work.

Denial of the Old: Rejection of Contextualization

Past missionaries often made the decisions and tended to reject most of the old customs as "pagan." Drums, songs, dramas, dances, body decorations, certain types of dress and food, marriage customs, and funeral rites were frequently condemned because they were thought to be directly or indirectly related to traditional religions, hence unacceptable for Christians.

Sometimes this rejection was rooted in the ethnocentrism of the missionaries, who tended to equate the gospel with their own culture and consequently judged other cultural ways as bad. Sometimes, however, the missionaries even realized that in traditional cultures it is hard to draw a sharp line between religious and nonreligious practices. In many societies religion is the core of the culture and permeates all of life—there is no division between sacred and secular beliefs, behaviors, and institutions, as there is in modern societies. Yet these missionaries felt that most customs, because they did have religious connotations, had to be rejected indiscriminately.

This wholesale rejection of old cultural ways created many problems. First, it left a cultural vacuum that needed to be filled, and too often this was done by importing the customs of the missionary. Drums, cymbals, and other traditional instruments were replaced with organs and pianos. Instead of creating new lyrics that fit native music, Western hymns and melodies were translated into the local idiom. Pews replaced mats on floors, and British- and American-style churches were built, although they appeared incongruous alongside wickiups and mud huts. Western suits were often required of pastors preaching in hundred-degree temperatures to scantily dressed audiences. It is no surprise, then, that Christianity was often seen as a foreign religion and Christian converts as aliens in their own land.

It is also no surprise that Christianity was often misunderstood. For example, missionaries in India rejected red saris for brides, for this was the color worn by Hindus. Instead, they introduced white saris to symbolize purity, not realizing that in India red stands for fertility and white for barrenness and death.

A second problem with suppressing old cultural ways is that they merely go underground. It is not uncommon in Africa, for instance, for the people to conduct a formal Christian wedding in the church and then go to the village for the traditional celebrations. In the long run, when pagan customs are practiced in secret, they combine with public Christian teachings to form Christopaganism—a syncretistic mix of Christian and non-Christian beliefs. For example, African slaves in Latin American homes taught the children of their masters the worship of African spirits. When the children grew up and joined the Roman Catholic church, they combined the Catholic veneration of saints and the African tribal religion into new forms of spirit worship that had a Christian veneer.

A third problem with the wholesale condemnation of traditional cultures is that it not only turns missionaries and church leaders into police, but keeps converts from growing by denying them the right to make their own decisions. A church only grows spiritually if its members learn to apply the teachings of the gospel to their own lives.

Acceptance of the Old: Uncritical Contextualization

A second response to traditional practices has been to accept them uncritically into the church. Here, old cultural ways are seen as basically good, and few, if any, changes are seen as necessary when people become Christians.

Those who advocate this approach generally have a deep respect for other humans and their cultures and recognize the high value people place on their own cultural heritage. They also recognize that the "foreignness" of the gospel has been one of the major barriers to its acceptance in many parts of the world. Consequently, they call for an uncritical contextualization that minimizes change in the life of the converts.

This approach, too, has serious weaknesses. First, it overlooks the fact that there are corporate and cultural sins as well as personal transgressions. Sin can be found in the institutions and practices of a society in the form of slavery, oppressive structures, and secularism. It is found in the cultural beliefs of people and exhibited as group pride, segregation against others, and idolatry. The gospel calls not only individuals but societies and cultures to change. Contextualization must mean the communication of the gospel in ways the people understand, but that also challenge them individually and corporately to turn from their evil ways.

Because first-generation converts often feel this call to change most deeply, they are adamant in rejecting specific customs in their past. They are all too aware of the meanings of these old ways, and they want to have nothing more to do with them now that they are Christians. These rejections by the people themselves, however, are radically different from changes imposed upon them from without.

A second weakness in uncritical contextualization is that it opens the door to syncretisms of all kinds. If Christians continue in beliefs and practices that stand in opposition to the gospel, these in time will mix with their newfound faith and produce various forms of neo-paganism. Obviously, new converts bring with them most of their past customs, and they cannot immediately change all those things that need to be changed. Even mature Christians have many areas of their lives that need to be examined in the light of biblical truth. But they must all grow in their Chrisian lives, and this demands that they continually test their actions and beliefs against the norms of the Scriptures. In naive contextualization, it is precisely this critique that is missing.

Dealing with the Old: Critical Contextualization

If both the uncritical rejection of old ways and their uncritical acceptance undermine the mission task, what should we and the Christian converts do about their cultural heritage? A third approach may be called critical contextualization, whereby old beliefs and customs are neither rejected nor accepted without examination. They are first studied with regard to the meanings and places they have within their cultural setting and then evaluated in the light of biblical norms (Figure 25).

How does this take place? First, an individual or church must recognize the need to deal biblically with all areas of life. This awareness may arise when a new church is faced with births, marriages, or deaths and must decide what Christian birth rites, weddings, or funerals should be like. Or it may emerge as people in the church recognize the need to examine certain other culturally based customs. Discerning the areas of life that need to be critiqued is one of the important functions of leadership in the church, for the failure of a church to deal with its surrounding culture opens the door for sub-Christian practices to enter the Christian community unnoticed. This can be seen in the way we in the Western churches have often indiscriminately adopted the dating practices, weddings, funerals, music, entertainment, economic structures, and political traditions around us. We must never forget that our faith calls us to new beliefs and to a changed life.

Second, local church leaders and the missionary must lead the congregation in *uncritically* gathering and analyzing the traditional customs associated with the question at hand. For example, in dealing with funeral rituals, the people should analyze their traditional rites—first describing each song, dance, recitation, and rite that makes up the ceremony and then discussing its meaning and function within the overall ritual. The purpose here is to understand the old ways, not to evaluate them. If we show any criticism of the customary beliefs and practices at this point, the people will not openly talk about them for fear of being condemned. We will only drive the old ways underground.

In the third step, the pastor or missionary should lead the church in a Bible study related to the question under consideration. For example, the leader can use the occasion of a wedding or funeral to teach the Christian beliefs about marriage or death.

This is a crucial step, for if the people do not clearly understand and accept the biblical teachings, they will be unable to deal with their cultural past. This is also where the pastor and missionary have most to offer, namely, an exegesis of biblical truth. It is important, however, that the congregation be actively involved in the study and interpretation of Scripture so that they will grow in their own abilities to discern truth.

The fourth step is for the congregation to evaluate critically their own past customs in the light of their new biblical understandings and to make a decision regarding their use. It is important here that the people themselves make the decision, for they must be sure of the outcome before they will change. It is not enough that the leaders be convinced about changes that may be needed. Leaders may share their personal convictions and point out the consequences of various decisions, but they must allow the people to make the final decision if they wish to avoid becoming policemen. In the end, the people themselves will enforce decisions arrived at corporately, and there will be little likelihood that the customs they reject will go underground.

To involve the people in evaluating their own culture draws upon their strength. They know their old culture better than the missionary and are in a better position to critique it, once they have biblical instruction. Moreover, they will grow spiritually by learning to apply scriptural teachings to their own lives.

A congregation may respond to old beliefs and practices in several ways. Many they will keep, for these are not unbiblical. Western Christians, for example, see no problem with eating hamburgers, singing secular songs such as "Home on the Range," wearing business suits, or driving cars. In many areas of their lives their culture is no different from that of their non-Christian neighbors, and much was brought from their pre-Christian past.

Other customs will be explicitly rejected by the congregation as unbecoming for Christians. The reasons for such rejection is often not apparent to the missionary or outsider, who may see little difference between the songs and rites the people reject and those they retain. But the people know the deeper, hidden meanings of their old customs and their significance in the culture. On the other hand, at some points the missionary may need to raise questions that the people have overlooked, for they often fail to see clearly their own cultural assumptions.

Sometimes the people will modify old practices to give them explicit Christian meanings. For example, Charles Wesley used the mel-

FIGURE 25

Dealing with Old Ways

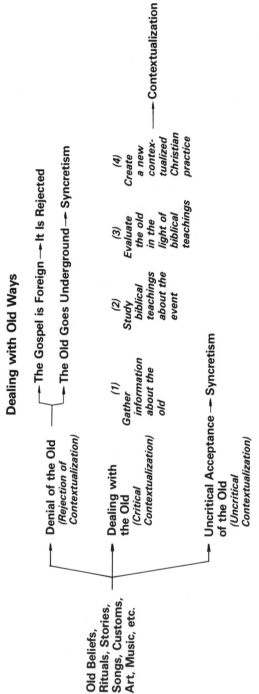

odies of popular bar songs, but gave them Christian words. Similarly the early Christians used the style of worship found in Jewish synagogues, modified to fit their beliefs. They also met on pagan festival days to celebrate Christian events such as the birth of Christ. In time the pagan meanings were forgotten. Contemporary Western Christians use bridesmaids as symbols of friendship and support. In our pre-Christian past they served as decoys sent ahead of the bride to attract the attention of those in the audience who might have an evil eye, thus drawing out their power. The people believed that since the maids were not being married, they were immune to such power. Brides, they thought, were susceptible to the evil eye and would become ill or even die if it struck them. On occasion Christians may retain pagan religious objects, but secularize them as the European church did with Grecian art.

The local church sometimes substitutes Christian symbols or rites borrowed from another culture for those in their own that they reject. For example, the people may choose to adopt the funeral practices of the missionary rather than retain their own. Such functional substitutions are often effective, for they minimize the cultural dislocation created by simply removing an old custom.

Sometimes the local church may add foreign rituals to affirm its spiritual heritage. All Christians live with two traditions, cultural and Christian. The addition of such rituals as baptism and the Lord's Supper not only provides converts with ways to express their new faith, but also symbolizes their ties to the historical and international church. Another example of this is an American bridal couple's decision to use the biblical practice of washing feet as a symbol of their mutual submission to each other.

The people may also create new symbols and rituals to communicate Christian beliefs in forms that are indigenous to their culture. For example, in one tribe the Christians decided to lift up their newborn babies to dedicate them to Christ. In India, when a seminary wanted to inaugurate a missions study center, the faculty, staff, and students looked for an appropriate way to express their commitment to ministry. They decided to plant some stalks of ripe grain in a bucket of earth and then have representatives from each group—faculty, staff, and students—cut sheaves as a symbol of their united dedication to missions.

Having led the people to analyze their old customs in the light of biblical teachings, the pastor or missionary must help them arrange the practices they have chosen into a new ritual that expresses the Christian meaning of the event. Such a ritual will be Christian, for it explicitly seeks to express biblical teachings. It will also be indigenous, for the congregation has created it, using forms the people understand within the own culture.

It is important for us to teach the explicit meaning of our Christian rituals to our children and to new converts, so these do not become empty forms and so they are not confused with the non-Christian customs from which they were drawn. We are always faced with the erosion of meaning in our symbols and rituals. The answer to meaningless and dead symbolism is not to eliminate symbols, but to preserve living symbols, which are constantly renewed through self-examination.

A final word of caution is needed here. The missionary may not always agree with the choices the people make, but it is important, as far as conscience allows, to accept the decisions of the local Christians and to recognize that they, too, are led by the Spirit of God. Leaders must grant others the greatest right they reserve for themselves, the right to make mistakes. The church grows stronger by consciously making decisions in the light of Scripture, even when the decisions may not always be the wisest, than when it simply obeys orders given by others.

A Case of Contextualization

The process of critical contextualization can best be seen by way of illustration. We could, for example, by looking at the case of the weddings of the Bhotiya of Tibet described earlier, try to understand how Bhotiya Christians should respond to their cultural practices in the light of biblical teachings. We will, however, examine a case of critical contextualization in the United States. We are often aware of the need for evaluating the practices of other cultures when the gospel is first introduced into them, but we too easily take it for granted that our own culture, with its long history of Christianity, has already been molded by biblical values. The result, too often, is comfortable accommodation between Christianity and Western culture, including an uncritical acceptance of Western cultural ways. This is true of many areas of life, one of which is music.

This case has to do with the young people in an inner-city Los Angeles church who faced the question whether as Christians they should listen to hard rock music. Most of them were new converts from gangs and drugs, and they knew both the messages and the power of contemporary songs.

The response of many Christian parents is to reject rock music altogether. When that happens, their children end up listening to rock at their friends' houses, and the parents serve as policemen. Other parents give up without a fight and permit their children to listen to rock indiscriminately. Their children learn no discernment and accept uncritically the ways of the world.

The youth leader in this Los Angeles church used critical contextualization to deal with the issue. He had the young people bring their rock records to a Bible study. There he discussed with them the meaning of Christian lifestyles and the place of music in their lives. Then the young people played each record and evaluated it. They smashed those they decided Christians should not listen to, keeping the rest and listening to them without guilty consciences. The following Sunday they triumphantly brought the records they had broken for their Lord and presented them to the church. There was no need, thereafter, for their parents to monitor their listening habits. They had learned discernment for themselves.

Theological Foundations

What are the theological foundations for critical contextualization? First, it affirms the priesthood of all believers. With critical contextualization, decisions are made not by the leaders for the people, but by all of the believers.

Leaders and missionaries throughout history have often felt threatened by this approach to biblical hermeneutics. Since they believe themselves better trained, they claim for themselves the exclusive right to make theological decisions. They are afraid things might get out of hand if the laity were involved in interpreting the Bible and in applying its message to their everyday lives.

What does keep matters from going astray when all are involved in the application of Scripture to the problems of life? Does not the process open the door for wild interpretations of the Bible and Christian practices? There are three checks on such excessiveness.

First, the Bible is taken as the final and definitive authority for Christian beliefs and practices. Everyone, therefore, must begin at the same place.

Second, the priesthood of believers assumes that all the faithful have the Holy Spirit to guide them in the understanding and application of the Scriptures to their own lives. It is all too easy for leaders to accept this belief in theory, but to shy away from it in practice. To deny young believers the right to be involved in biblical interpretation and decision making is to deny that the same Holy Spirit we know to be within us and guiding us into the truth is also within them.

Third, there is the constant check of the church. C. Norman Kraus (1979) points out that the contextualization of the gospel is ultimately the task not of individuals and leaders, but of the church as a "discerning community." Within that community, individuals contribute according to their gifts and abilities. The pastor and missionary have a greater knowledge of the Bible and therefore should provide the exegesis of the appropriate texts within their biblical context. The people, however, understand their own culture and problems and should play an important part in determining the hermeneutical application of the Scripture to their own lives. But they must be subject to the church as a whole.

The church is not an aggregate of individuals, each seeking his or her own interpretation of the Bible. It is to be a true community of people seeking to follow Christ and serve one another. Only then will it become what Kraus calls an "authentic Christian community," a hermeneutical community that strives to understand God's message to it and bears witness to the world of what it means to be a Christian, not only in beliefs but also in life. The church as a body is a "new order."

The Fourth Self

W e have seen how cultural differences affect missionaries as they identify with the people and influence the message as it is translated into the forms of a new culture. But what about theology? What happens when the Bible is seen through the eyes of people in another culture? How should we respond when they disagree with our interpretations of the Scriptures?

Behind these queries lies one of the most fundamental questions raised by modern missions, namely, the autonomy of new believers and churches. To what extent are they or should they be dependent upon missionaries? How fast and how far should missionaries encourage them to make their own decisions? Should they govern themselves? If so, do they have a right to change the patterns of church organization brought by the missionaries? Should they be encouraged to develop their own theologies, and what should the missionaries do when these theologies seem to be going astray? These are the most crucial dilemmas facing modern missionaries and mission agencies.

The Three Selves

During the first years of the modern mission movement, people were won to faith and congregations planted. The question then arose as to how the mission agencies and sending churches should relate to the new churches. It soon became clear that the paternalistic missionary attitudes common in that day were stifling the maturation and

193

growth of the young churches. Leadership remained in the hands of the missionaries. National leaders were suppressed and frustrated. In many cases they broke away and established churches independent from the missionary agencies, but that did not solve the problem for those who wanted to keep ties with the churches that had brought the gospel to them.

Around 1861, two outstanding mission leaders, Rufus Anderson and Henry Venn, proposed a plan whereby young churches would gain their independence on the basis of three principles: self-propagation, self-support, and self-governance. These were widely debated and finally adopted by mission agencies as their guidelines for establishing autonomous churches.

The first principle, self-propagation, pointed to one of the weaknesses of the early mission movement. The missionaries had planted churches, but often these churches had no vision for evangelizing their own people or sending missionaries to other cultures. Local leaders saw these tasks as the work of the original missionary. It became clear that young churches do not automatically become evangelistically minded. That vision must be as consciously taught and modeled as the rest of Christian life.

In defense of the early missionaries, it must be said that many of them did teach the young churches the need for evangelism. The first-generation converts, however, were still learning what it means to be Christians. Moreover, history will show that they did far more evangelism than we give them credit for. Missionaries wrote copiously about their work, but the national evangelists left few records, even though they did most of the evangelizing and bore most of the persecution that usually comes to the first believers in a community.

Anderson and Venn reminded the mission world that not only missionaries, but also the national churches must be involved in evangelism and missions. This raised little argument. Young churches were often deeply concerned about evangelism. Although they were too poor to carry on the expensive programs started by the missionaries, they did have their own indigenous ways of evangelizing their people.

The second principle, self-support, raised more debate. Missionaries argued that young churches should learn to support themselves, that continued reliance on outside support created a dependency that hindered their maturation and growth. Missionaries also pointed out that the young churches would gain a sense of autonomy and equality only if they were self-supporting. In a sense the missionaries were right.

The young churches argued that the foreign-funded programs the missionaries operated—the evangelistic teams, schools, hospitals, and even churches with paid preachers—did not fit their cultures and were too expensive for them to support. They could fund programs they themselves started, but not those the missionaries were now trying to turn over to them. They too were right.

In the end the mission agencies pushed hard for self-support, and the national churches, sometimes reluctantly, took charge of the institutions that the missionaries had built with foreign money. Some of these they closed, and some they continued to operate on levels more in line with their own financial abilities.

The third principle, self-governance, raised the most disagreements. Ironically, here the tables were turned. Young churches wanted the power to make their own decisions, arguing that they would never mature until they had self-rule. The missionaries were reluctant to give up their power for fear that inexperience and local politics would ruin the church.

As we shall see in chapter 9, there is no simple solution to the transfer of power. As missionaries we must recognize that natural leaders emerge even in the simplest of church communities, and they are capable of leading their churches. They may not be educated in the Western sense, but they are often wise and experienced in their own cultural ways.

We must also allow local leaders the greatest privilege we allow ourselves, namely, the right to make mistakes and learn from them. The story is told of a young missionary who asked a great missionary statesman how he came to be so successful. "By making good decisions," the senior leader said. "Yes, but how do you learn to make good decisions," the young man asked. "By making bad decisions," the old man replied.

Leaders of young churches, on the other hand, need to be sensitive to the concerns of the missionaries who love the church and have invested deeply in it, and to recognize that they are human.

The three "self" principles continue to guide much of contemporary mission planning. They make an important point—that young churches are equal and independent members in the worldwide community of churches. Today, however, many are arguing that we must move beyond autonomy to partnership. In the name of self-support, mission agencies too often withhold funds that would help young churches carry on effective evangelism. Our goal is not to establish isolated churches that work alone, but to sustain churches that share a unity of fellowship and a common mission to the world.

Self-theologizing: The Fourth Self

After much discussion about the three "selves," there has emerged a general consensus that young churches must be allowed to ma-

ture and take responsibility for the work of God in their regions as
soon as possible. But little is said about the fourth self—self-theologizing. Do young churches have the right to read and interpret the
Scriptures for themselves?

When a new church is planted, the first years are characterized by
warm fellowship, emotional expressions of faith, and a concern for
evangelizing relatives and neighbors. Most of the converts have simple
theologies and accept with little question the theological teachings of
the missionary. There are exceptions, of course, particularly among
well-educated converts who were formerly leaders in other religions.

After two or three generations, there emerge leaders who have been
raised with Christian teachings and trained in biblical exegesis. It is
these leaders who often raise difficult theological questions. How does
the gospel speak to their culture? What is the relationship of Christianity to the non-Christian religions in their land? And how does
Christianity answer the basic questions being asked by the people?
For example, in Africa what does the gospel have to say about ancestors or polygamy? And in India how should Christians respond to
beliefs in transmigration or the caste system or meditation as a way
to salvation?

Most mission movements have led to theological crises. Three or
four generations after a church is planted in a new culture, local theologians arise and truggle with the question of how the gospel relates
to their cultural traditions. How can they express the Good News in
terms the people understand, and yet retain its prophetic message? In
answer to these questions they develop new theologies. Today, for instance, we hear of Latin American theology, African theology, and
Indian theology.

How should we respond when national church leaders develop theologies that they claim are more relevant to their culture? If we encourage them, are we not opening the door for theological pluralism
and, eventually, relativism? If we oppose them, are we not guilty of
the worst form of ethnocentrism and of stunting their growth? These
are central questions we are forced to ask by the very nature of our
task, and we dare not take them lightly. This proliferation of theologies
in different historical and cultural settings raises important issues
about the nature of theology.

Theological Shock

Most of us were raised within a church and taught its theological
confessions. We were monotheological and assumed that there is only
one way to interpret the Scriptures, that all deviations from this ap-

proach were false. It comes as a shock, therefore, when we find honest, deeply committed Christians interpreting the Bible in different ways.

If we have not faced this pluralism of theologies before, we certainly will when we become missionaries. In much of the world, Christian communities are small, and the need for fellowship and mutual support is great, so missionaries of different church backgrounds relate to one another far more closely than we would in our home countries. Moreover, national church leaders abroad raise difficult theological questions that emerge out of the gospel in a new cultural setting, and they begin to formulate new theological responses.

The first time we truly confront theological pluralism, we experience theological shock. As in the case of culture shock, our old absolutes are challenged, and the unquestioned certainties we hold are put to the test. We are faced with the fact that there are different ways to interpret Scripture and forced to ask why we think our own interpretation is correct.

Our initial reaction to theological pluralism is often to deny it. We simply reaffirm our theological convictions without examining their nature and reject all other interpretations as false. We hold on to the certainty that we have the whole truth. The price of this certainty, however, is great. We dare not examine our theological foundations lest they be weakened. Moreover, we dare not fellowship closely with other Christians for fear that our beliefs will be challenged. Consequently, we withdraw into an isolated community of like-minded believers.

In time, however, most of us face up to the fact of theological pluralism and seek to deal with it. Initially, as in culture shock, we are confronted with a feeling of relativism. Since everyone seems to have his or her own theology, how do we know ours is correct? Then we realize that relativism undermines the concept of truth and of meaning itself. But how can we accept pluralism in theology and remain committed to biblical truth?

Bible, Theology, and Culture

As evangelicals we hold to the truthfulness of the Bible. We also have strong theological convictions. How do these two relate?

At first we are tempted to equate the two. After all, our theology is rooted in our study of the Bible. Further examination, however, forces us to distinguish between the Bible and theology. The Bible is a historical document of God's revelation to humans. Theology is the systematic and historical explication of the truths of the Bible.

Here it is important that we distinguish between two different definitions of the term *theology*. Sometimes we use the term when we

FIGURE 26

Theology Is Divine Revelation Understood in Human Contexts

talk about absolute truth. Theology is a systematic description and explanation of the way things really are, the way God sees them, and we will speak of this as "Theology" with a capital *T*. At other times we use the term when we speak of human descriptions and explanations of reality that arise out of our study of the Bible. We will speak of this as "theology" with a small *t*.

Too often we confuse the two. We think that our studies of the Bible are unbiased, that our own interpretations of the Scriptures are the only true ones. It disturbs us, therefore, when we begin to discover that theologies are also influenced by culture. The very fact that we phrase our theology in English can prejudice our understandings of the Bible. There is no theologically unbiased language (see Figure 26)!

The fact is, all theologies developed by human beings are shaped by their particular historical and cultural contexts—by the languages they use and the questions they ask. All human theologies are only partial understandings of Theology as God sees it. We see through a glass darkly.

Moreover, all theologies are flawed by human sinfulness. Just as the rich young ruler who came to Jesus did not want to hear what he said, we often turn away from the hard messages of the Bible.

But the fact that we are humans and see through a glass darkly does *not* mean that we do not see at all. We can read the Scriptures and understand them. The central message of the gospel is clear: creation, sin, and redemption. Of these we can be certain. It is the fine details that we see less clearly.

Kalonda of Kangate

Paul B. Long

The African sun poured upon us as we climbed the mountain path to the village among the trees. The people of Kangate, in the wild Babindl section of the central Congo, had seldom seen a white man. Excited cries greeted me and my three Congolese friends as we entered the dusty country to answer a strange request from an old chieftain among these isolated people.

Several days previously a runner had appeared at our mission station. "Teller of the Word," the runner had said, "Chief Kalonda wants to talk with you."

"What does this old rascal want to see me about?" I wondered, and the question remained in my mind as we drove with difficulty through the mountainous country over dangerous roads. Now at last we would know.

In the shade of the chieftain's hut, surrounded by the smaller huts of several wives, a very aged, emaciated man sat, wrapped in an old blanket. This broken, sick old chieftain, enthroned on a cross-legged stool bedecked with leopard skin, lifted a feeble hand and greeted us with the customary salutations of the land: "*Muoyo wenu*—life to you."

"*Wuoyo webe,*" we replied, "life to you."

I remembered the tales I had heard of this once-powerful chieftain. Twenty years ago Kalonda was feared and respected for a hundred miles or more around his realm. As a ruler, bold and savage, he freely exercised the power of life and death over his subjects, and death or slavery over his captives. His renown as a chieftain was surpassed only by his great power as a medicine man. Leaders came from distant villages to buy his charms and curses.

One day the chief of a neighboring realm, Kasenda of the Balubal people, arrived in the village of Kangate. The visiting chieftain was worried and needed help.

"I have killed the money messenger of the Mission and taken the money he was carrying to their preachers and teachers," he recounted. "Now the dead man has come to life and returned to the white men to tell what I have done. Give me medicine to make me invisible when the soldiers come!"

"Return to your country," replied Kalonda. "Get twelve she goats, six young, strong women, ten spears and ten knives, then come back to buy my medicine. This is my price for medicine powerful enough to make you invisible."

Complaining of the high cost of this protection, Chief Kasenda returned to Balubal to round up goats, women, and weapons.

Chief Kalonda proceeded in the meantime to compound his promised medicine. Sending out his bodyguard, he directed the capture of a young woman from a neighboring tribe. She was brought before the chief. With elaborate ritual the chief's warriors cut off the captive's head, which was needed for Kalonda's "invisible charm." Cannibal ritual was involved in the proceedings. On the appointed day, the medicine was presented, the goats and women and weapons were exchanged, and the deal closed to the satisfaction of both leaders.

When the soldiers arrived several weeks later to capture the ruler of the Balubal, Kasenda quietly entered his hut, picked up the head that would make him invisible, and stepped out into his courtyard to laugh at the baffled troops who would not be able to see him. To his surprise, anger, and consequent regret, they surrounded him, bound him securely, and marched him off to the white man's jail. Still holding his high-priced medicine, Kasenda became enraged with his former friend, Kalonda, whose charm had failed. He cursed Kalonda and gave his name as the murderer of the woman whose head he held in his hands. Kalonda, too, was arrested.

Fifteen seasons ran their course thereafter, and the peoples of Babinda and Balubal had all but forgotten their former chieftains. Condemned at first to die in jail, both were saved when their executions were three times postponed; finally the sentences were changed to fifteen years in prison at hard labor. To the chieftains, this judgment was as harsh as death.

Now, released after fifteen years of captivity, old Kalonda had at last come home to die. I looked across the council ring at this old man, remembering what I knew of those years of the past. After the customary silence of respect, I began the conversation: "*Nfumu,* Chieftain, your runner says you want to talk with me. I have come. What do you want?"

Kalonda's reply startled me. "Tell me about the white man's God."

"The God I follow is not a white man's God. He is the Father of the New Tribe, His people. Jesus Christ is the great Chieftain of the New Tribe, and He accepts anyone who will follow Him. My friends here are also members of the New Tribe. They will tell you about it." And I turned to my Congolese colleagues who really understood the battle old Kalonda was facing. One of my companions was an old witch doctor turned Christian and now an effective pastor among his people. I accompanied with deep concern the battle taking place between the powers which are real and the liberation which is possible.

Copper charm bracelets adorned the once-strong spear arm of the old chief. "You still trust in your medicine," observed Pastor Mutombo. "Why do you ask about another God?"

With great reluctance, the old man slipped the bracelets from his arm, dropped them in the dust, and said, "Now tell me, 'Teller of the Word,' about your powerful God."

With those copper bands lying at our feet, I began to realize something of the price he was having to pay for what he asked. He had just renounced his potency, and I heard him mutter, "I used to have eight good, strong wives, and all but three old ones ran away while I was in jail. All I have left are old women who are too weak to work."

My eyes followed his glance toward three old women crouched close to a nearby hut. They were agitatedly mumbling to each other and evidently unhappy with the events taking place.

"Your medicine couldn't hold your women while you were gone?" the pastor questioned; and he answered with a grunt.

"Now," the pastor continued, "the war medicine on your belt shows where you look for power."

After a long, thoughtful pause, the old warrior cut the small skin bag from his belt and dropped it in the dust.

"Now the 'counter-hex' packet at your neck." The old man put a trembling hand to the thong around his neck. This little charm held his protection against all his enemies and made their magic of no power. Silently we waited until, at length, he broke the thong and let his "security" fall at our feet. Grunts of respect for his courage echoed around the ring of watching tribesmen.

"Your *Buanga bua Bunfumu,*" the pastor reminded, "your medicine of chieftainship."

Wearily Kalonda arose, entered his hut and returned with a large antelope horn filled with assurance of his power over his people. (I have never been sure just what makes up such powers, but have been told that horns hold bits of hair, the eye of a frog, the tooth of a lion, and the claw of a bird.) Lightning medicine followed, and a host of other protective charms which give forest people some respite from their constant fear of living.

"This is all the protection I have," Kalonda said. But the pastor was evidently waiting for another, more costly surrender. "Now get your 'life charm,' Kalonda, and I will tell you about the God of the New Tribe."

The old man trembled, broke out in perspiration, shook his head and wrapped his tattered blanket across his bony chest. The three old wives had remonstrated with his renunciation of his medicines, and, with this last demand, they commenced the death wail, and started tossing dust in the air over their heads. At this acknowledgment of his impending death, Kalonda roused from his fearful reflections, re-entered his hut, and returned with a little packet of skins. With all the dignity of a great leader, he silenced the wailing wives and surveyed his council ring.

"Teller of the Word," he said, holding out his little packet in his bony hands, "you have asked the life of Kalonda! This medicine has protected my life from all my enemies for many years. Many still live who hate me and have curses on my life. When I throw down this medicine all their curses will fall on me, my spirits will withdraw their protection, and I will die. But Kalonda is not afraid to die."

As the packet dropped in the dust, the old chieftain straightened to his full height, lifted his old eyes to the distant hills, and waited for death. We sat in silence as the seconds grew into minutes and tension mounted in the ring of onlookers who waited for their chief to die.

After a long while, the old chief looked at us, and his lips parted in a relieved grin. "I'm still alive! Kalonda has not been struck dead!"

It took a long time to answer questions from old Kalonda and his people. Questions about the God, he said, he had always feared but never known. As the afternoon shadows lengthened, the old chieftain arose with dignity before his people. In a quiet, confident voice he announced, "Kalonda has a new chieftain. I follow 'Yesu Kilisto' and He will help me across the river, lead me through the dark forest, and take me to His village where I can sit with His people. I belong to the New Tribe. Kalonda wants all his people to follow *Nfumu Yesu,* [Chieftain Jesus], and go with Him to the Village of God."

Not many days after my visit to Kangate, a messenger arrived with the brief report: "Kalonda has gone on his journey to meet his new Chief."

The theological bridge. Because human theologies are rooted in the Bible on the one side, and in particular cultures on the other, they are bridges by which the gospel speaks to us today. To make sure our theologies are sound we need three things. First, we need a careful exegesis of the Bible. This must include not only a study of the biblical texts, but also the historical and cultural contexts within which these were given. God revealed himself and his work to us, but he did so within the history and culture of a specific people. The more deeply we root our theologies in Scripture, the more certain we can be of their trustworthiness.

Second, we need a careful exegesis of our own cultural and historical contexts. Through this, we become aware of how our culture and its world view influence our theology. We also become aware of the needs in our culture that the gospel must address.

Finally, we need a good hermeneutics in which the messages of the Bible that were given in other times and cultures are made relevant for the cultural environments of today.

Tests of truth.   But how do we test the truthfulness of our theologies, and how do we deal with theological pluralism? Obviously, there are disagreements over the interpretation of Scripture. The answer is not to accept all human theologies as equally correct, but to bring them all closer to the absolute truth, to Theology as God knows it to be. All theologies are incomplete, and all have biases that color their understanding. Moreover, all human understandings are flawed and need to be examined and tested.

The first test is the Bible itself, for through it God has revealed to us knowledge of ultimate realities that we cannot gain by human experience alone. The Scriptures, not our theologies, are our starting point. Consequently our theologies must be molded to fit Scripture, rather than Scripture bent to fit our theologies. This means that solid biblical exegesis is essential at every stage in formulating our theology. Moreover, if others convince us that our interpretation of the Scripture is wrong, we must be willing to change our theology.

A second test is the ongoing work of the Holy Spirit instructing believers in the truth. We need a humble and open spirit that is sensitive to the leading of God in our study of Scripture. As one writer put it, we must do theology on our knees. We need also to recognize that the same Holy Spirit at work in us is also at work in the lives of other believers. If we do so, we will not take a stance of militant confrontation against those who disagree with us. Rather, we will seek to examine with them our differences in the light of Scripture.

A third test is the Christian community. As priests in the kingdom of God, we have a right to interpret God's Word. As members of the body of Christ, we are responsible for listening to one another. As Kraus points out (1979:71), the interpretation of the gospel is ultimately not the task of individuals or of leaders, but of the church as a "discerning community":

> Thus the Scripture can find its proper meaning as witness only within a *community of interpretation*. Principles of interpretation are important, but secondary. There needs to be an authentic correspondence between gospel announcement and a "new order" embodied in community for Scripture to play its proper role as a part of the original witness. The authentic community is the hermeneutical community. It determines the actual enculturated meaning of Scripture.

We in the West, with our extreme forms of individualism, need to rediscover this corporate nature of the church, whereby the body checks the errors of the individual and the community of churches checks the errors of the individual congregation. Just as others see our sins more clearly than we do, so also do others see our heresies more clearly.

Testing our convictions with other Christians does not weaken them. It strengthens them. We are more sure of beliefs that stand up under careful examination. We are less sure of those that we are afraid to put to the test, lest they crumble. After putting our beliefs to the test, we may be less certain about some of the details, but we will be more certain about the central truths of the gospel that stand out so clearly.

In the end, even these steps do not always lead us to theological unity. What then? We have a right to hold firm to our own convictions and share them with others. We must, however, speak the truth in love, seeking not to conquer those who disagree, but to win them. We also have a responsibility to examine our beliefs closely.

Why theology? Why should we be concerned about theology, anyway? It can lead to wars between Christians and to a questioning of truth. Many argue that it is a waste of time, that all we need do is read the Bible and apply it directly to our lives.

There is a measure of truth in this appeal, for we are always in danger of building theologies for their own sake, as a purely academic exercise. Such theologies can deaden our spiritual lives and distract us from the essential call of the gospel to repentance and discipleship. In the end, Christianity is a whole way of living, not just a pattern of thinking.

Moreover, learning to apply biblical truths to our lives is essential to Christian growth. Wayne Dye (1982) found that the missionaries most successful in building mature churches are those who teach young Christians to take their problems to Scripture to find an answer there. For them, the Bible becomes a living reality in their everyday lives, not something they merely study in the classroom.

In another sense, however, we cannot avoid developing theologies. As we read Scripture we automatically link together different passages and form basic ideas about the nature of God, the Bible, humans, sin, forgiveness, grace, and redemption. We weave these concepts into a single tapestry in which they take their meanings not so much from formal definitions as from their relationships to one another and to the whole picture. For the most part, we do this implicitly. We are often not conscious of our own theologies until they are challenged. In developing a theology, we consciously examine our religious beliefs.

Furthermore, solid theological foundations are needed to keep a church true to Christian faith in the long run. Too often we think in terms of the immediate growth of the church and overlook the long-range direction in which it is going. In our concern about leading people to Christ, we neglect the discipling needed to keep them faithful unto death. We may be concerned about evangelism, but overlook the theological foundations that are needed to keep a church true to the gospel, particularly in times of persecution. We are in danger of planting large churches that go astray. Missionaries and church leaders must think of evangelism and church planting not only for a five- or ten-year span, but in the time frame of fifty and a hundred years and beyond, for they are laying the foundations of the church.

Types of Theology

There are two kinds of theology, each of which serves a different purpose. One kind examines the basic structures underlying reality. It asks questions about the nature of God, the world, humans, sin, salvation, and so on. These theologies, like most scientific theories, are concerned about the unchanging order underlying the universe. Both are "synchronic paradigms."

A second type of theology is interested in "the story" of reality. Theologies of this kind ask questions about the ultimate origins, purpose, and destiny of the universe, of human societies, and of individuals. They find meaning in cosmic and human history. Such theologies are "diachronic paradigms."

One way to compare synchronic and diachronic studies is to examine an automobile. If we approach it synchronically, we will look at the way it is put together and how it operates. We will examine the electrical system, the fuel system, the motor, the drive train, and so on. Notice that on this level we are interested in cars in general, not in this particular one. And we are interested in how they work, not what happens to them. In other words, we are interested in the *structure* and *functions* of cars.

A second way to study a car is to study its history. We find that it was bought in Seattle by a wealthy couple, that it made trips to Philadelphia and Toronto, that it was involved in an accident in which the couple was injured, that it was repaired and finally sold to a college student. We trace its history until it was junked. In such a diachronic study, meaning lies in the *story* of this particular automobile.

Which of these types of explanation should we use? We need both. If we want to understand how cars operate in order to repair them, we need a synchronic theory. If we want to know why and how they are used, we need a diachronic analysis. Similarly, when we study the nature of God and the universe, we need a systematic (synchronic) theology. But when we want to know what is going on, we need a biblical (diachronic) theology.

While both approaches are needed, meaning ultimately lies in diachronic studies. We may examine how human beings work—their blood, lungs, muscles, minds, and souls. In the end, however, we want to know the stories of their lives.

The Bible is basically a diachronic account, a history of God's work in the universe and in humanity. In it, of course, God progressively reveals to us his nature and that of ultimate reality. The story, however, is the drama of human creation, sin, and redemption.

Functions of Theology

Clifford Geertz (1972:169) has pointed out that explanation systems such as theologies serve two important functions. In the first place they are maps *of* reality. We use them to organize and make sense out of our experiences. In the second place they are maps *for* guiding our behavior. We use them in choosing a course of action.

Maps "of." We all need explanation systems. Without them we see the world not as evil, but as chaotic and incomprehensible. It is meaningless. Geertz points out that there is no greater human fear than to lose a sense of understanding. It is greater than the fear of death itself. Martyrs die willingly because their deaths take on meaning and purpose.

Above all we need a system of ultimate explanation that provides us with a basic framework within which we fit our other models and theories. As Christians, this is our theology.

As maps of ultimate realities, our theologies serve several important purposes. First, they provide us with a comprehensive picture of what is going on. This includes both a synchronic view of the nature of things and a diachronic view of what is happening. The latter provides us with a sense of purpose and destiny and of God's providence in our everyday lives. Unfortunately, we too often focus on the details of the

Bible and lose sight of the bigger story. In Sunday school we study various passages, but rarely take time to give students an overview of redemptive history. In missions we focus on specific doctrines and assume that people know the larger picture, an assumption we dare not make. Consequently, for many theology is made up of bits and pieces of unconnected information.

A second use of theology is to make explicit the implicit theological ideas we all have and to put them to the test. Poor theology is often rooted in the unexamined assumptions we hold. For example, we are generally unaware of the extent to which our world view colors our theology. Only as we make these explicit can we examine and correct them.

A third use of theology is apologetics, which undergirds our faith and helps us to make the gospel clear to non-Christians. Moreover, it can help us defend Christianity against the attacks of secularism and other religions.

A fourth use of theology as a model *of* reality is to combat heresy. The church, in every time and every culture, must seek after the truth and discern those critical errors that might lead it away from the gospel. Here we need a great deal of humility, for we dare not let our concern for heresy blind us to the fact that our personal understandings of the Scriptures are incomplete and often wrong. Nor should we use it as a game to gain status in the church. Our concerns must be the glory of God, a love for the truth, and a redemptive love that seeks to win back those who stray.

It is important here to distinguish between immaturity and heresy. People come to faith as they are, as drunkards, adulterers, divorcées, and self-righteous Pharisees. The church must begin with them there, not from where they should be. The same is true theologically. Young believers come with their Hindu, Muslim, or secular world views, and their conceptual categories do not change overnight when they are converted. Even their concepts of God are limited and distorted. Nevertheless, they can be saved. The molding of an individual's theology and world view to fit biblical teachings is a lifelong process.

A young church, too, begins with a simple theology that is deeply influenced by the local culture. But it must mature in its theology so that it will remain true to its divine calling. This was the experience of the early church, which began in a Jewish setting. When Christianity spread to the Greeks, the early church fathers had to wrestle with legitimate ways of expressing the gospel in Greek thought and deal with the heresies that emerged in the process. As R. H. Boyd (1974:47–52) points out, this was one of the main reasons for the emergence of systematic theology in the Western church. A church needs a living theology to be a truly Christian witness in the world. Such a theology must be constantly formulated to make the gospel meaningful in new settings and to guard against emergent new heresies. A church with a static or immature theology is easily led astray. In missions we must always keep this long-range view of the church in mind.

Maps "for." Maps not only give us a picture of a place; they also help us to choose a course of action. For example, we may use a map to get to the airport, since we plan our mode of transportation and set a time schedule accordingly.

Charles Nyamiti, an African theologian, points out that theology should not be done as an abstract exercise divorced from real life. It must always have a pastoral concern that seeks the well-being of people (Taber 1978:63). It must be a tool to help the church *be* the church, to help Christians grow, and to help non-Christians come to Christ. It should both tackle real problems in theology and deal with the problems people face. A theology has little value if it does not prove useful in the conversion and edification of persons in Christ.

The pastoral nature of theology must be expressed first in the life of the theologian and missionary. Ours must be a living theology that transforms our own lives and demands of us great sanctity. Only then will it be credible to our listeners.

It is easy to separate our theology from our lives and to place on others burdens we ourselves are not willing to bear. We must constantly wrestle with making our faith explicit in our daily living. Only then will we be able to understand the struggles of others and help them as they seek to fulfill Christian lives.

Theology in Context

The history of the church cannot be understood apart from its cultural and historical setting. The early church sought both to make the gospel understood and to preserve its authentic message in the context of a Greek culture that was in many ways foreign to the Bible. In the process it had to fight the heresies that emanated from the dualistic Greek world view, which made Christ either man or God, but not both. Protestant orthodoxy of the seventeenth and eighteenth centuries countered the degenerate nature of the church in its day and formulated a theology meaningful to the people of the Enlightenment. Since then, pietism, evangelicalism, liberalism, neoorthodoxy, and other theologies have emerged as attempts to make the Christian message relevant and meaningful for modern secular humans. Not all of these attempts to contextualize theology, however, have been equally successful in preserving the authentic message of Scripture.

Do churches in other cultures have the same right to understand and apply the gospel in their own settings? Is there not a danger that they will go theologically astray? The answer to both of these questions is yes. To grow, spiritually young churches must search the Scripture themselves, and if—for fear that they will leave the truth—we do not allow them to do so, we condemn them to spiritual infancy and early death. On the other hand, to allow people to study the Scriptures for themselves always entails some risk.

Levels of Centextualization

How will African, Asian, or Latin American theologies differ from our own? Certainly the core of the biblical message—the story of creation, sin, and redemption—remains the same. Changes, however, will take place on several levels.

Religion, Drives, and the Place Where It Itches

Jacob A. Loewen

A group of Lengua Indians was sitting around a fire outside one of the newly erected temporary shelters in a recently settled village in Paraguay. The group was in the process of changing its nomadic hunting way of life to one of sedentary agriculture.

The author, sitting with them, was making an anthropological investigation of the situation, hoping to find ways and means to facilitate this difficult transition for the tribe. He had been entertaining the group with accounts of his early missionary experience among the Chocó Indians of Colombia. Among other things he had told them about some of the cultural errors he had made when he first tried to reach that tribe with the gospel. After exposing his own mistakes at some length, he suddenly stopped and asked, "Have the missionaries who brought you the message about Jesus Christ also made mistakes like this?"

A painful silence followed. It was finally broken by the host who felt obligated to answer, "It is very hard for Lengua Indians to say if missionaries have or have not made mistakes." The visiting anthropologist well understood the truth of this assertion, for the Lengua concept of the "good innermost" did make it very difficult to criticize others. However, not wanting to lose this excellent occasion for discovering some of the attitudes of the Lengua toward the existing missionary program, he continued to press: "Maybe you could mention at least one of the areas in which there have been mistakes." After another period of silence the host answered in the Low German vernacular highly influenced by Lengua syntax, *"Es krautze woa nich es yeiche,"* which freely translated said, "They are scratching where it doesn't itch. . . ."

In order to understand why the missionary message often has not scratched as the missionary intended it to, we must consider several predisposing factors.

Faith and religion

All too often the American-trained, evangelical missionary approaches Christianity from the point of right belief. The missionary task is thus seen as replacing a wrong belief with the right belief. The right faith is *the* answer to man's problems. "Faith," in its current North American connotations, has undergone some subtle changes from New Testament times. For many deeply evangelical people it essentially involves mental acceptance of a set of premises or doctrines as truth, and it frequently lacks the concomitant ingredients of commitment and obedience. This means that faith has largely been separated from life.

Such an attitude is very frequently reflected in translation. In a number of the South American tribal languages the words "to believe" and "to obey" come from the same root word. In trying to distinguish between these two concepts missionaries have then translated "to believe" as "to accept as true." This, however, translates only the "static" component of faith and leaves out the most important dynamic component of personal commitment which the Biblical use of the word emphasizes.

Religion and the totality of life

Frequently, and possibly as a consequence of faith being interpreted as right belief, religious experience has been so completely separated from the totality of life that people have developed a kind of remote "spiritual" interpretation of how God works in the lives of men. Dr. Eugene A. Nida has pointed out the fallacy of this view:

> Some Christians tend to think of church growth almost entirely apart from the cultural contexts in which it has taken place, as though it were some special supernatural phenomenon involving only the struggle between the forces of God and the wiles of the devil. There is no doubt that church growth is directly related to the total plan and purposes of God; but at the same time it is equally true that God has evidently determined to work within the structures and patterns of human society, even as He works out His purposes for an individual's life in accordance with the physical and psychological principles He has created to govern it.

Conversion and culture change

Since religion is viewed by our missionary as involving only man's soul, conversion and its concomitant change of life is seen as a merely spiritual manifestation, without realization that such change of behavior at once involves a change of culture. "Whether missionaries are inclined to admit it or not, they are professional agents of culture change, for there is no other way of establishing, consolidating, and perpetuating the Church in a society than through its culture."

However, it is not merely a change of outward form that the missionary seeks to establish, but a basic change of heart and fundamental values. Man is to become a new creature. [Louis] Luzbetak [says]:

Especially in spiritual matters the transformation sought is meant to be more than the mere adoption of externals that might be accepted one day and discarded the next. The transformation sought is meant to be more than the recitation of a creed and a theoretical acknowledgement of certain articles of faith or the mere adoption of a ritual. "Conversion" means a "turning" away from old ways toward new ways, a basic re-orientation in premises and goals, a wholehearted acceptance of a new set of values affecting the "convert" as well as his social group, day in and day out, twenty-four hours of the day and in practically every sphere of activity—economic, social, and religious. The changes effected must become *living* parts of the cultural "organism."

Change needs a "reason"

The willingness to change religion will often depend on how well the present religion meets the daily needs. Because religion is so thoroughly integrated into the total fabric of life, there will be motivation for change only when a system frustrates an individual or a whole society at some rather crucial point. Every culture tries to achieve harmony between its parts, but such harmony is never complete. Again, all cultures are changing and very frequently even minor changes can lead to changes in the completeness with which man's needs are met by the religious system of his culture.

If and when severe frustrations, imbalances, or conflicts arise, a man will not only be willing to consider change—he will actually be looking for relief. These areas of frustration in a culture can become open doors for the gospel, for they represent, as it were, "the places where it itches." Therefore, in order to ascertain those places which would readily predispose men to listen to the Good News, it is of utmost importance to investigate the fundamental needs of man and to find out how these needs are being met by the given system.

From Jacob A. Loewen, *Culture and Human Values: Christian Intervention in Anthropological Perspective* (South Pasadena: William Carey Library, 1975), pp. 3–7. Used by permission.

New questions. As we have seen, people live in different cultures. Consequently they ask different questions. For example, Africans and Asians ask, "What shall we do about our ancestors?" Western theology gives little attention to ancestors, although much is said about them in the Bible. Jehovah is called the God of Abraham, Isaac, and Jacob. The fifth commandment, the first with promise, calls us to respect our parents.

What should we say when people ask about their ancestors? Are they saved? Should the people feed them or put flowers on their graves? We dare not brush such questions aside lightly, for ancestors are important in the lives of the people.

There are other such dilemmas. Churches in Africa must answer questions about polygamy, witchcraft, spirits, and magic; those in India are asked about the caste system, dowry, and the evil eye; and those in China must deal with parental authority, clan responsibilities, and the ethics of Confucianism. Western churches, too, need to look at the issues raised by their own culture, such as secularism, modern entertainment, and affluence in a poverty-stricken world.

According to Charles Taber (1978:69), finding Christian answers to human problems is the first task of the theologian: "[T]he theologian is called upon, long before doing any kind of systematic theology, to assess the life and testimony of the church, and to address himself, in the communion of believers, to the issues and problems that face the church and to the opportunities and challenges that it will try to meet."

New cultural categories. Theologians must do more than answer new questions. They must make the message of the gospel clear in cultural categories that do not correspond even remotely with those used in the Bible. For example, in Africa they must ask whether the concepts of sacrifice used in traditional African societies can be used with reference to Christ's death on the cross. In India they must decide whether the term *avatar* can be used for Christ's incarnation. As we have seen, the Indian world view makes no categorical distinction between God and humans. Consequently, when a Hindu god becomes an *avatar* or human, it is like a rich person helping a poor beggar. In Southeast Asia theologians must contrast the Buddhist idea of *nirvana* with the Christian concept of heaven.

One of the most crucial concepts in Christian theology is that of God. Theologians must decide which of the terms in the local culture can be used to refer to God and what needs to be changed to make the traditional concepts more biblical. People in many parts of the world refer to a High God who is the creator and ruler of all. Taber (1978:60) writes:

> When missionaries first arrived in the area of the Baoule of Ivory Coast and started talking about the Creator, they found immediate recognition: "Of course, we know him; his name is Nyamien." And when the missionaries proceeded to describe the attributes of the God they knew, they again found almost impatient agreement: "Of course, Nyamien is all-powerful, of course he's benevolent, of course he's eternal, etc. When you've said Nyamien, you've said it all. Only children don't know that."

Richardson (1981) maintains that missionaries can use such generalized High God concepts, particularly if they have little specific content, since we can usually fill them with meaningful Christian references. This is what happened in Korea, where the people had a High

God whom they called Hananim, and the Protestants were able to use this term for the God of the Bible. Richardson argues that this is one important reason for the rapid growth of Christianity in that land—the people already knew about the God about whom the Christians preached.

The question becomes more difficult when the concepts of god are closely tied to non-Christian religions. In Muslim countries missionaries by and large have adopted the term *Allah* because it is close enough to the biblical concept of God to be usable. But they must make clear that a Christian "Allah" is love, a notion foreign to Islamic thought. Indian theologians must choose between a number of terms, none of which is truly adequate. There is the ultimate reality *Brahman*, but it is a force, not a person. There is *deva*, a personal god who is part of this illusory world. And there is *Isvara*, a term associated primarily with the Hindu god Siva.

New world view. The most difficult theological problems have to do with world views. They are the core of a culture, and if we do not critique them theologically, we are in danger of ending up in syncretism or Christopaganism (Tippett 1979). On the other hand, because they are the foundations on which a culture is built, it is hard to change them.

Many non-Western world views are closer to that of the Bible than is our modern, secular world view. They understand the tribal ties and rituals of the Old Testament and are more aware of the spirit world. For example, the Japanese have a strong group consciousness, and the person who lets the group down experiences a deep sense of shame. We in the West, however, with our strong emphasis on individualism, often experience guilt when we do something wrong. These two feelings stand in contrast to one another.

Shame is a reaction to other people's criticism, an acute personal chagrin at our failure to live up to our obligations and the expectations others have of us. In true shame-oriented cultures, every person has a place and a duty in the society. Self-respect is maintained not by choosing what is good rather than what is evil, but by choosing what is expected of one. Personal desires are to be sunk in the collective expectation. Those who fail will often turn their aggression against themselves instead of using violence against others. By punishing themselves they maintain their self-respect before others, for shame cannot be relieved, as guilt can be, by confession and atonement. Shame is removed and honor restored only when a person does what the society expects of him or her in the situation, including committing suicide if necessary.

Guilt, on the other hand, is a feeling that arises when we violate the absolute standards of morality within us, when we violate our conscience. A person may suffer from guilt even though no one else knows of her or his misdeed; this feeling of guilt is relieved by confessing the misdeed and making restitution. True guilt cultures rely on an internalized conviction of sin as the enforcer of good behavior, not, as shame cultures do, on external sanctions. Guilt cultures emphasize punishment and forgiveness as ways of restoring the moral order; shame cultures stress self-denial and humility as ways of restoring the social order.

In the Bible, sin is tied to both shame and guilt. The former is emphasized in the Old Testament, where sin is seen primarily as a break in relationships that occurs when people violate their covenants with God and with one another as the people of God. Sin, therefore, has a corporate dimension to it, and one person's sin can bring punishment upon the whole group. The answer to sin is *shalom,* or the mending of broken relationships and the restoration of peace and harmony. This is a message well understood by the Japanese, who live in a shame-oriented culture.

The Bible, particularly the New Testament, also speaks of sin as a violation of the righteousness of God, and of the need for punishment and restitution. This message makes sense to Western people, who live in guilt-oriented cultures. In fact, we need both concepts, guilt and shame, to fully understand the biblical meaning of sin and salvation.

While some world-view assumptions can serve as bridges for people to understand the Good News, others run contrary to Scripture and distort the biblical message. For example, many people have a cyclical view of time that undermines the Christian message of creation and eschatology. Others believe that the world does not really exist. It is an illusion. There is no real history. This contradicts the biblical doctrines of creation and divine involvement in a real world. In such cases we must make clear the world-view assumptions of the Bible. If we do not, the people will misunderstand the gospel.

Steps in Contextualization

The development of a theology for a new cultural context does not take place overnight. As we have seen, the attention of a young church is focused on its growth and its immediate response to old beliefs and practices. The deeper problems of contextualization and of keeping the churches true to the Christian faith in the new setting often arise only with second- and third-generation leaders in the church.

The first efforts at contextualization are usually made by the missionary as he or she tries to make the message intelligible and relevant to the people. The danger here is that missionaries are often unaware of the cultural biases of their own theologies. Moreover, they tend to import Western ways of doing theology, which have been influenced by a Greek world view that stresses highly rational and synchronic systems of thought. But this emphasis on detailed systematic theologies is foreign to many societies. Holth (1968:18) points out:

> There are certain features of traditional Western theology which many Asians find objectionable. Generally speaking, Asians do not attach the same importance to formulated doctrines. Our keenness for analysis and system is something they find quite incomprehensible. . . . Our demand for definite and precise formulations of faith is a source of irritation. The rigidity of much of Western theological dogmatism leaves the Asian man of religion cold.

In these societies the church often develops biblical theologies that focus on the acts of God in history, particularly in the lives of his people.

In time, however, it is important for a church to wrestle with the question of contextualizing the gospel in its own cultural setting. Every church must make theology its own concern, for it must face the challenges to faith raised by its culture. And when this happens, the results will be more profound and enduring.

Young churches can learn much from theological debates, for these are part of their Christian heritage. But Western theology is not the final standard against which they should measure their own. That standard is biblical revleation. Widjaja (1973:42) writes:

> But it can be said that the Scripture is the basic source from which theological knowledge comes. It is also the sole authority by which theology should be judged. Therefore, the Scripture has to be explored afresh. Western conceptualization of the biblical theology should be reviewed critically, and if necessary set aside. . . . In doing so, we may have a deeper understanding of God's message as we ponder directly upon all the original material of the Bible.

Are there no limits, then, to contextualization? This is probably the wrong way to ask the question. The question is not how far we can go in contextualizing Christianity while still remaining Christian. Rather, our concern is how we can become more truly Christian while making the call of the gospel more clear and appealing to those in our cultural context. Visser 't Hooft (1967:6) adds a word of caution:

> Now in the history of the Church we find more examples of over-indigenization than of under-indigenization. The Christian message has

been often so uncritically adapted to the national cultures that its true distinctiveness became lost in the process. We have had the attempt at radical indigenization of the gospel in the so-called German Christian movement of the Hitler days. . . . I think of Will Herberg's lucid analysis of religion in America. . . . In fact, there are few of the older Christian nations which have not at one time or another produced curious syncretisms of Christian and national cultural concepts.

The message of the gospel must not only be expressed in the categories and world view of the local culture, it must also fill them with biblical substance and so revolutionize them.

Teaching New Christians

At the beginning of a work, it is the missionary who is responsible for making the gospel known and understood in the new culture, not only by bearing witness to the Good News of salvation, but also by modeling a Christian life. He or she is the only example the people have of what it means to be a follower of Christ. Moreover, at this stage the missionary must take the lead in contextualizing the biblical message in the local culture. Accordingly, it is vitally important that the missionary truly understand and appreciate the local culture.

New believers have little knowledge of the Scriptures and often cannot read. They are dependent upon the missionary for an understanding of what the Scriptures mean, and for guidance in dealing with the questions they face. It is the responsibility of the missionary not only to teach the people the Scriptures, but also how to study the Scriptures for themselves, and to apply them to their own lives. As they mature, he or she must make it clear that they must be obedient to the voice of God as it comes to them through the Word of God, not as it comes to the missionary nor even to the church that sent the missionary. New believers learn to be strong Christians by practicing Christian living, just as people learn a new language by speaking it.

Training National Theologians

After a church has been planted, it is important that the missionary encourage the rise of natural leaders within the young congregation, and support and train them. As much as possible, the local group of believers must take responsibility for the church from the very beginning. It is essential that we train leaders who can wrestle with the theological issues that emerge within their cultural context (2 Tim. 2:2). It is easier to train followers who merely believe what we say and imitate us. Since we have positions of honor, there is little disagreement. But followers are spiritually immature, and when we leave they are easily led astray by every false doctrine that comes along.

It is much harder to train leaders, for we must teach them to think for themselves, to disagree with us, and to stand for their own convictions. We must learn to accept debates and honest disagreements on tough theological issues without cutting off a national brother or sister. We must learn the humility of admitting we are wrong, and we must be willing to see young leaders receiving more honor than ourselves.

The Scriptures go even further. They speak of the priesthood of all believers. We need to teach all Christians to study and interpret the Bible for themselves and to apply its message to their lives. To deny them this is to keep them spiritually immature.

It is particularly urgent that we evangelicals encourage national leaders to be theologians. Too often in the past we have held on to the theology of a young church for fear of losing the truth. In the meantime liberal churches were training national leaders who today dominate the theological scene in many parts of the world.

There is no way to guarantee the preservation of our theological convictions. We can write them in creeds and constitutions and can police churches and schools. But those who succeed us will come to their own convictions. Each generation in the church must come to its own living faith. Secondhand beliefs will not do.

Finally, it should be noted that whether or not we "allow" national leaders to develop their own theologies, they will do so. Mission history is full of cases in which leaders suppressed by missionaries have gone out to start their own independent churches. Many would have remained in fellowship with the missionaries if they had been willing to listen to the new leaders.

Transcultural Theology

The fourth self, self-theologizing, recognizes that Christians need to develop theologies that make the gospel clear in their different cultures. At the same time, it raises tough questions about pluralism. How can we accept theological diversity and avoid a relativism that undermines truth, or a subjectivism that reduces theologies to human creations, or a particularism that allows Christians in each culture to develop their own theology, but denies that the gospel transcends cultural differences and that the church is one body?

The problem is not unlike the one we face in a local church, where it is accepted that individuals have a right to interpret Scripture for themselves. Consequently there are disagreements. But hermeneutics is the task of a community of believers as they share with and check one another. So also, churches in different cultures are part of a world community of believers. They, too, need to develop their theologies in discussion with that larger body. Although they have a right to interpret the Bible for their particular contexts, they have a responsibility to listen to the greater church of which they are a part.

Out of this dialogue can emerge a transcultural theology that transcends cultural differences—a metatheology that compares theologies, explores the cultural biases of each, and seeks to find biblical universals (Figure 27).

Characteristics of a Transcultural Theology

What are the characteristics of an evangelical transcultural theology—the theological consensus that emerges as people from different cultural settings share their understandings of biblical revelation? The details are not all clear, for dialogue between theologians in different cultures has only recently begun. Several principles, however, must be taken into account.

Biblically based. Like contextualized theologies, a transcultural theology must be biblically based. This may seem obvious, but we must constantly remind ourselves that the standard against which all theologies must be measured is biblical revelation.

The biblical message must be understood within its cultural settings, and it must also be seen in its historical progression. The Old Testament is a record of God's taking a people and molding their world view and beliefs so that these would be capable of conveying his divine message to humans. For example, beginning with Abraham's concepts of God, righteousness, sin, sacrifice, forgiveness, and time, God then shaped and enriched them through his revelations to Moses, David,

FIGURE 27

A Transcultural Theology Transcends Cultural Differences

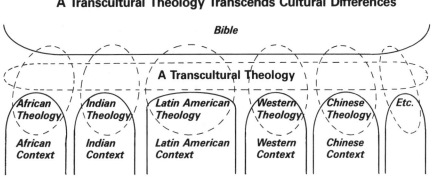

and the prophets. He taught the people these new meanings through the tabernacle, temple, sacrifices, festivals, and priestly orders. Consequently, the Jewish world view at the time of Christ was an adequate vehicle for communicating God's supreme self-revelation to humans.

Theology must also be biblical in another sense. While responding to human agendas for God, its ultimate concern is God's agenda for humans. Theology must ask the ultimate questions that the people may not be asking. Its deepest concerns are with sin and salvation and with God's rule in the lives of his people.

Supracultural.   Here we face a paradox. A transcultural theology must seek to transcend the limits and biases of human cultures, but it must be expressed in languages that are molded by specific cultural environments. If we deny that theology can transcend its cultural settings, we deny that God can break through to humans. Then we are left with culture-bound churches that cannot understand one another.

How can theology surmount the biases of different cultures? First, we need to keep in mind that cultures are not totally different from each other. There are fundamental similarities underlying all cultures because they are rooted in the common humanity and shared experiences of all people. All people have bodies that function in the same ways. All experience birth, life, and death; joy, sadness, and pain; drives, fears, and needs. All create categories, languages, and cultures. And all have sinned and need salvation. Without underestimating the differences that do exist between cultures, we need to recognize the basic commonalities in human existence. Since these unifying factors make it possible for people in one culture to understand those in another, they also allow us to develop metacultural frameworks that transcend cultural differences.

Second, outsiders often see things that insiders do not. For instance, others often see our sins more clearly than we do, because we tend to hide these from ourselves. Similarly, people in other cultures often see more clearly than we the cultural biases of our theologies. We are largely unaware of the deep, implicit assumptions of our culture and of their influence on our theologies. Outside views can help keep our systems of knowledge from becoming totally subjective in nature.

We need, therefore, to listen to Christians from other cultures, for they can point out the cultural biases in our theologies. In turn, we need to point out the cultural biases in theirs. In doing so, we can build theologies that are more truly biblical.

Historical and christological.   A transcultural theology must focus on God's acts in history. At the center of these stands Christ. His incarnation is the center of the gospel. His death and resurrection are the heart of redemption. It is around the person of Christ that all theologies must unite, for he is Lord of all cultures as well as of all people.

As Christians we affirm a real history that is the same for all people. Our knowledge of events may be incomplete, and our interpretations of them may vary, but the facts of history are universally true. For instance, we may disagree about the causes, but the reality is that Europeans fought two major world wars in this century. This fact is true for all cultures, whether or not they took part. Similarly, the Bible gives us a record of historical facts that transcend human cultures, and any transcultural theology must deal with these facts.

Spirit-led. Finally, the unity of a transcultural theology must depend on the work of the Holy Spirit. It is he who must lead us all into an understanding of the truth. Theology must therefore be done in a spirit of humility, not self-righteousness; of redemptive love, not condemnation; of sharing, not commanding. Again, we need to do theology on our knees.

Functions of Transcultural Theology

Why should we seek a transcultural theology? Are not contextualized theologies enough? One reason is to build a worldwide fellowship of believers. We belong to one body. Christ prayed that we be one, as a testimony to the world of God's love, which breaks down the barriers that divide human beings.

A second reason is to share in the mission of the church. The task of evangelizing the world is so great that churches in different parts of the world must work together to accomplish it. We dare not let cultural and national differences lead us into a Christian isolationism that blinds us to the needs of the world. We are called to bear witness to the Good News to all peoples.

Finally, the process of formulating a transcultural theology can help us see more clearly the cultural biases in our theologies and help us avoid the syncretisms that emerge when we contextualize our theologies uncritically. Although we all see through a glass darkly, through common study of the Scriptures we arrive at a better understanding of Theology as God knows it to be. In dialoguing with theologians from other parts of the world, we must be careful not to impose our Western theologies. The Bible is the criterion against which we measure all theologies.

Christianity and Non-Christian Religions

We experience a second theological shock when, for the first time, we come face to face with other religions. While preparing for missionary service, we may have studied Islam, Hinduism, and Buddhism and concluded that they are obviously false. We are certain that it will not be hard to convince people of the error of their beliefs and persuade them to become Christians. It comes as a surprise, then, when we meet good and thoughtful people who are deeply convinced that their own religion is true, and we fail in our well-prepared attempts to refute this religion.

Within us arises a question: Why do such people remain Muslims or Hindus? Then another question: Why are we Christians? How do we know that Christianity is true? We may have faced these questions before, but they return with greater intensity when we personally come to know believers in other religions who claim that their religions satisfy all their needs.

One young missionary candidate experienced this shock while traveling on a ship. Seeing an old Muslim on deck, he decided to witness to him. The candidate drew up a deck chair and began visiting with the old man, hoping to win him to Christ. After a time, the young man began to talk about the Bible. And the old man began talking about the Koran. Then the young man began to talk about Christ, and the old man about Muhammed. The missionary candidate suddenly realized that while he was trying to convert the Muslim to Christianity, the old man was trying to make him a Muslim. His immediate reaction was, "He can't do that. I will never become a Muslim." And then the real question arose: "Why, then, should I expect him to become a Christian?"

Our first reaction to this shock is often to reject other religions and their believers—to avoid relationships with Muslims, Hindus, and Buddhists. That way we can avoid the questions raised by religious pluralism. But this also closes the door for a Christian witness to them. Can we love them as persons, yet reject their religious beliefs? How we answer this question will deeply affect our relationships to non-Christians around us and our effectiveness as missionaries.

Christianity and Other High Religions

When we think of "other religions," we normally refer to Islam, Buddhism, Hinduism, Shintoism, and so on. Like Christianity, these "high religions" deal with ultimate questions about the origin, purpose, and destiny of all things.

How should Christianity relate to them? The question is not new. The early church had to deal with Greek religions. Paul denounced their idols (Acts 19:26), and Peter their use of magic (Acts 8:20–21). On the other hand, Paul appeals to the "unknown god" of the Greeks

(Acts 17:23), and John uses the word *Logos,* the Stoic term for what they considered the highest expression of nature, namely, reason.

Since then the church has struggled with the question. Some leaders have argued for a total condemnation of other religions. Others see good as well as evil in other belief systems, but call for people to choose between Christianity and their old religions. Some see common themes or redemptive analogies in other religions that can be used to communicate the gospel to the people. Others see non-Christian religions as a preparation for the gospel and seek seeds of truth in them on which they can build. Still others see Christianity as the evolutionary fulfillment of all other religions.

We do not have room here to explore the implications of these positions for the missionary task. Young missionaries, however, must be prepared to face the question. We will examine only one or two key issues that must be kept in mind.

The uniqueness of the gospel. One thing is clear—the Scriptures declare that there is only one way to salvation, and that is through Jesus Christ (John 14:6, Acts 4:12). This claim to uniqueness lies at the heart of the gospel and of the relationship of Christianity to other religions. Some call this claim arrogant, and it would be if Christianity were a religion created by humans. But Christianity is rooted in divine revelation. To deny that revelation, and to ignore the uniqueness of Christ who stands at the center of that revelation, destroys the foundation of Christian faith. To claim that Christianity is only one of many ways to God is to build on the foundations of Hinduism, which claims that all religions lead to God.

The uniqueness of Christianity does not lie in any particular form or expression of worship, but in the gospel as a whole. In prayer, Hindus kneel and Muslims raise their hands. Chukchi shamans and Hindu mystics speak in tongues. And people of all religions claim that their gods can heal them and raise them from the dead. Nor are the ideas of sin, sacrifice, forgiveness, and salvation only Christian. The uniqueness of Christianity is found in the biblical message of God's redemption of sinners through Jesus Christ.

The truth of the gospel. All high religions lay claim to truth, and all must be tested against reality. In affirming the truthfulness of Christianity, we do not claim ourselves to be superior. The superiority lies not in us, but in the gospel. Stephen Neill (1961:17–18) writes:

> Naturally to the non-Christian hearer [these claims of Christianity] must sound like crazy megalomania, and religious imperialism of the

very worst kind. We must recognize the dangers; Christains have on many occasions fallen into both of them. But we are driven back ultimately on the question of truth. It is not crazy megalomania for the science of chemistry to affirm that the physical universe has been built up in one way and not in another. . . . The Christian claim is very close to the claim of the chemist. It states quite simply that the universe under all its aspects has been made in one way and not in another, and that the way in which it has been made has been once for all declared in Jesus Christ. When Jesus stated that he *was* the truth (John 14:6) he did not mean that he was stating a number of good and true ideas; he meant that in him the total structure of the universe was for the first time and for ever disclosed.

When we declare the truthfulness of the Christian message, we must do so in humility and love (Eph. 4:15). We must recognize the highest insights in other religions and not take cheap shots by comparing their worst with the best of Christianity. We must rejoice in everything they possess of beauty and high aspiration. We must listen with respectful patience to the criticisms they have of Christian thought and practice. From their human insights we can gain new perspectives. But, in the end, we have a right to claim that Jesus Christ, and he alone, is the Way, the Truth, and the Life.

Christianity and Folk Religions

As missionaries we prepare to witness to people who are tied to Buddhism, Hinduism, Islam and other high religions which deal with questions of ultimate truth and meaning. We are surprised, therefore, when we find that most of the common folk do not know much about their own high religions, and that they are often more deeply involved in such folk-religious practices as magic, astrology, witchcraft, and spirit worship. We find that we are not prepared to deal with such practices.

Folk religions deal with the problems of everyday life, not with ultimate realities. Through omens, oracles, shamans, and prophets, they provide guidance to people facing uncertain futures. Through rituals and medicines, they counter such crises as droughts, earthquakes, floods, and plagues, as well as help bring success in marriage, in producing children, in business, and the like (Figure 28).

All people also have their own folk sciences which they develop on the basis of their everyday observations. South Sea Islanders know how to make outrigger canoes and how to sail them across vast stretches of the Pacific Ocean. African Bushmen know how to poison their arrows and track down a wounded giraffe until it dies. All societies have

FIGURE 28

High Religion, Low Religion, and Science

Cosmic religions that deal with beings and forces of other worlds, and with questions of ultimate origin, purpose, and destiny of the universe, of societies and of individuals.	**High Religions**
Folk religions that deal with beings and forces of this world, and with questions of immediate meaning, well-being, and direction for groups and individuals.	**Folk Religions**
Sciences that deal with this world using natural explanations, and with questions dealing with human relationships to nature and to one another.	**Folk Sciences and Folk Social Sciences**

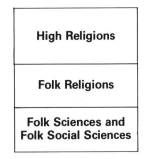

folk social sciences that tell them how to rasie their children and how to get along with cantankerous people.

Given our Western view of things, we do not take folk religions seriously. Consequently, we do not provide biblical answers to the everyday questions the people face. For example, we often have no answer when a new African Christian wants to know whether he should hunt to the north or the east, and whether he should go today or tomorrow. It should not surprise us, therefore, that many young Christians continue to go to shamans and magicians to deal with such questions (Figure 29).

Christians have given many answers for everyday problems. Roman Catholics have often turned to the doctrine of saints as intermediaries between God and humans. Protestants have stressed the doctrines of prayer and the providence of God—the fact that all events in our lives are in his control and that we can bring him our petitions in prayer. Charismatics have emphasized the work of the Holy Spirit in the daily

FIGURE 29

Young Christians May Turn to Traditional Folk Religions If They Are Given No Christian Answers for their Everyday Problems

Their Old High Religion *(Hinduism, Islam, etc.)*	*They find a better way*	**Their New High Religion** *(Christianity)*
Their Old Folk Religion *(magic, astrology, and spirit worship)*	*No Christian answer is given*	**Their Old Folk Religion** *(magic, astrology and spirit worship remain)*
Their Old Folk Science	*Modern science is introduced*	**Their New Modern Science**

lives of God's people. It is no coincidence that many of the most successful missions have provided some form of Christian answer to these kinds of questions.

In dealing with Christian responses to problems of everyday life, however, we must guard against syncretism. One danger is to make Christianity a new kind of magic in which we seek to use formulas to manipulate God into doing our will. The Bible always calls us to worship, and in this we subordinate ourselves to his will and learn from the experiences he sends our way. The difference between magic and worship is not in form, but in attitude.

A second danger is the lack of discernment. Not all that we do as Christians is of the Holy Spirit. In Israel there were true and false prophets, righteous and unrighteous rulers. It should not surprise us, therefore, to find many forms of Christian expression duplicated in other religions. Shamans and oracles speak in tongues, Hindu sadhus and Muslim fakirs claim to perform miracles, and all religious groups attest to healings and resurrections. Scripture repeatedly warns us to be on our guard in the last days, when Satan will counterfeit the work of God.

A third danger lies in setting wrong priorities. The gospel does deal with God's care and provision in the everyday lives of people, but its central focus is on their salvation and eternal destiny. We, too, must be careful to make our central message the reconciliation between God and humans, and then between humans themselves.

The greatest questions in missions today have to do with theological and religious pluralism. And no answers we give will have greater long-range consequences for the church than the answers we give to these questions. The easiest route is to reject all theologies other than our own and condemn all non-Christian religions. But this approach closes the door to evangelism and the maturation of the church. If we put our trust in Christ, we can listen to others without fear of losing our faith. And we can share with them the new life that we ourselves have found in him.

PART 4

Cultural Differences and the Bicultural Community

The Bicultural Bridge

 W e have looked at the messenger and the message as they move from one culture to another. But what about those who hear the gospel—how does the gospel take root in another culture?

In our day of mass media and modern technology, we are tempted to think of communication as synonymous with public meetings, radio and television broadcasts, and the printed page. The fact is, the transmission of the gospel across the chasms that separate cultures rests primarily upon personal communication between humans, especially between the missionary and the people he or she serves. This is affected by two things: (1) the ability of missionaries and national leaders to translate the message of the gospel from one culture to another, and (2) the quality of the relationship between the individuals involved. In the previous chapters we have looked at the first of these. Now we will turn our attention from cultures as systems of ideas to social structures as systems of organized human relationships, and we will see how these affect the communication of the gospel.

Building Cross-Cultural Relationships

Communication between people in different cultures does not take place in a vacuum, but always occurs within the context of social relationships. At first these may be casual, such as when a missionary

227

passes through the village and hands out tracts or visits with someone in the tea stall.

The most effective cross-cultural communication, however, takes place between people who are involved in regular, enduring relationships in the context of a social community. A missionary meets with new converts and helps them organize a church. Later, he or she visits them regularly. Or a missionary organizes a hospital or school in which relationships and roles are clearly defined. In either case we have the beginnings of a *bicultural community*.

The Bicultural Community

A bicultural community is a localized society in which people from different cultures relate to one another on the basis of well-defined social roles. It begins when people from one culture move into another, set up house, and start to interact with the local people. In time, social patterns emerge and a new type of community is formed, one made up of people from two cultures. As the community develops, it creates a new culture that draws upon the ideas, feelings, and values of both, a culture that is neither "native" nor "foreign," but is made up of both natives and foreigners.

When missionaries go abroad, they take their cultural maps with them. They have ideas of what is food and how to cook it, who should raise the children and what values they should be taught, how to worship properly and many other things. No matter how hard they try, they cannot completely "go native," since the earlier culture of their childhood can never be fully erased. On the other hand, it is impossible for missionaries to import their total culture, although some try to do so. They are influenced to a great extent by the environment they enter—their second culture.

To the extent that local people interact with the missionaries, they too become part of the biculture. They have their own ideas of food, child rearing, values, and worship. Even though they may not leave their country, they are exposed to new ideas and beliefs. But as members of the society within which the biculture emerges, they and their culture contribute a great deal to its formation.

In order to relate to each other, missionaries and nationals must create new patterns for living, working, playing, and worshiping—in short, a new cultural frame. Because this is created by people from different backgrounds, it is made up of elements from both.

While the biculture borrows from the different cultures of its participants, it is more than the sum or synthesis of those cultures. New patterns often emerge in the interaction. In the end, if the communication of the gospel is to take place between people of different cultures, a satisfactory bicultural community must be worked out, so that both sides find a measure of mutual understanding, trust, and satisfaction. The success of mission work to a large extend depends upon the quality of this bicultural bridge.

Culture Brokers

The bicultural bridge is only one stage in the multistage communication of the gospel from one culture to another. The missionary has been trained by parents, pastors, and teachers before going to a new society. There he or she works closely with national Christian leaders who are part of the same biculture. These leaders, in turn, will communicate the gospel to other people throughout the land. The greatest share of village evangelism and church planting will then be done by national workers.

Building the bridge between cultures is, however, the central task of missions, and it is this that we will look at in greater detail. It is crucial in bringing the gospel for the first time to areas where no churches exist.

The bicultural community is where the two worlds meet. It is made up of people who retain ties to their original cultures, but who meet and exchange ideas. Such people are "culture brokers." Like money changers who trade dollars for yen or rupees, they are essential to the communication between two cultural worlds. Missionaries are such brokers. Although they do not trade in money or political power, they do bring the gospel from one culture to another. Moreover, they negotiate between their churches at home and the new churches they serve.

Culture brokers are often lonely because they are caught between two worlds. The people in each world have only vague and often strange notions about one another. Moreover, each group expects the culture broker to be loyal to its interests and becomes suspicious when the missionary sides with the other. For example, many missionaries have been unable to convince Americans that much of other cultures in the world is good, or to persuade the people among whom they work that not everyone in the West is fantastically wealthy.

Finally, people in both worlds often distrust the culture broker. Neither side knows fully what is going on, and both suspect that the broker no longer represents their interests. The sending churches know only what the missionary tells them, and they are concerned because he or she no longer seems to be the same person they sent out. The national church sees the missionaries go home on furlough and wonders what secret arrangements they are making there.

Missionaries and national leaders are marginal people. They are simultaneously members of two or more different cultures and do not identify fully with any of them. They live on the boundary between them. "Marginal," however, does not mean unimportant, without influence, subordinate, or inferior. The prophets in the Old Testament were marginal persons. Their call by God put them in a special relationship with their people that was characterized by tension and conflict. A clear example is Jeremiah, who looked at his people with the eyes of God. When he spoke up, he was regarded as a disturber and a traitor.

Jesus, too, was a marginal person, out of tune with what the Jewish leaders wanted or expected of him. He related to people on the fringes of society—lepers, tax gatherers, Samaritans, and sinners (Kuitse 1983:4). He was crucified outside the city with two robbers. Paul also was a marginal person who lived his life between the Jewish and Gentile churches.

In a sense all Christians are to be marginal people, for they live in the world, yet they are citizens of the kingdom of God. They are no longer fully at home on earth, for they know of a better life. But they are not yet participating fully in their heavenly culture.

Marginal people have a significant contribution to make to any group. In a sense they are prophets who speak from outside. Missionaries, for example, represent the worldwide fellowship of the church. They make visible the ties of the local church to the church in other parts of the world. They also provide the broad perspective and critique that can help a young church struggle with its identity within a non-Christian setting.

Generationalism Among the Missionaries

All people must learn how to live in a culture. The same is true when dealing with a biculture. Young missionaries and national leaders must learn the beliefs, values, and social behavior expected of those who participate. If they do not, they are ostracized.

There is a fundamental difference between learning a primary culture and learning a biculture. We are raised in the first and *enculturated* into its ways as we grow up. Then we learn by observing and imitating and are taught informally and formally how to think and act. Later, as adults, we are *acculturated* into the biculture. We already have at our core social and cultural ways to which we add the overlay of the biculture. The result, as we have already seen, is a bicultural person who must deal internally with the tensions of two cultural worlds.

Just as we go through stages in learning our first culture, so also we do in acculturating to the biculture. John and Ruth Useem and

John Donoghue (1963) have traced the stages for people entering a biculture, referring to them as "generations." There are newcomers—the missionaries and nationals who have recently entered the biculture. And there are old-timers—those who have spent much of their lives in the biculture (Figure 30).

First-generation missionaries. First-term missionaries belong to the first generation of the biculture. For the most part, at this time we are idealistic and have taken an assignment because we have tremendous zeal and a great vision of the work. Consequently, the goals we set for ourselves are high—at times unrealistic. We are ready to evangelize a whole city or state, or build a large hospital or Bible school. At this time, too, we are prepared to sacrifice an established community that will try to acculturate us to the way it thinks missionary-national relationships should be structured. This, in fact, is one of the major dilemmas of new missionaries entering bicultural communities that began during colonial times. If we try to change the established ways of doing things and identify more closely with the local culture and people, those in power within the community are threatened and may send us home. Changing existing cultures—even bicultures, which are relatively unstable—is a difficult thing to do.

Our success or failure as first-termers depends to a considerable extent on our place within the social structure of the bicultural community. If we find ourselves at the top of a new venture, such as open-

FIGURE 30

The Bicultural Community

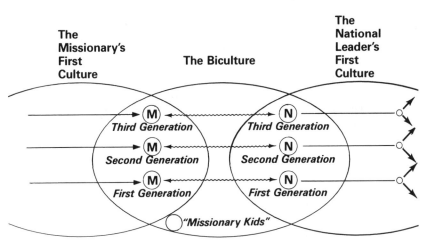

From Paul G. Hiebert, "The Bicultural Bridge," *Mission Focus* 6 (1982): 5.

ing a new field, starting a hospital, or building a Bible school, we can have tremendous success. After all, we begin with nothing and we leave something—a church or institution. Since there are no precedents to hinder us, we have the power to build a program largely according to our own plans. For example, when the first missionary doctor moves to an area, there is often only an empty field. When she or he leaves, there is a hospital with operating rooms, admission offices, and wards. We can also have tremendous failures, because there are often no peers or institutional constraints to check our bad decisions. One thing is clear; founders set the direction for new programs and institutions that are difficult to change later.

If, as first-generation missionaries, we are placed at the top of old established programs, we have a potential for moderate success. We have the power to institute our own ideas, but we inherit traditions from the past. When we try to change existing procedures, we are reminded, "That is not the way the founder did it!" or told, "We always do it this way." Nor can we ever measure up to the remembered image of the founder, whose picture usually hangs on the wall in the central hall. What the founder established as an *ad hoc* procedure becomes law under the second leader and a sacred rite by the third.

While as first-termers we can be only moderately successful in initiating programs, we can also be only moderate failures. We are guarded from making great mistakes by the institution, which has begun to acquire a life of its own. Once established, an organization has a way of staying alive and of tempering the failures of its leaders. By then, too many people have vested interests in the institution to let it die easily.

If we are placed as newcomers at the bottom of old programs, there is little possibility for either success or failure, at least as these are measured in community terms. We have little power to begin programs or change old ones. Since this, considering our vision and zeal, generally leads to frustration, it takes a special type of person to serve in such positions with joy and a sense of fulfillment.

Finally, as we have already seen, one of the primary characteristics of a missionary's first term is culture shock. The attitudes and relationships into which we are acculturated during this time generally color our ministries for the rest of our tenure in the biculture.

Second-generation missionaries.   We are second-generation missionaries when we are on our second, third, and fourth terms of service. By now we have become acculturated to the new culture and feel at home in it. And we have gained valuable experience in our ministries.

Second-generation missionaries share certain characteristics. For one, we tend to be more realistic in our assessment of our work. We have now come to grips with the fact that we cannot evangelize all of Japan—or even Osaka—in five years. But we realize that it is worth our lives to build up a Bible school, train a number of good leaders, and/or plant four or five strong churches. We begin to think in terms of long-range strategies for facing the problems not only of planting churches, but also of helping those churches grow into independence and maturity.

As mid-career missionaries we are also more realistic about our personal lifestyles. We become increasingly aware that we have only one life. If we are going to have time with our children, we will have to do it now, before they are grown. If we are to have rest and relaxation, we must do so at the expense of some other activities. We are no less committed to the task. In fact, our commitment has become a long-term one. At the end of our first furlough, we had to make the crucial decision to return, and we now see missions as our life's vocation. However, we are no longer willing to pay an unlimited price to attend meetings, classes, and wards. We begin to realize that our children and ourselves are part of the greater work of God. So we take time for family picnics and vacations and work to make our homes a little more livable.

Second-generation missionaries and experienced national co-workers jointly do the greatest share of mission work. By now, for the most part, we have solved the logistics of keeping alive. We know the language and customs of the biculture. Consequently, we are able to give ourselves to the long, hard labor required to plant and develop churches.

One of the important tasks of experienced missionaries is to help first-termers adjust to the field. When a first-termer is in culture shock and writes a letter of resignation, we need to listen to the young missionary and encourage her or him to wait a week before mailing it. And we need to take time to orient newcomers to the culture and the work.

Third-generation missionaries. This group is sometimes referred to as "the old-timers." In the study by the Useems and Donoghue (1963), in which the concept of bicultural generationalism was first presented, the old-timers were those who served abroad during the colonial era. Many of them, with some notable exceptions, accepted the notions of Western superiority and colonial rule. They assumed that missionaries should be in charge of the work and live like foreigners within their compounds and bungalows.

We need to be careful in judging missionaries of previous generations, for we rarely understand the world in which they lived. At that time, "colonial" and "imperial" were words of which one could be proud. Moreover, living conditions in most parts of the world were much more difficult than they are today. In the mid-1800s it took three or four months to sail to India and several weeks by horse or cart to go a few hundred miles inland. Terms of service often stretched seven years or more without a furlough. And without modern drugs, sickness and death took a high toll. For example, between 1880 and 1891, ten Lutheran couples went to South India. By the end of this period, seven of the men, nine of the women, and thirty-two of the children had died.

One Lutheran missionary doctor in that region had a coffin made and a grave dug near his house in the village so that he would at least have a proper funeral. When the roof of the house leaked badly, he slept in the coffin. On leaving the area, "he burned the coffin, filled in the grave, and standing over it, triumphantly exclaimed: 'Oh, death, where is thy sting? Oh, grave, where is thy victory?' " (Drach and Kuder 1914:81).

Most of the old-timers sacrificed a great deal more than do most modern-day missionaries. Many spent thirty, forty, or even fifty years in the work. Most of them buried spouses and children where they served. They seldom could take vacations in cool hill stations, because a journey by car, train, or boat was too long and difficult.

But times have changed, and so must missionaries. No longer do we live in a world in which colonial rule and foreign superiority are accepted. Today we must identify with the people and their aspirations. The shift, however, has resulted in a generation gap between those who look back with nostalgia to the colonial era, when missionaries played a central role in the life of the church, and those who see the task of missions as one of an incarnational ministry and partnership in the planting of new churches.

Generationalism Among the National Leaders

Generationalism is also found among the national leaders in the biculture. The first generation often has a great vision and zeal for the work. In our day of increasing nationalism, this is often linked to strong convictions that the national church should take total responsibility for its own affairs.

Like their missionary counterparts, young national leaders are usually willing to pay almost any price for the sake of the work. In many cases they have to sacrifice the support of families and kinfolk who may have planned more traditional careers for them. And, like first-term missionaries, when given responsibility for important tasks, they can be great successes—and great failures. If placed in positions of little authority and not allowed to lead, some of the best of them leave in frustration to join other churches, often independent national churches, or to start movements of their own. This is particularly sad, for a church or a mission has no greater resource than its young national leaders.

Second-generation national leaders are those who have committed themselves to the long-term work in the church or mission. They have learned to operate within the biculture and to find time for themselves and their families. Paired with experienced missionaries, they carry out the major share of the work, and it is they who must ultimately take responsibility for the churches.

Third-generation national leaders are those who grew up during the colonial era. For many of them, the rapid movement toward nationalism is frightening and unsettling. They look back with nostalgia to the day when the mission was in charge and there was a great deal of security. Like the older missionaries, they are often in conflict with the young leaders who are emerging within the churches around the world.

Bridging Relationships

So far we have spoken of missionaries and national leaders as separate groups. So long as they remain so, the bridge is incomplete. In the end, the most effective cross-cultural communication takes place when missionaries and nationals form intimate relationships and work as a team. Such shared efforts accomplish the major portion of the missionary task.

Stress Points in the Biculture

Bicultures emerge wherever people from two cultures interact over long periods of time and develop stable patterns of relating to one another. They are cultures in the making. They have little time depth and are created by people from different backgrounds who have little or no idea of what the new cultures will be like. It is not surprising, then, that bicultures are creative places within which a great deal of innovation can take place, particularly if the cultural patterns have not already been rigidly defined. Neither is it surprising that bicultures have unique problems emerging out of the stress of change.

Stress will remain part of most bicultures for some time, because few areas of life in the world have changed so rapidly as have international relationships. The shift from colonialism to nationalism—and now to internationalism—and the change in world powers, as one nation and then another rises and falls in power, influence bicultures greatly. Moreover the nature of a biculture and the tensions within it will vary markedly from country to country.

The Creation of the Biculture

One area of stress has to do with the creation of the biculture itself. What shape should it take? What types of clothes should the missionaries and nationals wear? Should they each wear their own type of dress? Should they all wear Western clothes, or the clothes of the local culture, or both, depending on the setting? What type of food should they eat? What type of houses should they build? Should missionaries have cars, and if so, should national leaders also have them? Where should the children of the two groups go to school, and what should be the medium of instruction? How should missionaries and nationals relate to each other? These and a thousand other questions must be answered in building a stable biculture that enables foreigners and nationals to communicate and work together.

Some of the most difficult questions have to do with basic attitudes and relationships between missionaries and nationals. Should missionaries treat local leaders as parents, as contractual partners, as undifferentiated equals, or as what? Should national leaders in developing countries receive the same salaries as missionaries? If so, will they not be alienated from their people? And will not many be attracted into the ministry merely by the affluent lifestyle? On the other hand, if there are differences, are we not guilty of perpetuating social distance and segregation?

Identification. Throughout our study so far, we have assumed that the ideal model for cross-cultural relationships is the incarnation. If so, the guideline for creating the biculture is identification. As missionaries we need to identify as closely as possible with the people among whom we serve, for in so doing we are able to carry the gospel farther across the bicultural bridge. The distance between cultures is often great. The farther we bring the gospel, the more effective will be its acceptance and the less distance the national leaders must carry it to make it indigenous in their culture.

Stephen Neill, a veteran missionary, calls us to become adopted members of the society we serve. We would then not be "missionaries," but members of the local church and brothers and sisters to the local Christians. We would be "missionaries" only when we return to the countries we have left. There we would serve as advocates for our adopted church.

We have already seen that identification can take place on several levels. On the surface it is a question of lifestyle. We can learn to like local foods, travel by native modes of transportation, and wear the national dress. We can adapt our time schedules and pace of life to that around us, taking time to listen and learn from the people.

All this is important, but in the end we must recognize our human limitations. It may be psychologically and physically impossible for us to adopt the local lifestyle in full, although we can usually go further in doing so than we normally expect. Moreover, living like the people does not lie at the heart of identification. We can adopt the local ways, yet still maintain attitudes of authority and superiority. If we assume that missionaries must be the heads of institutions, we may refuse to serve under local administrators, doctors, or church officials.

At a deeper level we can identify with the people in their varying roles. We can take our place within the social organization of the local church as teachers, doctors, nurses, and preachers in positions assigned us by the national church and working with and under other local leaders. This identification, too, is important, since it helps break down the segregation between missionaries and national leaders that has characterized much of North American missions.

This, however, is not the whole answer. In old institutionalized churches, missionaries may be assigned to routine tasks that have little or nothing to do with the outreach of the church, and this effectively kills their ministry. If missionaries do assume roles within the local institutions, they have the same rights as national leaders in deciding their assignments. They may also become rivals with those leaders for important positions within the church.

Even when we assume native roles within the society, we may still carry unconscious feelings of superiority. At the deepest level, identification must begin with attitudes: with a sense of love and oneness with the people and an appreciation for their culture and history. If these feelings are present, identification on the level of roles and lifestyle is much easier. If they are not, the people will soon know it, no matter how much we identify with them on the other levels. Our para-messages will clearly communicate to them any attitude of distance or superiority, which reflects a hidden contempt for them and their culture.

Change. There are people in most societies who look for and welcome change. It should not surprise us that these are often the first to relate to a missionary. At first they are curious about our new technology, the axes, saws, guns, radios, and cars we bring. Later, as they learn to know us, they ask questions about our culture and beliefs.

Missionaries, in fact, have introduced people in other cultures not only to the gospel but also to many foreign goods and ideas.

We are not called to introduce cultural innovations, except as these help the people and the churches. On the other hand, we should not stop culture changes when the people themselves choose them. We must identify with the people in both their existing culture and their aspirations for a better life. Our value to them, in part, is as a source of new ideas and as a bridge to the outside world.

Tribal cultures and peasant societies around the world are being absorbed into national and international markets and political systems. Often the people lose out because they do not know how to defend their lands and cultures from external exploitation. In many cases it is the missionaries, since they understand these outside systems, who can best defend them and their societies against oppression.

Search for Identity

We who live in the bicultural community are generally marginal people who in many ways do not fit anywhere. Since we live on the borderline between different worlds, we find that no matter where we are, we are not quite at home. We are never fully assimilated into our second culture, but after a while we no longer fit our first culture either, because we have been changed and influenced by our experiences.

One important question facing members of the biculture has to do with identity. To a great extent, people know who they are because of their statuses within a society. When missionaries and national church leaders enter the biculture, they acquire new statuses and new identities. Here they interact with each other and acquire a bicultural world view. Here they seek to gain honor and recognition from their peers.

As we have seen, missionaries are often unaware of the profound changes that take place within them through their participation in a second culture. We often think of ourselves merely as Americans or Canadians living abroad for a time, and we expect to assimilate back into our first culture with a minimum of adjustment. We are shocked to find that relationships with our relatives and first-culture friends are strained and distant. We expect them to be excited to hear about our many experiences, but after an hour or less, conversation drifts off to local affairs about which we know little—sports, church matters, or family issues. The people at home have their own social order, and we begin to realize that we no longer have a place within it. Old associates do not know what to do with "missionaries on furlough" after we have given a church report or two. In their uneasiness over how to relate to us, they begin to ask when we are going back to "the field."

This loss of identity in our first culture is not only social. It is also cultural. When we return, we can no longer identify uncritically with our home culture, nation, or even denomination. Consequently, when we criticize them, we so arouse the suspicions of our relatives and friends that they accuse us of disloyalty and even heresy. Distanced from our own kin, we often find our closest friends among other "biculturals"—people who are perceived in the home society as culturally alienated and marginal.

We often forget that national leaders who participate in the biculture face a similar identity crisis. In their relationships with missionaries they adopt foreign ideas and practices. They may even be accused of being foreign agents! Some travel abroad and become part of a world community of leaders, but in so doing they leave their traditional cultures and feel more at home with air travel, modern hotels, and international cuisine than they do with carts, huts, and village foods. When these leaders return home, they are often treated with suspicion and indifference. In the end, they too feel most at home with other bicultural people.

Both missionaries and national church leaders often find their primary identity within the biculture. It is here they have social status and specific roles to play. Here they can relate to other people who understand the fundamental assumptions of an international world view. But the biculture is a transient culture, dependent upon the whims of international politics and the comings and goings of missionaries and national leaders. Our children cannot grow up and spend their entire lives within it, and we ourselves must often find some other place to go for retirement. In this sense, bicultural people lack a primary culture in which is rooted their identity.

Psychologically, because we internalize two persons belonging to two worlds, we face an identity crisis and need to find out who we really are. As we have already seen, we may choose to reject one or the other of our two identities, but thereby we kill part of who we really are. We can compartmentalize our existences, living as one person in one world and as the other person in another world. The result is cultural schizophrenia. Or we can seek to integrate our two selves into a single integrated whole, but this is a difficult process, for we must find a resolution to the fundamental differences that do exist between our two cultural selves.

All of us need periodically to reaffirm our sociocultural identities by participating in what they represent. After a time of service, the missionary longs to return to "a taste of home." For bicultural people, prolonged detachment from either of the two cultures creates a psychological need to participate in it, if only in some symbolic forms. If they do not, identity within that culture begins to weaken. Consequently, it is not surprising that missionaries abroad often have symbolic ways of identifying with their Western culture. One missionary in India, for example, was happy to live there so long as he had Wrigley's gum, which was for him a necessary psychological tie to his first culture. On the other hand, like other missionaries returning from India, he looks for Indian restaurants in the United States where he can find special ritual meals to satisfy his "Indian self."

Symbols of identification with both cultures are important for most bicultural people. Western missionaries in Africa tend to talk about Western politics, greet all passing Americans and Canadians as old friends, and go to North American-style restaurants when they are in the cities. In earlier days they received packets from "home" with special foods that they could not purchase locally, such as cheese and Spam. These were put away for special occasions, to be eaten with American friends in a sort of ritual meal of identification with the West. On furloughs or retirement in the West, these same missionaries discuss African politics, hail all passing Africans as old friends, and eat African food whenever possible. Suddenly cheese and Spam have no symbolic value.

African, Indian, Latin American, and other national leaders who have become part of a biculture also have the periodic need to identify with their original culture. If they serve abroad they may long to go home for a visit to recreate their cultural selves. Sadly enough many of them, like many missionaries, end up with dual cultural identities and are torn between them. In a sense bicultural people often have no real cultural home.

Alienation

Closely related to the problem of identity is that of alienation. As people become part of a biculture, they are alienated from their first culture in varying degrees.

In the case of missionaries this is less obvious so long as they are in their field of service. Although they are away from their native culture, they fully expect to find their place withhin it again once they return. Moreover, the grinding of psychological gears as they move from one culture to another is minimized by geographic separation. Only when they go home on furlough must they face the full shock of cultural transition.

The problem is more severe for national leaders, for while they participate in the biculture, they continue to be physically involved in their first culture. It is impossible for them to separate the two cultures geographically. Daily they must shift gears as they move from one culture to another. Moreover, since their task is to bring the gospel to their native culture, they must retain close ties with it. If they identify too closely with the biculture, they become alienated from their people and are mistrusted as foreigners.

International leaders. A serious problem throughout the world is the emergence of a cultural gap between national leaders who have become part of an international network, and their people who continue to live in specific cultures. (See Figure 31.) This is true in politics and business as well as in the church. As leaders around the world learn new languages, travel the globe, and form friendships with people of other countries, they become members of an international community.

These international figures can plan broad strategies for world evangelization, but they often find it hard to minister to the people of their own countries. They can no longer serve as local pastors, village evangelists, teachers, or health workers.

In missions we need to train international leaders. In fact, although today many of the churches in countries around the world are self-governing, the world mission scene is still controlled largely by Western leaders. Until churches in the so-called Two-Thirds World are fully

FIGURE 31

Networks of International Leaders

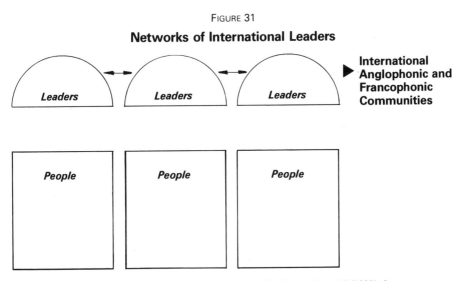

From Paul G. Hiebert, "The Bicultural Bridge," *Mission Focus* 10 (1982): 6.

represented in the networks at this level, the church will not be truly international.

Support.   Alienation in the case of leaders in the Two-Thirds World creates another problem, that of dependency on outside support. Many of the top leadership positions in developing countries are dependent on foreign funds. When such funds are cut off—an increasing possibility in our age of political turmoil—leaders in these positions are vulnerable. Missionaries generally can return to their home countries and find other jobs. When national church leaders lose their positions, they find it hard to locate suitable jobs within their traditional society, because the work they have done is often tied to the bicultural community. Moreover, they have become politically identified with the West, and if some anti-American government comes to power, as happened in Vietnam and Ethiopia, they may be marked for punishment or death. Unlike the missionaries, they cannot simply leave.

In planning mission strategies we must be particularly sensitive to the difficult position in which we may place national leaders and be properly appreciative of the tremendous sacrifice they often have to make.

Children

Some of the most difficult decisions faced by missionaries and national church leaders have to do with their children. To what culture do they belong? Where should they be educated? And where will they ultimately find a place in life?

Missionary kids.   The children of missionaries, in particular, face questions of cultural identity because they are geographically removed from their parents' culture and raised almost totally within the biculture. Unlike some of the earlier mission movements, when missionaries actually migrated to the countries they served, most modern missionaries see themselves and their children as citizens of their native country. They raise their children with glowing stories of the "homeland," and on furloughs they show them the greatness of their heritage. They assume that in times of crisis and retirement they will return home and that their children will marry and settle there.

Here, however, is a fundamental misconception. While we may think that missionary kids are Americans or Canadians, in fact they are not. Nor are they Africans, Asians, or Latin Americans. Their first culture, the one in which they truly feel at home, is the biculture within which they were raised. They belong to the community of "Americans living abroad." Similarly, the children of Indian or African missionaries belong to the culture of "Indians-[or Africans-] living-abroad." Failure to recognize this leads to false expectations on the part of parents and identity crises on the part of children. We must accept the fact that our children will never be full citizens of our home culture.

When missionary children go (not "return") to their parents' first culture, they experience a great deal of culture shock. On the one hand, they have glorified images of that culture based on the parents' stories and their own brief visits. On the other, it is a foreign country to them. Their problem is accentuated by the fact that their grandparents, relatives, peers, and sometimes their own parents see them as Americans and are upset when they do not fit quickly into that culture. They see the "eccentricities" of missionary kids as active rebellion or social deviation. Psychologically, these relatives and friends cannot accept the fact that their family member or former playmate does, in fact, belong to another culture. They are like the orthodox Hindu parents of an Indian couple who worked in the United States. When the couple returned to India for a visit, their children wanted television and hot dogs. The grandparents, who were strict vegetarians, were shocked that their grandchildren did not speak Hindi and horrified that they ate meat—especially "dogs." We must make it clear to our relatives and our sending churches that our children, in many respects, are foreigners.

Recognizing that our children belong to a third culture that is neither American nor foreign can help us understand and solve many of the problems our children face. We can be on guard, lest our dreams of "going home" present our children false images of what they will face. We can also prepare them for entry into a culture that in many ways is strange to them.

Schooling.   One of the most critical questions for missionary parents has to do with education. It is here, to a considerable extent, that the child's identity will be decided.

What schools should missionary children attend? At the beginning of the modern missions movement, missionaries often left their young children in their homeland with relatives for reasons of health and education. Now most children go to schools closer to their parents. Some are sent to local schools. Generally, however, these do not correspond in either language or curriculum with those of the parents' first culture. Consequently parents who expect their children to return to their home culture are hesitant to use them.

Many missionary kids now attend bicultural schools, usually boarding institutions. This means that they must be away from home at a relatively young age for long periods of time. The effects of this on the children vary according to the nature of the school, the personality of each child, and his or her relationship with the parents. Some do well, and others leave with deep psychological scars.

One problem young missionary kids face is that they often view God as a rival for their parents' love. They are not yet old enough to understand the nature of missionary work and the problems their parents encounter regarding their education. All they know is that they are often separated from their parents because of God. It is not surprising, therefore, that a significant number of missionary kids reject Christianity when they are grown.

To keep ties with their children, many missionaries are now schooling their children at home, at least during the early years when family contact is most needed. There are available a number of home instruction courses, such as the Calvert Course, that enable parents, even those not trained as teachers, to educate their own children. This provides an important alternative to formal schools, but leaves open the question of friends for the children. This can be solved by helping them form friendships with youngsters in the local community.

A second problem missionary children face is rootlessness. As Paul Tournier points out (1968), everyone needs a sense of place, of belonging to a location, a culture, and a community. But missionary kids have had their roots torn up, and some suffer unconsciously because of it. Others are quite well aware of the fact. Most continue to look for a place that is "home." And when the children are young, this home must to a large extent be a place outside of themselves, for they have not yet formed their own sense of identity.

The problem of rootlessness is overcome in part by the closeness of most missionary families. Torn from outside relationships, they tend to build relationships within the family unit. In many parts of the world there is more time for family activities in the evenings and on vacations than in the modern American home, where it is sometimes even hard to find time for family devotions. Moreover, lacking many of the toys and modern forms of entertainment, the children are often forced to be more creative and self-entertaining. Far too often, missionary parents lament openly over the "deprivations" (meaning lack of toys and entertainment) their children suffer because they are raised abroad. Rarely do they realize that they have given their children some of the greatest advantages of life through their international experiences. Most missionary children would not trade these for the material pleasures of life in the West.

Reentry. Many missionary children later have trouble adjusting to Western life. They arrive in America thinking that they will feel at home. It comes as a shock when they find they do not really fit in. The result is an identity crisis. Who, then, are they? And where is home?

Missionary children upon reaching early adulthood often feel a strong need to return to their childhood settings abroad, but if they do, they are disillusioned. First, it is not the same as they remembered it, since adult perceptions are never the same as childhood memories. Second, although they had a place as children within the biculture, there may be no place for them now to work as adults. Finally, old friends, both native and missionary, are gone, and the biculture itself may have disintegrated because of changes in the world scene.

In time, most missionary kids adapt to their parents' original culture, but for them this will always be a secondary home. The cultural imprint of their childhood can never be erased, and a significant number find jobs that take them abroad, whether in missions, government service, or business.

Foreign experience provides missionary kids with certain advantages in the West. They are exposed to the adult world quite early and often learn a sense of self-reliance and social grace that enables them to deal with adult relationships with dignity and confidence. They know how to cope in new settings. For the most part they are highly motivated and have had an education that well prepares them for college and adult life. Studies of missionary kids have shown that many of them become high achievers. Compared to graduates of average Western high schools, a greater percentage become leaders in academia, medicine, or the other professions. As parents we need to rid ourselves of the notion that somehow we have deprived our children by not providing the toys or entertainment their peers have in the West, a notion that unfortunately we too readily transmit to our children.

However, missionary children also face particular pressures. Compared to American high-school graduates, a greater percentage of them have psychological problems that require counseling.

If migrating to their parents' home culture creates problems for missionary children, so does "going native." Foreign children abroad have a somewhat unusual role in the society. They generally attend special schools, speak a different language, and have bicultural values—factors which set them apart from the local people. With some exceptions, they suffer serious culture shock if they later adopt local citizenship, marry into the society, and compete for local jobs. They are still outsiders. In spite of this, a small but growing number of missionary kids marry and migrate permanently to their childhood countries. Their adult adaptation to those settings depends to a considerable extent upon the attitudes their parents take to such moves.

Increasingly we are learning that our children are part of the missionary task. To "leave our children" for the sake of Christ does not mean neglecting their physical well-being or spiritual growth. How can we be witnesses of the gospel to others when we have not won our own children?

National children.   The children of national leaders who work closely with missionaries are bicultural, although to a lesser degree than missionary kids. While they are influenced by their contact with another culture, they remain closely related geographically and socially to their parents' first culture. Consequently adjustment back into the local culture is not so difficult. In some cases, however, they are branded because of their association with foreigners and may be treated as outsiders.

More serious are the tensions that arise when these children seek to advance themselves to higher positions. Too often we missionaries are anxious for native Christian children to study through high school, but resist their going for higher education. Daniel Wambutda notes, "It is all right for a missionary to go for further studies while on furlough, but it is unthinkable that the African should want to build his education as high as he can" (1978:725).

Perhaps we fear that such training will alienate the national leaders from their people, but we tend to overlook several important facts. First, we do need nationals in the highest positions of the church on both the national and international scene. Unfortunately, evangelicals have been slow in training non-Western Christians as theologians and international statesmen. Consequently the Asian, African, and Latin American theologians and leaders who today control the thinking in their countries come from more liberal churches.

Second, national leaders, like missionaries, can and often do identify with the people in incarnational ministries. Since abilities to work across cultural boundaries are not confined to Westerners, attention should be given to furthering the education of any local leader who shows potential.

Finally, much of the world is changing, whether we like it or not, and leaders in churches around the world must deal today with people who are widely exposed to modern ideas. This is particularly true in the cities. If we fail to train pastors who can minister in such settings, the church will stagnate in the midst of changing societies.

Transfer of Power

Another point of tension in the biculture has to do with power and authority. Like all cultures, the biculture develops a system of social statuses and assigns more power to some than to others. The result is a social hierarchy.

The missionary community. Missionaries often form a subcommunity within the biculture. We visit one another and discuss our unique problems and interests. Sometimes we are formally organized into councils that have the power to administer the mission work, and in such cases there is a sharp distinction between missionaries and national leaders in the biculture.

Missionary communities often act as extended families. Children learn to call the adults "Auntie" and "Uncle," and adults are careful to inquire about each other's children. Visiting is common, and families are automatically invited to eat and sleep in another's home, often for several days or weeks. In fact, networks among missionaries provide an entrée into new settings or communities, places to stay so that we can travel inexpensively throughout the world. This means, however, that missionaries must accommodate others just as we in turn count on being made welcome. Consequently we must be ready for unexpected house guests, and these reciprocal obligations extend not only to personal acquaintances, but often to strangers who are involved in missions.

Such visiting poses some problems. Sometimes it interferes with the missionary's work, although normally this is accepted as part of life in the field. More serious is the question of the guests' obligations to the hosts. In the past visits by other missionaries or guests from the West were extremely rare and highly welcomed. With today's modern air travel, there are many visitors, whose stays may be long. Because missionaries often live on small budgets, the question of cost arises. Guests in the past often felt uncertain about whether to give their hosts a gift or at least offer some kind of payment, but were uncertain about how much and what kind. Some missionary communities now suggest certain rates for visitors, and others provide guest houses for a modest fee.

Although some visits are a source of personal enjoyment and fellowship among friends, others are obligations dutifully carried out. And, as is the case in all communities, visits from strangers can be used at times to "check them out." Inquiries are made about where they come from, their work, the seminary or Bible college they attended, and mutual friends. This enables the missionary to evaluate their credentials and judge their orthodoxy. Those who "fit" may be informally invited into the fellowship of the missionary community.

All societies have hierarchies: parents and children, senior workers and juniors, office holders and staff. The missionary community is no exception. It is not surprising that "generations" in the missionary community often translate into a social hierarchy. Young missionaries are expected to respect and learn from experienced missionaries and to refrain from asking questions that challenge traditional ways of doing things. Senior missionaries are expected to hold offices of importance.

One critical question missionaries often ask involves who has the authority to administer the work in the field—the senior missionaries or the home mission office in the West. In the past, because of poor communication technology, most field decisions were made by the missionaries, but today's jets, regular mail, phones, and radios make it possible for many mission agencies to have centralized decision making in the home office. This, however, remains a sore spot in many missions.

The status symbols in the missionary community are often longevity of service, ability to speak the language well, invitations from the national church, and familiarity with the local culture. These may also include the houses we live in, the cars we drive, and the furniture we have. Because missionaries have modest budgets and move often, and because houses, cars, and furniture are often expensive in other countries, the question of who should own them becomes a central point of discussion. If they are thought of as personal property, senior missionaries with wide circles of friends can raise special funds for such items, while junior ones may not be able to do so. On the other hand, if these items are owned and allocated by the mission agency, the question of who gets what becomes a major consideration and, at times, a bone of contention.

The national community.　Local people involved in the biculture also form a subcommunity with its own generations and status levels. Within it they find their identity and self-esteem and also compete for authority and honor.

One source of power and respect during the colonial era of missions was access to the missionary. Consequently, someone who worked in a missionary home often had more power than his or her status would normally have allowed. In many areas the local adage "The way to influence missionaries is through their servants" was not altogether false.

Missionary-national relationships.　Over the past three centuries, one of the most crucial and frequently debated issues in missions has had to do with the relationships between missionaries and nationals. Because the modern mission movement began during the time of colonial expansion, missionaries often emulated the practices of the Western administrators. They adopted similar types of housing and dress and often treated the local people as uncivilized subordinates.

One particularly harmful attitude was that of segregation. Unlike the Spanish and Portuguese Catholic missionaries of the sixteenth and seventeenth centuries, Western Protestant missionaries, particularly those from northern Europe and North America, had a strong sense of racial identity that was manifested in social segregation. Missionaries in some parts of the world refused to let local people enter their houses and sit on their chairs. In other areas they would not take the Lord's Supper from the same cup as the natives—and it was generally unthinkable that their children would marry and settle down locally.

Today with the spread of nationalism, a growing awareness of the value of different cultures, and a recognition that missionary service must be incarnational, these barriers of colonialism and segregation are being torn down. But too often they remain in subtle forms that need to be discovered and rooted out. For example, while the missionaries no longer are in authority, they often control the funds that come from abroad. This gives them great power behind the scenes. While the more public forms of colonialism are disappearing, new hidden forms of it frequently appear through the control of resources and information.

Church-Mission Structures

Although relationships between missionaries and nationals take place between individuals, these relationships are deeply influenced by the structures within which people find themselves. What are some of the organizational formats underlying the relationships between mission agencies and national churches, and how do these affect the mission task? There are many different types of missionary-church structures. Here we will look at only a few to gain some idea of how structural analyses can help us. (See Figure 31.)

Missions as part of the church. In some churches, mission work is seen as one of the tasks carried out by the church or denomination as a whole. These bodies organize mission boards and send out and support their missionaries. The missionaries abroad become members of the churches they plant and take offices within it, such as pastor and treasurer. These missionaries do not organize into a separate missionary council that is set apart from the national church. This has been one of the models used by the Anglican church at the beginning of the modern mission movement. (See first example in Figure 32.)

This model of mission organization has certain strengths and cer-

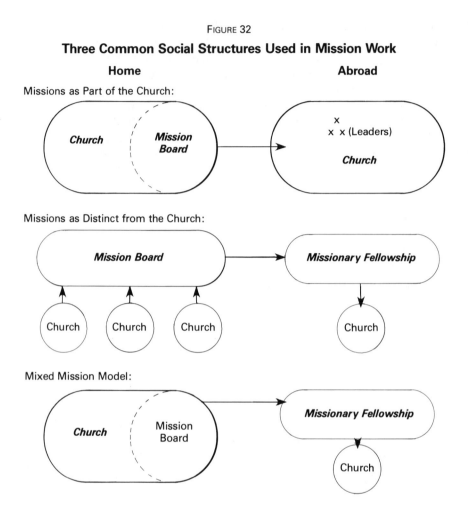

Figure 32

Three Common Social Structures Used in Mission Work

Home   **Abroad**

From Paul G. Hiebert, "Social Structure and Church Growth," in *Crucial Dimensions in World Evangelization*, ed. Arthur F. Glasser et al. (Pasadena: William Carey Library, 1976), p. 68.

tain weaknesses. It tends to have a strong concept of the church, because it is deeply rooted in the church as a unit and is committed to planting new churches. It also tends to minister to the whole person, for it sees mission as part of its larger responsibility. This model for missions has little problem with indigenizing the work and transferring responsibility to the nationals. The missionaries are part of the church structure, which remains intact. Transfer of authority takes place as national leaders replace missionaries in the church offices, but there is no mission structure that must be broken down.

The danger of this approach is that the parent churches may lose their vision for missions. There are so many activities and needs at home that they cease to be missionary in nature.

Missions as distinct from the church.   Because many churches had no vision for missions, another structural model was developed. Here missions were seen as an activity distinct from the normal tasks of the church. There arose independent faith missions boards that recruited missionaries from the churches, but the boards themselves were never subject to any corporate church.

Abroad, this led to a pattern in which the missionaries formed a "missionary fellowship" distinct from "the church." They saw their task as planting a church and then turning it over to national leaders when it was ready. These missionaries normally did not become members of the national church or hold offices in it. Their primary ties and memberships were with the individual sending churches. (See second example in Figure 32.)

The primary strength of this approach was a strong zeal for missions. Because there was only one focus—the evangelization of the world—there was less likelihood of distraction. Moreover, this model was particularly suited for such specialized ministries as translating and printing the Scriptures, radio and television broadcasting, Christian literature, and medical services. These ministries are used by churches from a wide range of denominations and therefore have an appeal in a great many churches of different kinds. In addition, specialized ministries are not directly involved with planting churches, which raises the delicate question of the denominational affiliations of the new churches and the difficult problems of indigenizing the work.

This model tends to have a weak concept of "church," for the mission is structurally distinct and independent from the church. Its strength lies in evangelization and specialized ministries, but it is often weaker in the long-range task of planting new congregations.

This type of organizational format also has a problem with indigenizing the work. There are two distinct structures, mission and church, which leads to a number of critical questions. When and how should missionaries transfer responsibilities to the national church? Can the church maintain the institutions formerly funded by the mission? And how does the mission relate to the national church once the transfer has taken place? Is there still a place for the mission; is it subordinate to the church; and what is its responsibility if the national church asks it to leave, even though the church has no evangelistic outreach of its own?

When transfer of responsibility and power does take place, it is often traumatic. One structure—the mission—must give the work to another structure—the national church. This requires a total administrative reorganization of schools, hospitals, evangelistic programs, and other institutions. It also involves a transfer of ownership of buildings and lands. Often the financing of programs is also expected to change. When a mission agency turns work over to a national church, it usually expects the church to assume responsibility for funding. If the mission does continue to subsidize the work, it must avoid the temptation to use funds to control the young church.

Finally, the dichotomy between mission and church tends to lead to a similarly dichotomous view of human beings, an approach that ministers only to the spiritual needs of man and not to the total person.

Mixed Mission Models. Like other human organizations, mission structures are in part a product of their histories. In many instances, denominations organized mission boards and sent out missionaries as part of the church's activity. This fits the pattern of the sending churches in our first model. But once abroad, the missionaries looked to missions already established for an example of how to do the work and then imitated the overseas patterns of our second model. In other words, the mission was structurally part of the church at home, but abroad the two were distinct. (See last example in Figure 32.)

Rooted in the sending church, this approach has often had a strong vision of the church and church planting and an emphasis on ministering to the whole person, though it faces the danger of losing the mission vision at home, as well as the overseas problems of transferring responsibilities to the national church. Moreover, like the second model above, it creates a structural differentiation abroad between the missionaries and the local Christians that makes identification with the local culture more difficult.

Post-colonial models. One of the greatest tasks now facing the church is to construct models for international church-and-mission relationships that have no vestiges of the colonial past. How do we recognize the autonomy and equality of churches in different countries, but still build organizational structures that will permit them to work together to accomplish the work God has given them to do? How do we overcome cultural differences, feelings of superiority, inequalities of wealth, and national loyalties, in order to become one in Christ? This oneness must find its expression not only in our theology, but also in the social structures we create.

Retirement

A final concern missionaries face, particularly as they grow older, is retirement. We are generally willing to accept simply lifestyles and low budgets in the field. But what about our later years, when we can no longer work or earn our support? While Western missionaries can count on governmental programs such as social security and possibly some additional assistance from retirement plans from their mission boards, most of them face old age with few financial resources. The problem is accentuated because most of their peers who remained at home are better off financially.

Many mission boards today are looking more closely at the retirement concerns of their missionaries, but the problem often remains a difficult one for the missionaries themselves.

Over the Bridge and Beyond

The bicultural community is the bridge by which the gospel crosses from one culture to another. It is only one feature of the long road that has brought the gospel to us from biblical times and that must continue to bring the Good News to the ends of the earth—but it is an essential part of that heritage.

The effectiveness of missions depends to a great degree upon the quality of that community and the relationships within it. Mass media and other modern technologies will never replace personal human relationships as the center of mission communication. The task would be much easier if technological advances alone were enough, for they cost us little when compared to the price paid by missionaries to build Christlike relationships with people in other cultures. God knew this, for he chose to bring us his supreme self-revelation as the person of Christ. The cost to God is beyond our imagination. So will it always be with missions, which calls us into relationships and demands that we be willing to pay with our lives.

10

The Missionary Role

Human relationships are at the heart of the missionary task, but not all relationships are effective in communicating the gospel. As masters we could force people to comply to our wishes, and as Westerners we could approach them with a spirit of arrogance. Neither of these tactics, however, will bring people to Christ. In order to persuade people, we must win them, and to that end we must build relationships based on love and trust. If the people distrust the messenger, they will distrust his or her message.

What relationships are effective in missionary service? Two key concepts—status and role—can help us to understand the nature of human relationships and to examine how they affect the missionary task.

Status and Role

Much of our behavior in interpersonal relationships is predictable. For example, we walk into a shop, select an item, give money to the cashier, wait for the change, and leave with the item, never stopping to think that we have carried out a transaction with a total stranger. Each party seems to know exactly what is going on. Only if the pattern of expected behavior is broken is the relationship called into question. If we walk out without paying for the items, leave before getting the change, or pay with the wrong kind of money, the salesclerk reminds us of our error, and the normal flow of events continues. But if we are

255

rude to the clerk or pull a gun or set up house in the store, the nature of the interrelationship is called into question. Our behavior has then violated the social norms and will not be tolerated. How can we account for this high degree of predictability in human relationships?

Status

A society is made up of people, but it is not defined by merely the number of individuals it contains. Members of a "society" form a social organization, a patterned way of relating to one another. They occupy a set of socially defined positions and interrelate in ways appropriate to that arrangement. In contrast, an uncoordinated aggregation of humans is a mob, not a society.

There are many social contests, and in each of these there are sets of positions or status assignments that complement one another. For example, in a grocery store there may be a manager, checkers, stock clerks, and customers. In a hospital there are doctors, nurses, administrators, sanitary workers, patients, and so on. To participate in either of these contexts, we must occupy one of the statuses associated with that setting. It will not work if we try to be a checker in a hospital and start selling what we find lying around.

To participate in a society, then, we must occupy one or more of the statuses within that society. In one social setting a man may be a husband, in another a shopowner, and in a third a layman at church. Some of these status assignments, such as being a daughter or son, an heir to the throne, or a member of a particular ethnic group, we acquire by birth. These we call *ascribed statuses*. Others, which we call *achieved statuses*, such as student, doctor, or missionary, must be earned. Taken together the statuses an individual occupies play an important part in his or her sense of identity and self-worth.

Role

When one occupies a social status, he or she is expected to act in certain predictable ways. A teacher, for example, is expected to lead the class, to give students instructions regarding assignments, and to evaluate their work. A mother, on the other hand, is expected to take full responsibility for her own children. We call the behavior patterns associated with specific statuses "roles." A little reflection shows that we all change our behavior and sense of identity as we move from one status to another. For instance, when a teacher leaves her job at school and returns home to be a mother, her behavior and her attitudes toward herself change markedly.

Each society has an ideal and predetermined role behavior for each of its statuses. For the most part, however, considerable variation in behavior is permitted, except in formal situations. Soldiers on parade, for instance, must follow the rule book, and little leeway is permitted in their behavior. But in the field or mess areas, their actions are less rigidly prescribed. Some horse around; others are reserved or cynical. Some go beyond the call of duty; others do only the bare minimum. These differences reflect diversity in personality, training, and situation.

There are, however, limits to the variation in behavior allowed to people occupying a given social status. At some point, if their behavior is too deviant, they are removed from their statuses. A teacher who, despite warnings, refuses to act as a "teacher" is fired. Or a son or daughter may be disowned. Those who refuse to meet even the minimum requirements of at least one of the acceptable statuses within a society are often ostracized (in the West we put them into jails or mental asylums), exiled, or killed. They are not functioning members of the society.

It may upset us to discover that much of our basic behavior is programmed by our society, that relatively few of our actions are based on personal decisions alone. In a sense, if we want to be a part of a society, we must play by its rules. The fact is, however, that human relationships would be impossible without such mutual understandings. We would live in uncertainty and chaos. Order in relationships enables us to predict within reasonable degrees how others will act. We can therefore interact with them, knowing what is going on, and can choose a course of action that enables us to pursue our goals. If no meaningful patterns of behavior exist, relationships and planning break down, and the society collapses.

Multiple Statuses

Most individuals occupy a number of different statuses at any one time in life. A person may be a teacher, a Presbyterian, a Democrat, a wife, and a mother at the same time. Each of these statuses is associated with a particular social context, and each has its own patterns of expected behavior. Moreover, those who have been socialized into a set of statuses—in other words, have learned to live in the socially acceptable ways—move smoothly from one status to another, changing their patterns of behavior as they go. In a work setting a man acts as a doctor or postman and even dresses to fit the status. In another setting he is a member of the church and may act as a deacon or lay preacher.

People also occupy a sequence of roles throughout their lives. We all start as children, but soon become students, Girl or Boy Scouts, actors in the school drama, and members of local churches, chess clubs, and a dozen other associations. Later we become missionaries, dentists, or business operators; husbands, wives, and parents; and members or officers in various institutions. In fact, much of our personal history is found in the statuses we acquire and later leave. Moreover, we mark the important changes from one status to another by rituals of transition. For example, we have weddings to mark the change from a single to married state, graduations to denote the end of studenthood, and funerals to show the transition from living person to ancestor.

Taken together the statuses in a society provide a complex social structure—a framework of interlocking and complementary positions into which people are placed (Figure 33). Status not only provides persons with niches within a society, they also determine to a considerable extent how each person relates to people in other statuses in the hierarchy.

Role Sets and Role Pairs

As mentioned, we occupy different statuses within a society. At the same time, within any one of them we relate to a variety of people in different ways. For example, a teacher must relate to the students, to their parents, to the school administration, to working peers, and to the public. The behavior expected of the teacher in each of these relationships is different and constitutes a separate role (Figure 34).

For purposes of analysis, all social relationships can be broken down into role pairs: teacher-student, teacher-administrator, doctor-patient, doctor-nurse, employer-employee, and so forth. In each of these pairings the people involved have some basic idea of how to act and respond, and this makes social relationships easier to initiate and sustain. It would be impossible to create a totally new type of relationship with everyone we meet. Not only would this require a great deal of

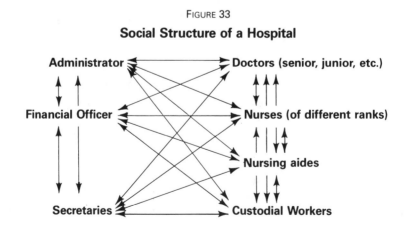

FIGURE 33

Social Structure of a Hospital

FIGURE 34

Several Roles May Be Associated with a Single Status

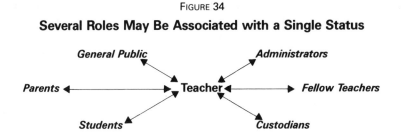

time and energy to define the nature of each relationship, but such unique relationships would not be parts of the larger social structure that integrates the interaction of a great many people.

The concept of role pairs provides us with a powerful tool for analyzing complex social relationships. For example, if we break down a typical North American family into basic relationships, we end up with eight possible role pairs:

husband-wife
father-son
father-daughter
mother-son
mother-daughter
brother-brother
brother-sister
sister-sister

Each of these pairs has its own ideal role behavior. A man is expected to act in one way toward a son, another toward a daughter, and a third way toward his wife. When any family member deviates too far from these expectations, the organization of the family is threatened.

The everyday behavior of the actors in these family role pairs varies a great deal according to a number of factors, such as the nature of the social context, the presence or absence of audiences, and the psychological attitudes of the actors at that moment. A husband treats his wife differently in church, at the store, in the home, or on the beach. He modifies his behavior when friends, children, parents-in-law, or strangers are around, and his actions are also based on how he feels at that moment toward his wife or the world in general. Despite such daily variation, however, there is a basic behavior pattern in the relationship and a corresponding set of social restraints.

Role expectations may change over time. The ideal American father of a century ago was an authoritarian figure, a man of strength, and the sole breadwinner. Today he is expected to be a companion to his son and a true partner to his wife. When such changes occur, social disagreements and confusion can arise.

Cross-cultural Role Confusion

So far we have looked at the roles in one culture, the United States. But societies are different, and so are the roles they create. Consequently we can expect a great deal of role confusion when people move from one society to another. This ambiguity is all the more damaging because we are rarely conscious of the roles we play—they are so much a part of our everyday lives that we do not stop to think about them.

One type of confusion arises when two cultures have similar statuses, but these are associated with different roles. For example, although the role "father," or biological progenitor, is found in all societies, what a father is expected to do varies greatly from society to society. In the West he is expected to provide for his children. Among the Trobriand Islanders he should give the yams he raises to feed his sister's children, while his wife's brother provides him with yams to feed his own family. In the West a father is expected to be with his wife during or immediately after she delivers their child. In India the wife goes to her mother's home for the delivery, and the husband should not show up until the third, fifth, seventh, or some other auspicious month after the birth.

A second type of confusion arises when the roles we play in our original society do not even exist in our new society. Because we are often unaware that this is the case, we continue to act out the roles familiar to us. The local people, however, do not know who we are, for we do not fit into any of their social categories. For instance, when we are abroad we generally think of ourselves as "missionaries." But this status does not exist in most of the cultures to which we go. The only thing the nationals can do in such cases is to observe our behavior to see which of their categories we most nearly fit. They may see us as government officers, secret-service agents, or—as was often the case in parts of Africa and Papua (New Guinea) when the first white people came—as spirits or ancestors returned from the dead. We are often placed by the people into an undesirable status without our knowing it.

To participate fully in another society we must be given a status within it. Otherwise we are "enemies" and must be speared, or strangers who cannot be trusted. Consequently the locals may adopt us into a tribe or clan, not necessarily because they love us, but because they do not want to kill us.

As we have seen with communication, what is important is not how we see ourselves, but how others see us. That in the long run will determine the effectiveness of our ministry, although we will know how we are viewed only if we are sensitive to the people's responses.

Defining Missionary Roles

The concepts of status and role as we have outlined them so far are very useful in the analysis of our work as missionaries. Being a missionary means being involved with people in many different contexts, and these concepts can help us examine more carefully the nature of these relationships. Let us begin by looking at the roles associated with the status called "missionary," and the images and expectations the people have of these roles.

A "missionary" relates to different kinds of people: non-Christians, national Christians, fellow missionaries, mission administrators, the people of the missionary's sending churches, and members of the missionary's family (Figure 35). We will examine each of these briefly, considering first some of the roles missionaries have played in the past that have hindered the effectiveness of their work, and then examining some of the roles we might fill so as to facilitate the spread of the gospel. In looking at former negative roles, we are not doing so to pass judgment on missionaries of the past. In those times and places most of us would have acted in similar ways. Moreover, there are also many examples of effective and sacrificial missionary service. We need, however, to learn from the mistakes of the past and to remind ourselves that people respond to the gospel not only on the basis of its intrinsic truthfulness, but also according to the nature of the relationship within which they hear it.

The Missionary and National Non-Christians

The relationship between missionaries and the non-Christians they seek to serve lies at the heart of the missionary task. It is also the one most likely to be misunderstood or misused. This relationship does not lie within the social organization of the church, and its nature is defined by both the missionary and the non-Christians, who may choose to see it in a negative light. Because the missionaries initiate the connection, it is they who must be most sensitive to the way the non-Christians perceive the relationship, to make certain the roles that emerge do not undermine the message of the gospel.

FIGURE 35

Roles Associated with the Status of "Missionary"

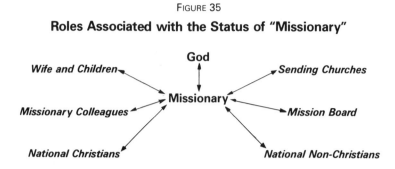

Colonial rulers or incarnational missionaries? Unfortunately missionaries are seen not only as Christians, but as representatives of their countries of origin. It should not surprise us, therefore, that during the era of Western colonial rule most missionaries, because they came from European countries, were seen as "colonial rulers." Whether true or false, the opinion of one African leader was widely held around the world: "The missionary came first, then followed the trader. Last came the soldiers with guns to kill, conquer, divide and rule. Missionaries were the means by which the white people lulled Africans to sleep while they took away our land and freedom. . . ." (Loewen 1975:434).

This is partly a misunderstanding, for many missionaries tried to draw a sharp distinction between Christian missions and the colonial administrations under which they served. But the misunderstanding is not surprising, because the missionaries were mostly white, and the only other white people most Africans and Asians saw were colonial rulers. Moreover, while the missionaries may not have wanted to be seen as colonialists, they were all too happy to make use of their relationship to the colonial administrations when it suited their purposes. For example, missionaries in much of the colonial world did not have to stand in long hot lines at railroad stations for tickets. They generally went to the stationmaster, who invited them to sit down for a cup of tea while he personally got the tickets behind the scenes. While missionaries often justified this as avoiding unnecessary hardship and increasing the efficiency of their work, the local people saw it as evidence that missionaries were indeed part of the colonial regime. Similarly, the use of cars identified missionaries with Western rule in countries where few nationals had access to such transportation.

Identifying the missionaries with colonial administrations was only partly a misunderstanding. In many instances the missionaries *did* see themselves as working hand in hand with the colonial rulers to stamp out such evil practices as headhunting and the burning of widows on funeral pyres—in short, to bring civilization to the people. In fact, one of the widespread mottos of the era was to "Colonize, Christianize, and civilize."

While the colonial connection opened doors for missionary service in many parts of the world, it also placed missionaries in roles that made it difficult for them to identify with the people and to present a gospel not tied to local cultural and political systems. It also meant that churches started in these countries were often branded as tools of the colonial government to suppress the inhabitants. National Christians, following the lead of the missionaries, were often opponents to the rising spirit of nationalism and self-rule that began to sweep many colonial outposts.

The colonial era is largely past, at least in its more overt political forms. But as today's missionaries, we must still struggle with the fact that we are commonly seen as representatives of our own country first and missionaries second. We are often forced to declare where our real loyalties lie. Unfortunately, if we side with our country of origin, we often close the door for any effective hearing of the gospel. But if, for the sake of the gospel, we identify with the local people in countries where colonialism once reigned, we need to take a more critical look at our native land and its economic and political policies. We must look at the needs of the world as a whole, not only at those of our own nation, although such a frame of reference often brings us under heavy criticism from our sending churches in the West. In the end, we may be forced to choose where our primary identity lies—with the West or with the people we have come to serve.

Landlords or servants? A second role missionaries fall into, often unknowingly, is that of "landlords." In Latin America they are frequently called patrons, the term for rich landowners who virtually own the serfs who till the soil (cf. Loewen 1975:436–439). In Hawaii many missionaries did end up as well-to-do farmers.

In a few cases missionaries consciously chose the role of landlord as a way to help the people oppressed by cruel local masters. They argued that missionaries could not help the serfs until the latter were given economic alternatives: jobs, their own land, and markets for their goods. Rarely, however, were these missionaries able to move beyond economic assistance to presenting the whole of the claims of Christ upon the people. Although the landlord role enabled some missionaries to help free the people from more oppressive landlords, it often closed the door for bringing them the gospel.

More often the identification of missionaries as landlords was a case of cross-cultural confusion. The missionaries were sometimes unaware that they were being so classified, and they saw themselves as "missionaries," not realizing that this is a Western status that does not exist in most other societies. When asked who they were, they said "missionary." Since this word had no meaning for the local people, they tried to guess what the missionaries were by observing their behavior. Their answer, of course, had to be related to one of the statuses in their own familiar culture.

In South India, for instance, landlords are *doras*. A good *dora* builds a bungalow and surrounds it with a compound wall. If he has second and third wives, he builds separate houses for them so that they will not quarrel with one another. On his land he also constructs quarters for his servants and possibly a Hindu shrine. When a missionary came, he bought land and built bungalows and compound walls. He constructed a separate house for the single women missionaries because they were not his wives. Finally missionaries also built servant quarters and churches on the mission lands (Figure 36). It is not surprising, therefore, that the people began to identify the missionaries as *doras*. Or that they thought that missionaries had two or three wives. After all, they were only being good *doras* if they built separate houses for each of them.

Learners.   What role will help rather than hinder a missionary in the communication of the gospel? There is no simple answer to this question, for each culture has its own sets of statuses and roles, and we must choose one that fits the society in which we minister. It helps us to know that we will be placed in such a role whether we like it or

FIGURE 36

Typical Compounds

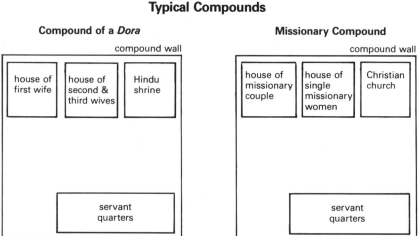

not, for then we can avoid the cross-cultural misunderstandings that have occurred so often in the past. Moreover, we can consciously look for roles in the society that enable us to carry on our witness more effectively.

What early role do we assume while we study the society and learn to know about the roles within it? Fortunately, as Loewen (1975:439) points out, many societies have a role for "learners," or strangers who are entering the society. The Waunana of the Choco, for example, have the role of "young man getting to know the world."

Accepting the role of learner enables a missionary to enter a new society and study its ways. It also opens the door for building close relationships, for most people are happy to teach others their own customs. Such relationships frequently provide the missionary with occasions for sharing the gospel on a personal basis with his or her hosts. In fact, from the perspective of the missionary task, the period of being a learner is often one of the most fruitful for sharing the gospel with non-Christians.

There are, however, limits to this role. In the first place, we must be sincere in our desire to learn the culture. The people soon know if we are simply using it as a quick way to build relationships with them so that we can win them. If they feel used, they will reject us and our message. As Christians we should love the people, and if we truly do, we will be interested in their lives and culture. In fact, learning to know more about people is one way to build our love for them.

A second limit to the role of learner is time. We can be learners only so long. Then people expect us to grow up and find our place as a contributing member within the society. This does not mean we stop learning about the culture, but only at some point—usually a year or two—we must find a more permanent role within the society.

Finally, while the role of learner does open the doors for building trust and for personal witness within a society, it may not be the most effective role for evangelism in the long run. After trust has been built, we may be more effective as "religious teachers," "prophets," or "doctors," as these are defined within the society. Or we may be adopted into a tribe and clan and given roles such as "mother," "father," "older brother," or "older sister."

In any case, we will have to choose a role within the local society, and we need to look carefully at the ones we are considering, to see which of them would hinder or help us in the communication of the gospel. We must also consider whether we can fulfill the people's expectations of that role. For example, as "older brother" or "older sister" we may be expected to share our material goods with our younger brothers and sisters when they ask us for help. If we do not exemplify the normal role expectations of the people, they will see us as dishonest and irresponsible.

The Missionary and National Christians

Our relationship with national Christians is different from that developed with non-Christians. As Christians we belong to one family. Yet even within the church we have statuses and roles that govern the nature of our interactions. Here too we need to examine the roles we take, for too often we find ourselves in ones that hinder our ministry. What are some of these roles, and how can we avoid those that are counterproductive?

Policemen or advocates? One role a missionary frequently plays is "policeman." We are concerned about the purity of the church and therefore are tempted to prevent converts from stealing, immorality, drinking orgies, witchcraft, and the like. And we do so by investigating the behavior of the Christians and by imposing punishment upon the violators.

One common problem is household "theft." Household workers in some cultures see themselves as part of the family, with the right to take small amounts of foodstuffs for themselves. Servants, therefore, help themselves accordingly. Missionaries tend to see this as theft and often have large rings of keys to keep everything locked up.

Another problem is premarital and extramarital sexual relationships. We see these as particularly evil, so we try to supervise the moral behavior of the Christian nationals. One missionary made it a point to visit the homes of Christian workers unexpectedly to see who was sleeping with whom. Another built a twelve-foot wall to safeguard adolescent girls in a boarding school. But, as Loewen (1975:437) points out:

> [T]he irony of the situation was that the missionaries had not realized that it was the female who chose the sex partner in that culture, and so when they put the braces of the wall on the inside of the enclosure, they provided an excellent ladder for the girls to climb out and rendezvous with the fellows. Watching the girls climb out of the "pen" was a major source of evening entertainment for adults and children who gathered around to watch. Then the rest of the evening was spent recounting the most interesting escapades of the past and laughing at the missionaries.

Church discipline needs to be exercised, but when it is enforced by the missionary, he or she soon becomes a police officer. Loewen (1975:437) elaborates:

Protestant legalism has often pushed missionaries into perpetrating "monstrosities" of justice, such as the excommunication laws used in one African church: the first illegitimate child—no communion for three months; the second child—no communion for six months; and the third—no communion for nine months.

Reyburn (1959:11) writes that in the Eastern Cameroons, the French passed a law making adultery a civil offense punishable with a fine paid to the aggrieved husband. For the Kakas who lived in this country, this became a way of making money. Husbands encouraged their wives to have affairs in order to collect the fines.

Although we must be concerned about the growth and purity of the church, church discipline is something we must help the national leaders of the church to exercise. If we enforce righteousness as "policemen," the gospel becomes legalism and our ministry to the people is undermined. The people will not learn to make Christian norms their own, but will merely obey the missionary's laws out of fear of punishment rather than personal conviction.

How do we avoid becoming policemen? We need to teach the awfulness of sin, but the people often know this. We need even more to be on their side by teaching and modeling the gospel message of redemption and forgiveness. We must identify with the people in their struggles with sin, for they—like us—fight not only against their own sinful nature, but against evil practices within their cultures.

Saints or saved sinners?   A second role in which it is easy for a missionary to fall is that of "saint." As bearers of the Word, we seek to model what it means to be a Christian. But when we sin, and we surely do, we are afraid to confess our failings to the national Christians. We are afraid that they may lose confidence in us and reject the gospel.

There are several problems with a saintly approach. First, the people are aware of our sins, often more than we are. They see behind the pious masks we wear and accuse us of hypocrisy. "Inside information" on the missionaries' relationships with one another, their tempers and their weaknesses, are widely discussed by the national Christians. Loewen (1975:59) relates one such case in which a missionary couple was having marital problems that were kept top secret in the missionary community. Unknown to them, the matter was being widely discussed in the local churches.

The question of sin in the life of the missionary is complicated by the fact that many cultures put great emphasis on sins that we tend to ignore. For example, our Western church has a great preoccupation with sexual sins. Although we usually reinstate pastors who commit theft or lose their tempers, after they have confessed their sin, we rarely do so if they commit adultery. In India, on the other hand, the cardinal sin is anger. Yet all too frequently missionaries get angry and think nothing of it. Loewen (1975:59) tells of an African houseboy whose "mama-boss" always lost her temper over his mistakes. After listening to his stories, the group concluded that since she always got "mad as the devil," she probably was not a Christian.

A second problem with presenting ourselves as sinless saints is that we cannot model for the leaders the way of confession and forgiveness. Festo Kivengere (Loewen 1975:60) forcefully illustrates this in an account of an encounter between a missionary and a national leader in Uganda. The missionary pleaded with the leader to be open with him so that they could pray together about the latter's problems. The national replied, "Brother, my box is open, but your box is not only closed but locked."

A missionary is often the first leader a young church has, and therefore is its model for leadership. If we are not examples in the confession of sin, it should not surprise us that national leaders often feel they need not do so either. In one part of the world the Christian leaders concluded that the unpardonable sin was to sin after ordination. Consequently, the leaders did not want to be ordained until they were about to die, since they knew that they could not remain sinless for long.

A third problem with playing the role of saint is that it builds a barrier between the missionary and the people. It is hard to live with a saint! Most people are all too aware of their sins and understand one another's temptations. But saints are above temptation and do not comprehend the moral struggles of ordinary people. When we try to relate to people as saints, we can only do so by putting on empty masks of holiness.

But what are missionaries if not saints? Does not Paul speak of Christians as saints, and are not missionaries the elite among Christians? Too often we think of "saints" as those who do not sin, and we strive hard for a time to fit that definition. All too soon, however, we realize that we are just as tempted and as sinful as we were before we became missionaries. We may have fewer temptations of the flesh, but certainly more of the spirit. We try to hide our sins and put on a mask of piety. This deceives no one. It only encourages others to do the same.

What is the alternative? We need to think of "saints" as saved sinners—as those who are righteous before God not because they are sinless, but because of the righteousness God gives them through Christ. Even Paul, that great missionary, said, "Christ Jesus came into the world to save sinners, of whom I am [not "was"] chief" (1 Tim. 1:15, NIV). Our task is not to stand in condemnation of young Christians, but to help them overcome the sins that so quickly beset us all.

Seeing ourselves as saved sinners has two important implications for us as missionaries. In the first place, it means that we need to be transparent—that we let people see who we really are. Paul Tournier (1957) distinguishes between the social and the real person. Tournier calls the former the "personage," the statuses we occupy in social relationships. By contrast, the "person" is who we really are inside. The danger is that we hide our real selves behind social masks to impress others. People then do not see us as real human beings. The greatest danger is when we try to act as if we never sin. The only cure is to let others see our weaknesses and sins as well as our strengths.

Does this not destroy our credibility? Of course, we are not called to publish our sins in the local paper, as they are best dealt with in a small circle of church leaders. But our willingness to admit to others that we are weak usually increases their trust in us. Since they already know we are weak, they will respect our honesty and humility and recognize that we are not trying to play games.

Showing others who we really are can also open up communication with people. Jacob Loewen (1975:54–55) narrates one experience in which self-exposure by the missionaries became the bridge across the moat that separated them from the national leaders. The missionaries had heard that one of the Panamanian leaders had committed adultery, but he had denied it. When asked, the other leaders had shrugged their shoulders and said, "Who knows?"

Finally, after weeks of uncertainty, prayer, and heart searching, the missionaries opened their own lives to the national leaders in a small prayer meeting. They revealed their own sexual tensions when they were away from their families, and they confessed that on occasion there had been tension between husband and wife because of sex. They admitted, as Peter warns, that their prayers had been hindered when they as husbands did not live with their wives in wisdom. Then they asked the leaders whether Indians had this kind of problem in their lives, too. Before much else could be said, the leader under suspicion burst out, "I got involved with one of my former wives."

The missionaries asked him, "Do you think that we can now 'throw stones' at you as the Pharisees wanted to when they caught the woman in adultery?"

"No," he replied, "for I know that you men have sex problems, too."

When the missionaries and the repentant leader knelt down to pray, the other two leaders asked, "But are you the only ones that are going to get forgiveness? Can we not get it also?" After they had confessed the tensions that had arisen in their own homes, the leaders and missionaries knelt down to ask God to forgive them individually and collectively for their many common shortcomings in the area of sex.

A South African Pioneer Missionary's Translation of 1 Corinthians 13

If I have the language perfectly and
  speak like a native
    and have not His love,
      I am nothing.

If I have diplomas and degrees and know
  all the up-to-date methods,
    and have not His touch of understanding love,
      I am nothing.

If I am able to argue successfully against
  the religions of the people and make fools
    of them and have not His wooing note of love,
      I am nothing.

If I have all faiths and great ideals
  and magnificent plans
    and not His love that sweats
      and bleeds and weeps and
        prays and pleads,
          I am nothing.

If I give my clothes and money
  to them and have not love for them,
    I am nothing.

If I surrender all prospects. Leave home
  and friends and make the sacrifices
    of a missionary career and then turn
      sour and selfish amid the daily
        annoyances and slights of the missionary life,
          then I am nothing.

If I can heal all manner of sickness
  and disease but wound hearts and hurt feelings
    for want of His love that is kind,
      I am nothing.

If I can write articles and publish books
  that win applause but fail to transcribe
    the word of the cross into the
      language of His love,
        I am nothing.

From a sermon by Stephen Brown, Key Biscayne Presbyterian Church (Fla.)

Spiritual parents or brothers and sisters? One role particularly difficult to handle is that of "spiritual parent." On the one hand, the missionary is often the "father" or "mother" who brings people to salvation and plants a new church. On the other, no one wishes to be treated like a child forever.

E. Stanley Jones (1957:211) points out that the relationship of many pioneer missionaries to their converts should go through several stages. At first it is one of *dependency*. The missionary, in fact, has been the parent of the church, and as such bears much of the responsibility for its growth. In time, the new Christians must stand on their own and learn *independency*. Only after they have established their personal identities can they really move on to a relationship with the missionary characterized by *interdependency*, in which they work together as equals.

The transition from dependency to independency is particularly difficult and needs a great deal of patience and understanding on the part of both missionaries and young Christians, especially the former since they are in the positions of power. The danger is for us to hold on to a parental role far too long because we fear things may go wrong. We need to learn that Christians must grow, and they can only do so by being allowed to make their own mistakes.

The second transition in the relationship is equally important. Our ultimate goal is not Christian individualism, but the church as a body of believers who are interdependent. We must learn to work as equals with those who were once our dependents, without reverting to a parental role when the relationship grows stormy.

Jones's three stages can help us understand not only our relationships with individual Christians, but also the relationship of the mission organization with the national church. Here too the relationship often begins with one of dependence, but this must soon mature to independence and eventual interdependence.

What, then, is the function of missionaries when national Christians and churches become independent? Certainly there are other fields to which they can go. But is there no place in the church for them to help and strengthen the believers? One important role suggested by Loewen is that of "catalyst." Missionaries are important sources of information about the outside world. Moreover they can be counselors with whom the local leaders can test their ideas. It is important in this role that missionaries avoid prescribing answers, no matter how strongly they feel about a matter. Their function is to suggest alternative courses of action and help the leaders think through the consequences of each. In the end, however, the decision should be made by the national leaders.

Paid preachers or self-supporting witnesses?   One of the more difficult questions facing missionaries has to do with their financial support. Although they do not take money from the national churches, the people know they are being funded by their sending churches. Consequently, the nationals often see the missionaries as paid preachers. Jacob Loewen (1975:432) reports one such instance:

> In 1962 a local resident missionary and two visiting Americans participated in a special service with the Choco church in Panama. Using the two American visitors as models, the speaker challenged the Choco congregation to emulate their example and to become witnesses for their Lord. "These men have left their homes and families. They have given up opportunities to earn money. Why? They did this in order to be able to come here and to tell their friends, the Choco, the message of Jesus Christ. We must learn from them, for we, too, must leave our work and our families to share this message with our people on other rivers."
>
> After this service was over the two visitors took the speaker aside and pointed out to him, "You mentioned the two of us in the message this afternoon, but why didn't you mention the resident missionary? Don't you think he will feel hurt? After all, he gives his full time to this work and we only give up our vacations."
>
> To this the leader replied, "But I cannot use him as an example. He isn't making any sacrifice. He doesn't work for a living like you and I do. In fact, there are people in your country who are paying him to live here!"

Many are the times when missionaries leading teams out for evangelism have been asked, "How much are we going to be paid?" The problem is one of perspective. The missionaries see themselves as having made a great sacrifice—they have given up profitable careers at home to minister in a foreign land. But in most parts of the world the people see missionaries as wealthy people paid by others to live relatively easy lives in their society.

There is no simple solution. It is helpful to have self-supporting missionaries, or "tentmakers," to show the people that laymen as well as paid clergy should be involved in evangelism. But the planting of churches in new cultures can rarely be done by financially independent or short-term missionaries. The former can rarely free enough time for sustained mission work, particularly if they work for a secular agency or institution. The latter do not stay long enough to help a church grow to full maturity. The long, hard task of identifying with the people and of planting churches and leading them to maturity still depends upon missionaries who give long periods of their lives to minister in one area—and these need external support.

In part, full-time missionaries must identify with the people as much as possible, so that the walls of economic difference do not hinder the communication of the gospel. In part, they also need to live with any financial misunderstandings without being defensive, knowing that the people have no way to see the broader picture. Fortunately this is changing as national leaders increasingly travel around the world.

The Missionary and Other Missionaries

One of the most rewarding yet most difficult set of roles a missionary has is with his or her colleagues. On the one hand, these co-workers form a community, sharing a common vision and task and often a similar cultural heritage. Visits by other missionaries are significant events, particularly when a missionary lives in prolonged isolation.

On the other hand, because we are part of small, tightly knit communities, our relationships with fellow missionaries are often intense. Consequently they are subject to feelings of rivalry, animosity over personality differences, and cynicism. Many missionaries report that their greatest problems are with other missionaries, not with the people among whom they work. This should not surprise us, for missionaries tend to have strong personalities and deep convictions. Otherwise we would not become missionaries. Moreover, we cannot choose associates. They are given to us. At home we can avoid those who antagonize us and find our friends elsewhere. Abroad, we are forced into tight communities of people not of our own choosing.

"Missionary" or colleague?   If there is one place we can play the role of "missionary" it is with our associates in the field. They know what the status is, and how a missionary should behave.

Being a "missionary" gives us a status and role within a mission organization. It gives us the power that enables us to do our work. For example, we can vote in missionary councils; exercise authority in the schools, hospitals, and churches in which we work; and raise support for our projects. This status also provides such resources as housing, salaries, vehicles, and money for various tasks. Without institutional structures, it would be almost impossible for us to do any work at all.

But social organizations also have inherent problems. One set has to do with the dynamics of day-to-day living. We work most closely with others in our social organization. We seek their approval, compete with them for status and resources, oppose those who disagree with us, and try to impose our will on others. One missionary is made the principal of a high school, another the chairman of the evangelism committee. Personal skills, seniority, and even politics enter into the assignment of missionaries to various tasks.

This may shock us at first, for we often have an idealized view of how missionaries relate to one another. We hope to find a strong, supportive community in which the petty infighting of ordinary people is missing. But missionaries are humans first. Moving into another culture does not change us. We face the temptations of all those involved in human organizations, and the interpersonal dynamics can become particularly intense because we are often a small, isolated group and feel so strongly about what we are doing.

Sometimes we are caught in rivalries with our missionary colleagues. If a missionary builds a grade school for the churches in another area, Christians in our area want one, too. To gain their approval we feel obligated to raise funds for a grade school and possibly a high school as well.

Although we need institutions to support our work, there is no way to fully avoid the tensions that arise within them between individuals and cliques. We need to remind ourselves of our Christian calling to live in fellowship, and we must consciously build a team spirit by spiritual fellowship and recreation together. We must also create ways to handle tensions and conflicts before they lead to personal attacks. Pastoral care must be provided for all our missionaries. Above all a missionary must cultivate a spirit of flexibility and love that enables the solving of problems for the good of the body, without tying them to his or her own personal identity.

A second set of problems has to do with the fact that the missionary role has become a profession. Since we think of missionaries as specialists, with esoteric training and highly technical skills, we may get the idea that missionaries are spiritual superstars. Consequently not only do ordinary people not feel that they can relate to missionaries as equals, but missionaries may even put on their formal masks when they relate to each other. They dare not admit their faults and weaknesses, lest the others think less of them.

One young missionary went through a spiritual crisis the first time he sinned against a fellow missionary. He was making a trip to the city to get some things for his family and the school in which he worked, and his senior colleague asked him to stop by at the railroad station to see if a certain box had come. The day was long and hectic, and the young missionary returned late at night, having forgotten to stop at the station. The senior missionary was at the gate and asked him about the box. What does a first-termer say to a senior colleague in such a case? Without thinking, the young missionary said, "No, it has not come." He immediately knew he had lied. But what should he do? Three days later, after much agonizing, he did what he knew he must. He walked the "thousand miles" to the next house and knocked. When the senior missionary appeared, the young man could think of a hundred other things to talk about. But he confessed his sin and asked forgiveness. Fellowship between the two was restored, and they later became warm friends, but the young missionary's image of himself as a "missionary" was shattered and fell like broken glass at his feet before the door.

We all need statuses so that we can work with others. The danger is that these become ends in themselves and not merely means to carry out our ministry. They can also become walls that divide us, rather than bridges of cooperation and fellowship.

Administrators, practitioners, and catalysts. One source of tension for missionaries is the conflict between doing and administering. Those who are most successful in evangelism and planting churches are often assigned to administrative posts, but this removes them from the work they do so effectively.

All missionary work requires administration, and all missionaries are caught up in it to some extent. Good administration can mobilize large programs that bring far-reaching gains, just as bad administration can seriously hinder the work of everyone involved. But not all have the gift of administration. For example, being effective village church-planters does not necessarily qualify us for administering a whole mission program. Administration can become an end in itself, and so rob us from the work that needs to be done. It is hard for those in power to view administration as the servant of the mission work and not let it become the master.

The Missionary and Mission Administrators

One sensitive relationship all missionaries maintain is with the administrators of their mission. They all work within the same institutional structure, and their interconnecting roles are prescribed by the nature of their organization.

Obviously we cannot examine the many different types of mission organization and the ways each affects the missionary-administrator role pairing. Young missionaries need to look at their own situations carefully, for it is this interaction, together with their relationships to their missionary colleagues, that will largely determine what is expected of them.

Several general comments can be made about these role dynamics. First, we may face the problem of role confusion. We may be close friends with members of the mission board or administration and find them personally encouraging and warm. But they also occupy official positions within the social structure. It should not surprise us, therefore, that what they say in formal business meetings may seem to contradict what they say to us in person.

Second, we may face the problem of power. One of the central questions for many mission organizations is who should make the decisions governing policies and practices in the field? Should this be done by the missionaries themselves, or by the home board? Unfortunately, disagreements on this have often led to a rift between the field personnel and the administration at home.

Finally, we may face the problem of divided allegiances. Missionaries belong to a group of people we have called culture brokers—they stand between two communities. They are important because they are the bridge across which communication passes from one culture to the other. But they are also suspect because neither side knows fully what the other is doing. In a way, a missionary is like a money changer at an airport. Customers must trust him not to cheat them when they exchange their currency.

Because they belong to two cultural worlds, missionaries have two allegiances. On the one hand, they have loyaties to the churches they plant. On the other hand, they are expected to be loyal to their sending churches and the administrative organization. When these two bodies disagree, the missionaries must choose their primary loyalties. Are they members first of the national church (which puts them in confrontation with their mission agency), or are they members of the mission (which puts them in confrontation with the national church)? Normally missionaries can serve as impartial mediators (even here each side believes its interests have been sold out), but there may come times when they must break with one side or the other.

The Missionary and Sending Churches

When missionaries return to their sending churches, they enter a new and poorly defined role, "missionary-on-furlough." The first week, the home church asks a missionary to speak on Sunday morning, the second week to show slides on Sunday evening, and the third week to give a Bible study on Wednesday night. After that, the people begin to ask when he or she will return to the field! We missionaries frequently dream about what we will do when we return "home," but when we do, we find ourselves in an uncomfortable position that we cannot endure for long.

One reason for our discomfort is that the status of missionary-on-furlough is temporary and therefore marginal in Western societies. Missionaries-on-furlough are outsiders. Our real place is abroad.

Another reason is that as missionaries we become increasingly estranged from our own society. Some missionaries are alienated from their cultural base even before they become missionaries, and this may play a part in their choosing this vocation. All are influenced by the fact that people tend to regard a missionary as a special person. The public has been conditioned to think of missionaries as the "cream of the crop," as people who have achieved a high degree of spiritual maturity and dedication. Loewen (1975:403) notes:

> Often the very act of volunteering as a missionary is motivated by a kind of other-worldliness that has become a part of the role expectations for truly evangelical missionaries. Such people turn their backs on the major concerns of their contemporaries in their own society, they step out of their social setting and ordinary living to engage in "winning souls" for a heavenly kingdom. In a society that ordinarily gauges the worth of a person in terms of measureable production, missionaries stand out as unique do-gooders whose work is to produce only unmeasurable "spiritual" returns. It is no wonder, therefore, that returning missionaries frequently feel themselves out of place, or at least out of step with the home society.

There is no easy scenario for living as missionaries-on-furlough. It helps to have frank talks with the church leaders, to clarify their expectations of us and to let them know that we want to fit back into the church as regular members as rapidly as possible. This is particularly important for our children, who desperately want to be accepted in the crowd of their peers, but often feel as if they are on display. It is also important for the family unit, because furlough puts great strains on the relationships between husband and wife, and parents and children, at a time when all these returnees are in a state of disorientation and need help.

We must be especially sensitive to the needs of our children, who are in culture shock and are trying to find acceptance among the local young people. Because they feel like strangers, some of them are withdrawn. We need to help them by inviting their friends over to our homes. Others are so determined to fit in that they overidentify with the local culture in order to gain acceptance. These we need to understand and love with great sensitivity.

For ourselves, we need realistic expectations. Furloughs are difficult times. As we live in temporary quarters or with relatives or travel across the country and hold meetings, we are being watched all the time. Through it all, we must set limits and schedule time alone for ourselves and our families.

The Missionary and His Wife

It may surprise us that marital problems are not uncommon among missionaries. Generally their commitment to Christ, to other Christian families, and to the pressures of their work often hold these partners together. But they are only human, and they also face a multiplicity of tensions through working together in difficult situations with few of the usual outside systems of support. It is important, therefore, that missionary husbands and wives give high priority to building strong marriages. Good marriages require hard work, and we simply cannot take them for granted.

The missionary setting adds several significant stresses to married life. Missionaries are isolated from family, friends, and familiar settings, and are thrown upon each other for support and encouragement. They face the unique problems of living in a new culture, with difficulties related to the kinds of houses they live in, the types of food they eat, and the expectations others have of them.

The greatest problems are faced by the missionary wife and mother. In most cases, it is the husband who has a clearly defined role within the mission. As an evangelist, a school principal, or a doctor, he can find a sense of identity and personal satisfaction in the work he does. After all, he preaches to large audiences, leads people to Christ, heals the sick, and/or educates the young.

But what about his wife? Unless she, too, is ordained, she usually has no specific role in ministry. She is expected to keep the house and raise the children as she would at home, but she must do so under far more difficult circumstances. One study showed that in many countries it takes five and a half hours to cook a meal that in the West takes an hour and a half—partly because the chickens are still running around when we buy them.

If the wife hires servants to compensate for the prepackaged foods and electrical servants she had at home, she faces other problems. In short, the wife does all that she does in her native land and more, but without any added rewards and without feeling directly a part of the work herself. She must be content to hear her husband's exciting reports and gain a vicarious sense of worth through his achievements.

Sometimes a wife is expected to distribute medicines and help the local women and children, but this does not really take into account her need to find fulfillment in ministry. Nor does her role usually give recognition to the fact that as a mother in a new setting she has far more responsibilities than in her homeland. She must be unofficial doctor, teacher, and friend to the nationals, as well as mother to her own children. She, even more than her husband, must struggle with the occasional conflict between her dual role as parent to her children and missionary to the people.

It is important for a missionary husband to recognize the difficult positions into which he may place his wife—and for both partners to work out roles in which each has a meaningful ministry and feelings of fulfillment.

Missionaries and Their Children

As we have already seen, children and retirement are two nagging concerns for most missionaries. We can and do choose to leave our communities, thereby to minister in foreign settings. But what about our children? How will our decisions affect their lives?

We have already looked at the status of missionary kids in the bi-culture. Here we will add only a comment or two about the place of these children in the missionary family. Fortunately, missionary service does provide many opportunities for building strong family ties. The absence of TV, Little League, and every-night meetings of all sorts means that the family usually has time in the evenings for family devotions. Winning our children, sharing with them our vision of the work and their place within it, helps them to understand their role within our broader ministry. Equally important are recreation and fellowship. Missionary children must often entertain themselves, and, with a little assistance in crafts and skills, they can become very creative. It should not surprise us, therefore, that many missionary homes develop strong family ties that last for life.

There is a second reason for us to take time with our children, namely, to show the young church a model of Christian family life. We often forget that how we live speaks louder than what we say. New Christians do not know the specifics of Christian living. We are often the only example they have. It should not surprise us, then, that they imitate us. Too often they learn by our actions that Christians must be so busy about the work of God that they neglect their own children.

Single Missionaries

A special word needs to be said about those going out as single missionaries, who in the modern missionary movement have made up close to one-half of the missionary force. Single missionaries have unique and important ministries that all too often go unreported and unrewarded, but they also face particular problems because of their unmarried state.

One common difficulty is that of loneliness. It takes special grace and gifts to live alone in a new society. Since many societies have no real place for adult singles, an unmarried missionary often finds it difficult to form intimate friendships with the people. Sometimes this problem is solved by stationing two single missionaries together. This raises questions of living arrangements. How should they coordinate their roles and divide the household tasks? It also requires finding suitable ministries in the same area.

Married missionaries need to be sensitive to the loneliness experienced by single missionaries and make a special point of including them in their circles of fellowship, perhaps by adopting the singles as "aunties" and "uncles" to their children. This provides supporting relationships for both the single missionaries and the children.

Another question that singles face has to do with their place in the local culture. What status should they occupy? This is particularly difficult to answer in societies where there are no cultural roles for single adults other than prostitutes, transvestites, and the like. In some societies there is a status for young single men as bachelors, and for old single women as revered "mothers." Other cultures have roles for singles as religious prophets. If singles do take roles within the local society, they need to be careful in analyzing those available to them, because these roles tend to have very specific images and expectations associated with them.

A closely related question has to do with the role of missionary widows and widowers. In some societies remarriage may be expected; in others this is looked down upon, particularly for older people. In India, for example, old men are expected to leave their families in order to serve God. If they remarry, the people see them as carnally minded and not spiritual.

Today in many parts of the world singles may take modern roles, such as doctor, nurse, and teacher. Unfortunately, these sometimes are associated with "loose living." On the whole, however, they do provide single missionaries with legitimate places within the local society.

One factor lessens the problem of being single in a foreign society. An outsider is seen primarily as a "foreigner," and his or her sexual identity is downplayed. The single missionary is perceived almost as an asexual person. Consequently, she or he can move between the respective worlds of men and women more freely than the nationals in that society. It is not uncommon, therefore, to see single missionaries serving in roles usually closed to people of their sex within the society. This is particularly true of single women, who are often permitted to work alongside men in the church, a nonacceptable practice for the local women.

A third issue missionary singles must face is their relationship to married couples. Unfortunately, singles are sometimes seen as peripheral to the mission task. Their needs are ignored and their voices unheard in the administration of the work. It is crucial that those in leadership build a sense of teamwork among the missionaries by including the singles as full partners.

Functional Roles and Locational Roles

Much more can be said about missionary roles and how they relate to a missionary's self-image (cf. Loewen 1975:412–427), to changes that take place during a missionary's long-term ministry (cf. Loewen 1975:349–369), and to their effect on the communication of the gospel (cf. Smalley 1978:701–836). We will look, however, only at missionary roles as these relate to the place where the missionary works.

Before the time of Western colonial expansion, the term *missionary* was not used. People spoke of mission and missions, but they did not categorize "missionary" as a professional role. For example, William Carey, Adoniram Judson, and others went out as traders, teachers, and doctors. They were guests of the countries that hosted them, and their roles were tied to functional occupations.

The specific idea of the missionary as one who served abroad emerged during the colonial era together with such other roles as colonial administrator. While these classifications included special functions, their primary definition had to do with location. For instance, "British colonial administrators" served in the colonies. They could not serve in Britain. Similarly "missionary doctors" were physicians who served in lands other than their homeland.

In time this identification of the missionaries' task with location rather than function led to a change in how the public viewed their work. Candidates were "missionaries," which meant simply that they went to serve abroad, with their specific tasks not clearly defined. Some became teachers; others became medical personnel. Many were "general missionaries," jacks-of-all-trades who fulfilled a variety of functions as the occasion demanded. They constructed buildings, dispensed some medicine, taught a few classes, repaired automobiles, and preached.

The category of general missionary was and still is an important one in pioneer work, and without it many churches would not have been planted. But the role does have its weaknesses. First, because it is so nonspecific, it often lacks focus. We can become busy doing so many different things that we do few of them well. For effective ministry, we need a clear vision of the mission task and a firm idea of our place within it. And that place should relate partly to our own gifts, to the functions we can best perform within the overall work. Even in pioneer missions, we are not Lone Rangers. We are members of a body, the church, to whom God has entrusted his work. So we need to see our ministry within the broader mission outreach of God's people.

Second, the role of general missionary creates problems when missionaries are forced for one reason or another to return to their homeland. Missionaries with functional roles can reenter similar roles within their home societies. A missionary doctor can return and set up a practice. A missionary teacher can work in a Western school. But general missionaries often fail to find a role in their own society. They may have preached abroad, but be unable to hold a pastorate at home. They may have been evangelists while overseas, but be unable to plant new churches at home. In the end many find themselves in menial jobs and struggle with the loss of meaning and status that this entails.

Modern missionaries must face the possibility of sudden reentry into their original culture. In the past it was possible for a missionary to serve for a lifetime in one field. Today, with rapid changes in world politics, this is often not a reasonable expectation. Nor is it always advisable. One of the keys to successful church planting is to know how to change roles within a young church as it matures and when to leave so that it can learn to stand alone. This does not mean we must cut ties with these churches, but only that our relationships to them should serve their good, not ours.

Does this mean that in the future the essential work in missions will be done through short-term ministries? The answer is no. Although it is clear that such ministries can perform special tasks, the heart of the work will continue to be done by missionaries who take the time to learn the people's language, to identify with them, and to nurture a young church to maturity.

What happens, then, to career missionaries when the doors close for ministry where they serve, or when they are no longer needed there? It is increasingly clear that missionaries whose roles are tied to locations—to specific countries—often have no place to go when work opportunities in those areas are closed. On the other hand, missionaries who have functional roles and cross-cultural skills become international specialists who can move from one country to another as they are needed. True, they may need to learn a new language and identify with a new people, but they already know from past experience how to do so.

Today the question of what roles missionaries should play is under a great deal of discussion. The colonial era has come to an end, and it is important that missionaries dissociate themselves from the more subtle forms of colonialism that still persist. Churches have arisen in most countries of the world, and missionaries must ask themselves how they can relate to these churches without being paternalistic.

Moreover, the growing networks of relationships between churches around the world is opening up possibilities for new and creative types of missionary service that were not possible in the past.

In these discussions it is important to remember that the multi-faceted role any missionary assumes will, to a considerable extent, mold his or her relationships with those people being served. And these face-to-face personal relationships are still the most crucial bridges across which the gospel passes from one culture to another.

11

The Unfinished Task

The Book of Acts is, in a sense, unfinished. It begins by referring to "all that Jesus began to do and teach," and ends abruptly with Paul in a Roman jail. David Howard (1979:61) points out, "Apparently no attempt was made to bring the book to a conclusion. It was recognized that the work of the Holy Spirit in spreading the gospel would go on continuously through the church and throughout the world."

What has happened since that early beginning? We need to understand the past in order to envision where we are headed in missions today.

Early Advances of the Gospel

The beginning of Christianity was unpromising. During the three years of his public ministry, Jesus wrote no book and created no elaborate organization to carry on his message and his work. His crucifixion seemed to mark the end of a well-meaning but unpractical visionary. Even after his resurrection Jesus' followers constituted only a small band of believers, one of several Jewish sects and one of the weakest of the many faiths that were competing in the Greco-Roman world. The Roman Empire itself covered only a small part of the world and was soon overrun by the barbarians. Nevertheless, within five centuries Christianity had won the professed allegiance of a large ma-

285

jority in the empire and had sent out missionaries to Europe, North Africa, Inner Asia, and India.

Christianity suffered from the fall of the Roman Empire, but even more so from the disastrous invasions of Arab Muslims that drove it out of North Africa and Western Asia and threatened its base in Europe. Internally the churches were suffering from a loss in numbers and morale. From A.D. 500 to 950, the fate of Christianity seemed to hang in the balance.

During this same period of time, however, the barbarian invaders of Western Europe were won to Christ, and by A.D. 1000 they had established a civilization in Europe that stemmed the Muslim advance and fostered the rise of vigorous new monastic movements and universities and the formulation of great theologies. During this era missionaries spread the gospel through the Balkans and Russia and across Asia to China's coast.

Between 1350 and 1500 Christianity became stagnant. It died out in China and Inner Asia and lost Eastern Europe and Asia Minor to Muslim Turks. The Western church was weakened by internal rivalries, and it had lost its missionary vision.

After 1500 the church experienced a resurgence of new life through the Protestant and Roman Catholic Reformations and, a little later, the renewal of Russian Christianity. Shortly thereafter the European countries began a series of geographic discoveries, commercial ventures, and conquests that spread their influence around the world. With this expansion often went the gospel. In the sixteenth to eighteenth centuries Christianity was planted in the Americas, on the fringes of Africa south of the Sahara, across the northern regions of Asia, and in much of South and East Asia and its bordering islands. Most of this was done by the Roman Catholics of Spain and Portugal. For the most part, the Protestants had little interest in missions at this time.

The Era of Protestant Missions

The Protestant mission movement began among the Pietists and Moravians in the beginning of the eighteenth century. Led by Count Zinzendorf, self-supporting Moravian missionaries went to Greenland, America, and Africa. They were told not to apply their own German standards to other peoples, but rather to recognize the God-given cultural distinctives of the people among whom they served.

Interest in missions spread to other churches with the founding of the Baptist Missionary Society by William Carey in 1792. During the first twenty-five years after Carey sailed to India, a dozen mission agencies were formed on both sides of the Atlantic, and missionaries were being sent to most parts of the world.

Carey's influence led women in Boston to form women's missionary prayer groups, and women eventually became the main custodians of mission knowledge and motivation. Single women began to go abroad as missionaries, and by 1865 they had organized mission boards operated entirely by single women.

This early era in Protestant missions was characterized by a high degree of love and sacrifice. Missionaries gave their whole lives for the work, and a great many missionaries and their wives and children died young. But their deaths inspired many more to go to outposts in the field. The era was also characterized by the high quality of those who went and by a great sensitivity to the cultures in which they ministered. Many of the missionaries were graduates of seminaries and medical schools, and most mastered the local languages and cultures. Some became renown poets and writers in these languages.

A second surge in Protestant missions occurred in the late nineteenth century. In 1865 Hudson Taylor led a movement into inland China, and in the 1880s and 1890s the Student Volunteer Movement led a hundred thousand volunteers to give their lives to missions. Of these, twenty thousand went overseas; the others mobilized to support them. By now, however, Western colonialism with its notion of the superiority of European and North American cultures had begun to influence the missionary movement. Many missionaries adopted the slogan "Civilization and Christianity" as their motto. Native peoples and their cultures had to be made over into the likeness of European culture, which was equated with Christian culture. From time to time there were dissenting voices, but most had no doubt about the inherent superiority of Western civilization.

In the nineteenth century a third *C, commerce,* emerged in the Protestant mission strategy. Missionaries concluded that the only lasting solution to such evils as slavery was to introduce legitimate trade that would make these evils economically unattractive.

The negative effects of this colonial attitude in missions survive to this day. As Wilbert Shenk (1980:37) points out:

> In some non-Western people it produced a prideful rejection of things Western and Christian. In others it destroyed their own self-esteem. Many Native Americans of North and South America embody the results of a long campaign which told them that their culture was worthless and they were subhuman. . . . This uncritical confidence in so-called Christian culture and equally uncritical rejection of other cultures blinded missionaries to the need to be critical of *all* cultures. At the same time it slowed the process of finding the positive values and points of reference

in a given culture to which Christian faith could relate and on which the church could build.

Despite their colonial approach, missionaries did plant churches in most parts of the world during the eighteenth and early nineteenth centuries. On the one hand, their love and sacrifice often won the hearts of the people whom they served. Many spent a lifetime in ministry abroad. On the other hand, God has chosen to do his work through ordinary people, with all their weaknesses. These missionaries were as much people of their times as we are of ours. While we may see their faults more clearly than they did, we need to remember that those who come after us will likewise recognize our shortcomings.

The rapid growth of the church during the modern era of missions is more a testimony to the work of God in the lives of people around the world than to the successes of human efforts. God took broken and dedicated people and accomplished his work.

The Contemporary Mission Scene

The twentieth-century world is being swept by massive changes that are altering the face of the earth and that also have profound implications for missions in the future.

Population Growth

The first significant change is population growth. The current increase in the world's population staggers our imagination. There are 90 million more people on the earth today than a year ago; 249,000 more than yesterday; 10,400 more than an hour ago. It took from Adam to 1830 for the world to reach a population of one billion. It took another hundred years to add a second billion, thirty to add a third, and fifteen to add a fourth. It will take twelve years to add a fifth, and nine to add a sixth billion to the world population (see Figure 37).

The impact of this increase is being felt in all parts of the world and in all areas of human life. Especially in certain geographic areas, it has led to overpopulation, famines, shortages of firewood and other fuels, disease, crowding, and even wars. This has greatly increased the missionary task. There are more than six times as many people in the world today than when William Carey went to India in 1793. In sheer numbers there are also more non-Christians than ever before.

Urbanization

A second wave of cultural change is urbanization. Never in history has there been such a massive movement of people involving so drastic

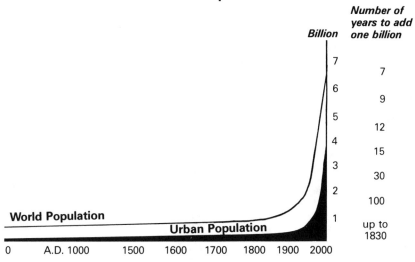

FIGURE 37

World and Urban Population Growth

a change in their lifestyles. In 1800 about 97 percent of the world's population lived on farms or in villages with populations of less than five thousand. By the end of this century, more than 55 percent will live in larger towns and cities (see Table 6). In 1800 only one city, London, had more than one million people. By 1972 there were over a hundred cities with a population larger than that, thirteen larger than five million, and four larger than ten million.

While urbanization was first a Western phenomenon, today it is occurring faster in the Two-Thirds World than anywhere else. By the end of this century, only one North American or European city will be in the top ten (see Table 7). By then there will be four hundred

TABLE 6

The Urbanization of the World

Year	Percent in Towns of 5,000+ Population	Percent in Cities of 100,000+ Population
1800	3.0	1.7
1900	13.6	5.5
1975	39.0	24.0
2000	55.0	35.0

cities with more than one million people, and sixty-five with more than five million.

TABLE 7

Super Cities by Year 2000

City	Population in Year 2000 (in millions)	Growth from 1980 (in percent)
Mexico City	31.0	+107%
São Paulo	25.8	+91%
Shanghai	23.7	+66%
Tokyo (including Yokohama)	23.7	+19%
New York (the greater metropolitan area, including parts of New York and New Jersey)	22.4	+11%
Peking	20.9	+ 83%
Rio de Janeiro	19.0	+78%
Bombay	16.8	+102%
Calcutta	16.4	+86%
Jakarta	15.7	+115%

Reprinted from *U.S. News & World Report* issue of August 2, 1982. Copyright, 1982, U.S. News & World Report, Inc.

What does this urban shift mean for missions? Most churches in the past have been negative toward city life. They see cities as evil, secular, and godless. Consequently, few missions have focused on working in urban areas, partly because it is hard to raise funds for this task. Somehow cities are not considered glamorous mission fields. Christians tend to think of missions as involving trips to distant tribes of people who have never seen a white man and never heard the gospel. The fact is, there are more unevangelized people in the city than in the jungle!

The modern city offers one of the greatest challenges for modern missions. Within it are found people who come and go from all parts of the world. If we follow Paul's example and win those in the city, the gospel will spread to other urban areas, to the rural regions that are dependent upon them, and then to other parts of the world. If God is in control of history, then there must be a purpose in this massive movement of people to metropolitan centers. Spreading the gospel is certainly part of that purpose.

But planting churches in cities calls for new strategies. Methods used by missionaries in evangelizing tribal and village societies often do not work in an urban society. Some principles, of course, remain: the need to understand the people and their problems; the need to identify with them in love and ministry; and, above all, the need to depend on the power and leading of God. But there are new dynamics we must apply, as they relate to the unique structures and cultures of the city. These we are only beginning to learn.

Cultural Crises

We live in a time of sudden cultural crises and growing social turmoil. Globally these trends open many doors for Christian witness through compassionate ministry—but they also make that witness more costly for those who would serve the world's millions.

Violence. Missions today and tomorrow must deal with the growing violence that is sweeping the world. Between 1900 and 1941, an estimated twenty-four international and civil wars were fought. Between 1945 and 1969, a far shorter time, there were no fewer than ninety-seven wars. In 1984 some forty wars of various magnitudes were being fought around the world (Kroeker 1984:5). To this we must add the growing terrorism, street violence, and kidnapping that pervades even the "civilized" world.

The implications of all this for missions are multifold. The church must evangelize and minister to those who are victims of this violence. There are more than seventeen million refugees around the world, most of them in great need and many of them open to the gospel message. The church must also play the role of peacemaker. Where it has done so, as in Indonesia, doors to witness have opened. Unfortunately missionaries themselves must be prepared to be kidnapped, suffer, and die, for the spirit of violence chooses victims indiscriminately and with no regard for cultural codes and moral standards.

Poverty and hunger. David Barrett points out that 780 million people today live in absolute poverty, a condition of life defined by the World Bank as a condition "so characterized by malnutrition, illiteracy and disease as to be beneath any reasonable definition of human decency" (Barrett 1982:5). Roughly 500 million of these needy are on the edge of starvation, and another 1.5 billion are malnourished. Growing resentment against the affluence of the West has made these people open to Marxism and its revolutionary goals.

The effects of poverty are particularly damaging to infants and children. Of the 125 million babies born in 1981, 12 million died before their first birthday, and another 5 million will not see their fifth birthday. One child in four suffers from malnutrition; four of every five children lack adequate health care. The poorest children are often parents themselves: 40 percent of the first births in the Two-Thirds World are to girls fifteen years old or younger.

In contrast to this, the 1.5 billion followers of Christ own two-thirds of the world's resources and have an average yearly income more than three times that of non-Christians. Not all Christians, however, are materially wealthy. Almost 200 million live in absolute poverty, while 750 million of their fellow Christians live in affluence. Although most well-off Christians support relief, on an average they give less than 3 percent of their income to Christian ministries. If they were to give even a tithe, Barrett concludes that "to a large extent, the global sharing by Christians of money, wealth, property, and goods could solve most of the problems of famine, poverty, disease, unemployment, dangerous water supply and so on" (Jantz 1984:4-5).

Missionaries from the West must be aware not only of the growing suffering around the world due to poverty, but also of the fact that they themselves are identified in many parts of the world with the affluent West.

Oppression and injustice.   People around the world are becoming increasingly conscious of oppression and injustice. The concept of human rights, which has its roots in Christianity, has gained wide acceptance in many modern nations, at least in rhetoric, if not in practice. As a result, most governments—whether they are based on Christianity, other religions, or secular marxism—decry injustice. In the Christian church, particularly in Latin America, there have emerged theologies that try to deal constructively with human oppression.

Today's missionaries must think through a biblical response to injustice and suffering and then take action accordingly. We can disagree with liberation theologies, but we cannot avoid the human issue which has become one of the agonizing questions of our day.

Nationalism

Another cultural phenomenon to sweep the earth is nationalism. We have seen a collapse of the colonial system that dominated the mission scene for the past two centuries. In a sense one age has died and another is struggling to be born, although the future of human political organization is still obscure. Herbert Kane and Ralph Covell (1981:347) write about the significance of nationalism for the missionary movement:

There is no doubt about it; we are living in a new day as far as the Christian mission is concerned. The last thirty years have seen more changes in the political configuration of the world than any previous period of similar length. Colonialism, the most powerful force in the world in the 19th century, has given way to nationalism, by far the greatest force in the 20th century. . . . [T]he missionary movement now finds itself in a political atmosphere sometimes favorable, sometimes unfavorable—at times downright hostile.

One problem is that we had it too good in the 19th century. In those days the Christian missionary could come and go as he pleased. Passports were seldom required and visas were unknown. The great European powers imposed their peace on whole continents, and the missionaries enjoyed the protection of their respective colonial authorities.

Today the situation has changed drastically. The United Nations began in 1945 with fifty-one charter members. Now the membership has approximately tripled. Most of the new members are ex-colonies that have gained their independence since 1960.

Naturally these countries have exercised their newfound sovereignty, which includes the right to exclude or expel anyone thought undesirable. Communist regimes and many Muslim countries have closed their doors to Christian missionaries. Others, acting in the name of national self-interest, have banned or restricted missionary activities. Today not only visas but also residence and work permits may be required, leading to endless paper work and frustrating delays for missionaries, even in countries where they are still allowed entry.

Revolutions complicate the picture. Countries once open to missionary work, such as Ethiopia, are closed after political coups. Others, like Uganda, are more open after a change in government. Missionaries must learn to work in the midst of revolutions and be willing to move wherever doors for service open.

Revival of Non-Christian Religions

Today, perhaps for the first time in history, the whole world is becoming pluralistic in terms of religions. The various religions were once generally confined to specific geographical areas. Hinduism was at home in India, Buddhism in East and Southeast Asia, and Islam in the Middle East, North Africa, and Indonesia. Now there are Muslims in Europe, Buddhists in England and Germany, and Hindus in the United States. The mission field has become the whole world (Table 8).

Moreover, there is a growing militancy and mission-mindedness in non-Christian religions, stimulated in part by a reaction to Christian missions. Islam, for example, has organized a mission movement funded

TABLE 8

World Religious Populations
(In millions of people and percentage of world population)

Year (A.D.)	30	1000	1800	1900	1985	2000
World Population	170	270	903	1,620	4,781	6,260
Christians	0	50	208	558	1,549	2,020
%	0	18.7	23.1	34.4	32.4	32.3
Muslims				200	817	1,200
%				12.4	17.1	19.2
Hindus				203	648	859
%				12.5	13.5	13.7
Buddhists				127	296	359
%				7.8	6.2	5.7
Chinese Folk Religions				380	188	158
%				23.5	3.9	2.5
Tribal Religions				118	103	101
%				7.3	2.3	1.9
Non-Religions & Atheists				3	1,016	1,334
%				.2	21.3	21.3

From *World Christian Encyclopedia*, ed. David B. Barrett (Nairobi: Oxford University Press, 1982), pp. 3, 6.

by oil money, and today it is growing more rapidly than Christianity. If the current rates of growth continue, it will overtake Christianity by the end of the next century. Reformed Hinduism is spreading rapidly in Europe, and Buddhism has mission centers in Germany and the Netherlands. No longer are Christian missionaries the only ones preaching on the streets of cities and in rural villages.

Strangely enough, along with this revival of non-Christian religions, there is a spread of secularism among the more educated populations of the world. This represents a turning away from questions of ultimate concern and an emphasis on aspects of this life only.

The Challenge of the Future

The changes sweeping our world today create many new problems for Christian missions. They also bring fresh opportunities. As colonial ties are severed, gone is our open access to much of the world. But also disappearing is the identification of Christian missions with Western colonialism. There is a growing sensitivity in modern missions to national and cultural pluralism and a concurrent search for post-colonial models for mission ministry.

The resurgence of traditional religions is matched by a growing vitality in young churches around the world. Today we need to face the fact that the church is truly international. The most rapid growth is taking place in the so-called Two-Thirds World, particularly in Central Africa, Northeast India, Korea, and Latin America. Freed from the paternalism of earlier days, many of these churches are showing new life and a vision for missions. The greatest increase in the mission force today is from the churches of Africa, Asia, and Latin America. Korean missionaries now serve in Los Angeles, and those from India venture into Europe. With the whole world becoming a mission field, churches around the globe have become missionary in character. Doors closed to church endeavors in one country are opening in others.

The question remains as to how the churches, particularly those in the West, will respond to the new challenges and opportunities. One thing made clear from history is that missionary action is first and foremost the work of God himself. And if any one church loses interest in that task, God will find other hands to do the work. Jerusalem, Antioch, Ephesus, and Alexandria each served for a time as a center of missionary outreach for the early church, and as one was side-tracked, God found a new base for his work. In the Middle Ages Constantinople, Rome, and France carried on this work of the church until each of them in turn lost the missionary vision. Then Spain and Portugal, Germany and England, and, in our century, North America became centers of outreach. The lesson is clear. If we are not faithful to God's calling to exemplify and represent the church in witness and life, God will move on to other agents.

We need to hear anew Christ's Great Commission: "As the Father has sent me, so I send you." And we must respond in a life of discipleship that is willing to bear the cost and suffering demanded by obedience to God's call. We dare not be sidetracked from that responsibility.

Canon Theodore Wedel told a parable of a dangerous seacoast where many sailing ships were wrecked and many lives were lost (Sweazey 1968:12–13). Volunteers from a nearby fishing village again and again braved the storm and rescued many from drowning, and those who were saved often joined the rescue corps.

One day a volunteer suggested that with practice they could do an even better job. So in summer the rescue crews practiced rowing and throwing life preservers and were later able to save more lives. Another volunteer thought they should build a boat house near the coast to keep the rescue boats. That way they would not waste time bringing their boats from the village. After a time, a third volunteer suggested that they build a shelter for the people they rescued, for they often died of the cold. And another recommended adding a kitchen to make soup to warm the storm victims. All these innovations added to the effectiveness of their work.

Later a rescuer suggested that they wait in the boat house during the storms so that they would be ready when a ship was wrecked. Another proposed adding a game room so that they would not be bored, and a third that they expand the kitchen so that they would have hot drinks and food while they waited in the boat house. The members took great pleasure in their building projects and added a lounge and a fine restaurant. The rescue station grew in prestige, and many more joined it on that account.

As time passed, one member observed that rescuing was a highly specialized task and that only those highly trained for it should be allowed to do the job. So they hired young men to go out in the storm while the rest cheered them on from the rescue complex. Finally the members had a meeting and decided to discontinue the lifesaving feature of the "club" altogether. It was too costly, and they all were too busy with related committee meetings and other activities.

A number protested that this abandoned their primary purpose, so they resigned and started a real lifesaving station down the coast. Once again they went out into the storm and waves to rescue those who were drowning.

One day a volunteer suggested that with some practice they could do an even better job. So in the summer the rescue crews practiced rowing and throwing life preservers, and they rescued more people. Soon the crews from the club up the coast challenged them to a contest, for although the group had given up actual lifesaving, it retained "rescuing" as a summer sport. And when a rescue station won, its members were given a trophy to take home.

Later someone in the newer group suggested that they build a boat house near the coast to keep their boats, and another added that they needed a kitchen and shelter for those who were rescued. After a time, they added a game room and restaurant for those waiting on the coast during the storms.

Eventually, rescuing became a highly trained skill and specialists were hired to do the job. And one day the members decided to discontinue the lifesaving because it was costly and they were all busy. A number protested and moved down the coast to start a true rescue station.

We know the rest of the story.

It is said that if we visit that seacoast today, we will find a whole series of exclusive clubs, up and down the coast. None of them is much interested in lifesaving anymore, although there are still many shipwrecks in those waters, and many people are drowning.

Meditations of a Missionary

Though I speak in the dialect of the people I serve and can preach with the eloquent power of a fiery evangelist; though as a surgeon I can operate with skill; though as an agriculturist I can raise high-grade river rice; though as a teacher I can deliver learned lectures, but do not have love, my message is empty.

And though I have the talent of a diplomatic organizer and administrator in councils and meetings; though I have all the confidence that I need to raise large funds, but do not have love, I am good for nothing.

And though I share my possessions and give money to the poor, but do not help my brother and sister to become strong, independent followers of Christ, I achieve absolutely nothing.

Love, if it is genuine in the life and work of a missionary, is patient and constructive; it does not seek for position and prestige. Love is glad to see a competent national in charge, and envies not. Love seeks to train an indigenous leadership; it does not cherish inflated ideas of its own importance; it is never anxious to impress. Love tries to identify itself with people and is never arrogant and ethnocentric.

Love that is genuine does not belittle. It does not compile statistics of another's mistakes. Love seeks to bear joy and sorrow, failure and success, in helpful ways. Love is not easily provoked when there is a difference of opinion or cultural differences arise; and when rumors are spread, love believes the very best.

Love that is genuine is a partnership. It is better to fail with a national in charge than to succeed without him. Love is not touchy; it never hides hurt feelings. Love never barricades understanding; it rejoices in sharing the truth.

Love keeps an open mind; is willing to attempt new methods and ways of doing things. Love does not consider the past so precious that it limits new vision. Love gives courage to change old ways when necessary; is flexible in adapting tried and trusted forms from the missionary's culture to fit the new cultural context of the national's society. Unless we are prepared to adapt and change, we shall have defenders of an old system but no new voice; institutional caretakers but no truth seekers; we shall have preachers but no prophets. We shall keep the bush primly pruned by hired gardeners using expensive equipment, but within the bush there will be no burning fire.

Love that trusts like little children never fails. Large institutions may cease; even heavily subsidized schools and colleges that impart knowledge may close. If wisdom gained there fails to lead students to Christ the Savior, it would be better to entrust such education to the government; for our knowledge is always incomplete without Him who is "the Way, the Truth and the Life." Love that has no other desire but to trust, never fails.

We are in a period of change and transition. The post-colonial era is upon us. And where is the person who knows where we are going or what will happen in the world of mission and evangelization? Here on earth, we can only vaguely comprehend.

When Christian missions were yet at the stage of childhood, the methods of proclaiming Christ's gospel were simple and sometimes naive. Authority was in the hands of a few. But now that missions have grown for over a century toward maturity, they must put away childish dependence. There must be planted deep within the soil of every people, a new, vibrant, indigenous church of the Master; one that is not only self-supporting, self-governing and self-propagating, but one that is also self-theologizing.

But whatever happens, whatever direction the winds of change may take, there is this certainty: Our Lord has not, and will not leave Himself without a witness. Through His creation and redemption He is perfecting His plan in and through history, though everything now looks confused, baffling and sometimes hopeless.

Be sure of this: institutions will pass away, but labor wrought by hands which have shared with those in need, and proclaimed the message of the saving love of Christ, who died and rose again and lives as Lord of life, will never, never pass away. In this life there are only three enduring qualities: Faith, Hope and Love; these three. But the greatest of these is Love.

Bibliography

Arensberg, Conrad M., and Arthur H. Niehoff
  1964   *Introducing Social Change: A Manual for Community Development.*
           Chicago: Aldine.

Arias, Mortimer
  1982   "Centripetal Mission or Evangelism by Hospitality." *Missiology*
           10:69–81.

Barrett, David B., ed.
  1982   *World Christian Encyclopedia: A Comparative Survey of Churches
           and Religions in the Modern World.* Nairobi: Oxford University
           Press.

Beeby, H. D.
  1973   "Thoughts on Indigenizing Theology." *South East Asia Journal of
           Theology* 14:34–38.

Berger, Peter, Brigitte Berger, and Hansfried Kellner
  1970   *A Rumor of Angels: Modern Society and the Rediscovery of the Super-
           natural.* Garden City, N.Y.: Anchor Books, Doubleday.
  1974   *The Homeless Mind: Modernization and Consciousness.* New York:
           Vintage Books.

Boyd, Robin H.
  1974   *India in the Latin Captivity of the Church: The Cultural Context of
           the Gospel.* London: Cambridge University Press.

Brewster, E. Thomas, and Elizabeth S. Brewster
  1982   *Bonding and the Missionary Task.* Pasadena: Lingua House.

Brislin, Richard W., and H. Van Buren
  1974   "Can They Go Home Again?" *Exchange* 9:19–24.

Burtt, E. A.
  1954   *The Metaphysical Foundations of Modern Science.* Garden City,
            N.Y.: Doubleday.

Carlson, Dwight L.
  1974   *Run and Not Be Weary.* Old Tappan, N.J.: Revell.

Condon, J. C.
  1976   "Cross-cultural Interferences Affecting Teacher-Pupil Communi-
            cation in American Schools." In *Intercultural Communication: A
            Reader,* edited by Larry A. Samovar and Richard E. Porter, pp.
            340–347. Belmont, Calif.: Wadsworth.

Condon, J. C., and Fathi S. Yousef
  1975   *An Introduction to Intercultural Communication.* Indianapolis:
            Bobbs-Merrill.

Dabner, Jack
  1983   "Notes on Communication." Singapore: Haggai Institute.

Drach, George, and Calvin F. Kuder
  1914   *The Telugu Mission of the General Council of the Evangelical Lu-
            theran Church in North America.* Philadelphia: General Council.

Dye, T. Wayne
  1982   *The Bible Translation Strategy: An Analysis of Its Spiritual Impact.*
            Ph.D. dissertation. Fuller Theological Seminary.

Elliot, Elisabeth
  1975   *These Strange Ashes.* New York: Harper and Row.

Engel, James
  1984   "Communicating the Gospel with Understanding." Atlanta, Ga.:
            Haggai Institute.

Firth, Raymond
  1973   *Symbols: Public and Private.* Ithaca, N.Y.: Cornell University Press.

Foster, George
  1965   "Peasant Society and the Image of the Limited Good." *American
            Anthropologist* 67:2 (April):293–315.

Geertz, Clifford
  1972   "Religion as a Cultural System." In *Reader in Comparative Reli-
            gion,* edited by W. A. Lessa and E. Z. Vogt. 3rd ed. New York:
            Harper and Row.

Glasser, A. F., et al.
  1976   *Crucial Dimensions in World Evangelization.* South Pasadena: Wil-
            liam Carey Library.

Hall, Edward T.
  1959   *Silent Language.* Greenwich, Conn.: Fawcett.

Hiebert, Paul G.
1967   "Missions and the Understanding of Culture." In *The Church in Mission,* edited by A. J. Klassen. Fresno: Board of Christian Literature, Mennonite Brethren Church.
1976   "Social Structure and Church Growth." In *Crucial Dimensions in World Evangelization,* edited by Arthur F. Glasser et al. South Pasadena: William Carey Library.
1982a   "The Flaw of the Excluded Middle." *Missiology: An International Review* 10:35–47.
1982b   "The Bicultural Bridge." *Mission Focus* 10:1–6.
1983a   "Anthropological Tools for Missionaries." Singapore: Haggai Institute.
1983b   *Cultural Anthropology.* 2nd ed. Grand Rapids: Baker.

Holmes, Thomas H., and M. Masusu
1974   "Life Change and Illness Susceptibility." In *Stressful Life Events: Their Nature and Effects,* edited by Barbara S. Dohrenwend and Bruce P. Dohrenwend. New York: Wiley.

Holth, Sverre
1968   "Towards an Indigenous Theology." *Ching Feng* 11:5–26.

Howard, David M.
1979   *Student Power in World Missions.* Downers Grove, Ill.: Inter-Varsity.

Hsu, Francis L. K.
1961   "American Core Value and National Character." In *Psychological Anthropology: Approaches to Culture and Personality.* Homewood, Ill.: Dorsey.
1963   *Clan, Caste and Club.* Princeton, N.J.: Van Nostrand.

Iwanska, Alicja
1978   "Some American Values." Cited by William A. Smalley in "The World Is Too Much With Us," in *Readings in Missionary Anthropology,* edited by William A. Smalley, p. 701. South Pasadena: William Carey Library.

Jantz, Harold
1984   "The Church of the Rich." *Mennonite Brethren Herald* 23, no. 20 (October 5, 1984): 4–5.

Jones, E. Stanley
1957   *Christian Maturity.* Nashville: Abingdon.

Kane, J. Herbert, and Ralph R. Covell
1981   "Missions in the Modern Milieu." In *Perspectives on the World Christian Movement,* edited by R. D. Winter and S. C. Hawthorne, pp. 347–354. Pasadena: William Carey Library.

Keidel, Levi
1971   *Stop Treating Me like God.* Carol Stream, Ill.: Creation House.

Kelly, Daniel P.
1982   *Receptor Oriented Communication: An Approach to Evangelism and Church Planting Among the North American Indians.* D. Miss. dissertation. School of World Mission, Fuller Theological Seminary.

Kivengere, Festo
  1962   "Personal Revival." In *Commission, Conflict, Commitment*,
          pp. 27–46. Chicago: Inter-Varsity.

Kluckhohn, Florence R., and Fred L. Strodtbeck
  1961   *Variations in Value Orientations*. New York: Row and Peterson.

Kraft, Charles H.
  1979   *Christianity in Culture*. Maryknoll, N.Y.: Orbis.

Kraft, Charles H., and T. N. Wisley
  1979   *Readings in Dynamic Indigeneity*. Pasadena: William Carey Library.

Kraus, C. Norman
  1979   *The Authentic Witness*. Grand Rapids: Eerdmans.

Kroeker, Wally
  1984   "The Deadly Race." *Direction* 1 (January/April): 3–15.

Kuitse, Roelf
  1983   "The Missionary: A Marginal Person." *AIMM Messenger* (Spring):
          3–6.

Loewen, Jacob A.
  1975   *Culture and Human Values: Christian Intervention in Anthropolog-
          ical Perspective*. South Pasadena: William Carey Library.

Loss, Myron
  1983   *Culture Shock*. Middleburg, Pa.: Encouragement Ministries.

Luke, P. Y. and J. B. Carman
  1968   *Village Christians and Hindu Culture*. London: Lutterworth.

Mayers, Marvin K.
  1974   *Christianity Confronts Culture: A Strategy for Cross-Cultural Evan-
          gelism*. Grand Rapids: Zondervan.

Mbiti, John S.
  1969   *African Religions and Philosophy*. New York: Praeger.

McElroy, Richard
  1972   "The New Missionary and Culture Shock." *Latin American Evan-
          gelist* 52 (May-June): inside cover.

Mehrabian, Albert
  1979   "Communication Without Words." In *Basic Readings in Commu-
          nication Theory*, edited by C. David Mortensen, pp. 193–200. New
          York: Harper and Row.

Minz, Nirmal
  1973   "The Freedom of the Indigenous Church Under the Holy Spirit
          and Communication of the Common Christian Heritage in the
          Context of this Freedom." In *The Gospel and Frontier Peoples*, ed-
          ited by Pierce Beaver. South Pasadena: William Carey Library.

Nakamura, Hajime
  1964   *Ways of Thinking of Eastern Peoples: India, China, Tibet, Japan*,
          edited by Philip Wiener. Honolulu: East-West Center Press.

Neill, Stephen
1961   *Christian Faith and Other Faiths.* London: Oxford University Press.

Nida, Eugene A.
1975   *Customs and Cultures: Anthropology for Christian Missions.* Pasadena: William Carey Library.
1978   "Mariology in Latin America." In *Readings in Missionary Anthropology II*, edited by William A. Smalley. South Pasadena: William Carey Library.

Nida, Eugene A., and William D. Reyburn
1981   *Meaning Across Cultures: A Study on Bible Translating.* Maryknoll, N.Y.: Orbis.

Nyamiti, Charles
1973   *The Scope of African Theology.* Kampala: GABA.

Oberg, Kalervo
1960   "Culture Shock: Adjustment to New Cultural Environments." *Practical Anthropology* 7:177–182.

Ong, Walter J.
1969   "World as View and World as Event." *American Anthropologist* 71:634–647.
1982   *Orality and Literacy: The Technologizing of the Word.* London: Methuen.

Osborne, Cecil
1967   *The Art of Understanding Yourself.* Grand Rapids: Zondervan.

Palmer, Parker
1977   *A Place Called Community.* Wallingford, Pa.: Pendle Hill.

Raab, Laura
1984   "Practical Tips for Coping with Culture Shock/Stress." Pasadena: Fuller Theological Seminary.

Radin, Paul
1957   *Primitive Man as Philosopher.* New York: Dover.

Rao, Raja
1967   *Kanthapura.* New York: New Directions.

Ray, Benjamin C.
1976   *African Religions: Symbol, Ritual, and Community.* Englewood Cliffs, N.J.: Prentice-Hall.

Reichel-Dolmatoff, Gerardo, and Alicia Reichel-Dolmatoff
1961   *The People of Aritama: The Cultural Personality of a Colombian Mestizo Village.* Chicago: University of Chicago Press.

Reyburn, William D.
1959   "Polygamy, Economy and Christianity in Eastern Cameroon." *Practical Anthropology* 6 (January-February): 1–19.
1978   "Identification in the Missionary Task." In *Readings in Missionary Anthropology*, edited by William A. Smalley. 2nd ed. South Pasadena: William Carey Library.

Richardson, Don
 1981   *Eternity in Their Hearts.* Ventura, Calif.: Regal.

Ryder, Arthur W.
 1956   *The Panchatantra.* New Delhi: Jaico.

Shenk, Joseph C.
 n.d.   "Joys and Frustrations of Going Home." Akron, Pa.: Mennonite
           Central Committee.

Shenk, Wilbert
 1980   "The Changing Role of the Missionary: From 'Civilization' to Con-
           textualization." In *Missions, Evangelism and Church Growth,* ed-
           ited by C. Normal Kraus, pp. 33–58. Scottdale, Pa.: Herald.

Smalley, William A.
 1978   "Culture Shock, Language Shock and Shock of Self-Discovery."
           In *Readings in Missionary Anthropology II,* edited by William A.
           Smalley. South Pasadena: William Carey Library.

Spradley, James, and Mark Phillips
 1972   "Culture and Stress—A Quantitative Analysis." *American Anthro-
           pologist* 74:518–529.

Stewart, Edward C.
 1972   *American Cultural Patterns: A Cross-Cultural Perspective.* Chicago:
           Intercultural Press.

Sweazy, George E.
 1968   "Hiding from God Behind Religion." *Presbyterian Life,* September 1.

Taber, C. R.
 1978   "The Limits of Indigenization in Theology." *Missiology* 6 (Janu-
           ary): 53–79

Taylor, John V.
 1977   *The Primal Vision: Christian Presence amid African Religions.* Lon-
           don: SCM.

Thurnwald, Richard C.
 1916   *Banaro Society: Social Organization and Kinship System in a Tribe
           in Interior New Guinea.* Lancaster, Pa.: American Anthropological
           Association.

Tippett, Alan R.
 1979   "Christopaganism or Indigenous Christianity?" In *Readings in
           Dynamic Indigeneity,* edited by Charles H. Kraft and T. N. Wisley.
           Pasadena: William Carey Library.

Tournier, Paul
 1957   *The Meaning of Persons.* London: SCM.
 1968   *A Place for You.* New York: Harper and Row.

Turnbull, Colin M.
 1968   *The Lonely African.* New York: Simon and Schuster.

Useem, John, Ruth Useem, and John Donoghue
1963   "Men in the Middle of the Third Culture: The Rites of American and Non-Western People in Cross-Cultural Administration." *Human Organization* 22 (Fall): 169–179.

Van Gennep, Arnold
1960   *The Rites of Passage.* Translated by M. B. Vizedom and G. L. Caffee. Chicago: University of Chicago Press.

Vicedom, G. F.
1961   *Church and People in New Guinea.* London: World Christian Books.

Visser 't Hooft, W. A.
1967   "Accommodation—True and False." *South East Asia Journal of Theology* 8:5–18.

Wallace, A.F.C.
1956   "Revitalization Movements." *American Anthropologist* 58:264–281.

Wambutda, Daniel N.
1978   "An African Christian Looks at Christian Missions in Africa." In *Readings in Missionary Anthropology II*, edited by William A. Smalley. South Pasadena: William Carey Library.

Warner, W. Lloyd, M. Meeker and K. Eells
1960   *Social Class in America: A Manual of Procedure for the Measurement of Social Status.* New York: Harper and Brothers.

Widjaja, Albert
1973   "Beggarly Theology: A Search for a Perspective Toward Indigenous Theology." *South East Asia Journal of Theology* 14:39–45.

Index

307